The Selected Correspondence of Aaron Copland

The Selected Correspondence of

Aaron Copland

Edited by

ELIZABETH B. CRIST AND WAYNE SHIRLEY

Yale University Press   New Haven & London

Publication of this volume was supported by a University Cooperative Society Subvention Grant awarded by the University of Texas at Austin.

Designed by James J. Johnson and set in New Caledonia type by Keystone Typesetting, Inc. Printed in the United States of America.

Library of Congress Cataloging-in-Publication Data

Copland, Aaron, 1900–

[Correspondence. Selections]

The selected correspondence of Aaron Copland / edited by Elizabeth B. Crist and Wayne Shirley.

p. cm.

Includes bibliographical references and index.

ISBN-13: 978-0-300-11121-7 (alk. paper)

ISBN-10: 0-300-11121-5 (alk. paper)

1. Copland, Aaron, 1900– —Correspondence. 2. Composers—United States—Correspondence.

I. Crist, Elizabeth Bergman. II. Shirley, Wayne D. III. Title.

ML410.C756A4 2006

780′.92–dc22

[B]

2005021094

A catalogue record for this book is available from the British Library.

The paper in this book meets the guidelines for permanence and durability of the Committee on Production Guidelines for Book Longevity of the Council on Library Resources.

10 9 8 7 6 5 4 3 2 1

The letter from Aaron Copland to Harold Clurman of May 8, 1945, is reprinted by permission of the Harry Ransom Humanities Research Center of the University of Texas at Austin. The letter from Ronald Caltabiano to Leonard Bernstein of May 3, 1988, is reprinted by permission of Ronald Caltabiano. All other letters are reprinted by permission of the Aaron Copland Fund for Music, Inc., copyright owner.

Contents

Preface

"I'm a pig! I'm a pig and a sinner and a wretch. But apparently I'd rather be all those things than write a letter." Every line of this book belies these words, which open Aaron Copland's letter to Nicolas Slonimsky of July 14, 1927. Perhaps Copland was simply joking, or perhaps, like many of us, he felt a reluctance to begin something, which he then enjoyed once he had started. What is sure is that Copland always wrote with confidence and élan. He was a gifted and natural letter writer with a knack for expressing himself clearly and colloquially. Even a standard business acknowledgment—there are none in this collection—reads graciously. Letters to friends are written with wit and warmth and an amount of self-revelation that Copland, conscious of his position as spokesman for modern music, did not allow in his more formal writings. In his later years Copland himself enjoyed his earlier letters, quoting from them often in his memoirs (co-written with Vivian Perlis), and they remain a joy to read today.

The letters in this collection have been selected for their readability, their interest, and the light they cast on Copland's thoughts about his career. There has been some attempt to represent the general flow of his life from the 1920s through the 1970s, but we have preferred to let the richer periods of the correspondence (especially the early 1920s and early 1940s) take up more space rather than to seek an equal representation of all years. We have not excluded anything as unsuitable for public print, nor have we included anything for sensational content. While we have striven to reproduce letters to a wide variety of correspondents, we have not published items simply to get

another name on the list: indeed, we have omitted letters of moderate interest to such notables as William Grant Still, Henry Cowell, and Walter Piston.
A composer's life, to a large extent, is lived in his or her compositions, and
we have allotted a generous portion of this collection to letters that deal with
the creation and reception of Copland's works. Not all are well documented,
however, and no mention is made of such obscurities as *The World of Nick
Adams* or *The Cummington Story*. We have not excluded letters because they
are available elsewhere or have already been widely excerpted. This is a collection of Copland's correspondence and should be the first place for a reader
to turn.

Every letter in this collection has been published intact. The only omission
has been the address of the recipient on the few letters typed by a secretary
that follow the convention of giving the name and address of the recipient at
the bottom. (We *have* included indications of secretarial aid—"AC:dw" and the
like—when they occur, as proof that a letter has been dictated.) Any ellipsis
dots found in the text of Copland's letters in this collection are Copland's own.
Ellipsis dots in the footnotes and commentary, including Copland's letters
quoted there, are editorial and represent omitted text. At the top of each letter,
we have noted the letter's recipient and physical description. If the original
paper has a letterhead, it is indicated here as well, in brackets. The date of
each letter appears in the upper-right corner—Copland's usual place for such
dating—with editorial additions given in brackets. Postscripts appear at the
bottom of the letter. Names of locations in annotations have been given in
English when an English form exists—Rome, not Roma. The single exception
is the letterhead for the letter of April 11, 1922, which caused Copland to try to
translate "Firenze" for his parents.

This collection reproduces Copland's somewhat informal punctuation, in
particular his habit of omitting the apostrophe in such contractions as "it's"
when he wants to sound conversational. (Copland rarely adds an incorrect
apostrophe.) We have also kept Copland's usage in citing the names of works.
Although Copland often placed periods and commas outside closing quotation
marks or parentheses, we have followed the conventions of contemporary
punctuation and tucked them back inside where appropriate. Likewise, we
have moved periods outside close-parentheses marks when they should be
there. Always, the goal is readability.

The few obvious slips of the pen and typos have been corrected. In most
cases, we have allowed Copland's own misspellings to stand without comment,
rather than clutter the text with "[*sic*]" or footnotes. Most of the misspellings
are fairly innocent—"appartment," "Teusday," "rehearsel"—but he found
proper names somewhat of a trap. It was many years before he learned that the
name of the conductor who most influenced his career was not "Koussevitsky."
We have left Koussevitzky's name as Copland spelled it. Other names he had

problems spelling include Damrosch, Honegger, Jan Peerce, and the always troublesome Isidor Philipp. We have identified these at their first appearance with proper spelling in a footnote. In the very few spots where Copland's syntax is obscure enough to cause difficulty for a reader, we have attempted to clarify his meaning, either in brackets or a footnote. In his correspondence with Leonard Bernstein, Copland would occasionally employ Koussevitzkyese, imitating the accent and phraseology of their beloved Russian-born mentor. When this is not clear, we have annotated such Koussevitzkyisms, but we have tried not to explain the obvious. Copland's French orthography is preserved as well, even with the occasional error. The occasional foreign phrase has been translated (liberally, not literally) in brackets if its meaning does not seem obvious, and the single letter in French has been translated by the editors.

Editors must choose what to annotate, but editors who have spent their lives studying and enjoying twentieth-century music may find themselves unsure of how much to explain. We have assumed that our readership will know the major figures in twentieth-century composition—those with many pages in *Schwann* and *The New Grove Dictionary of Music and Musicians*—but have not assumed detailed knowledge of their work lists. Thus we have identified *Oedipus Rex, Elektra, Le Poème de l'exstase,* and other works known to most musicians. One litmus test was *Les Six,* the group of French musicians endemic to undergraduate music exams. The spouse of one editor, a woman of wide general culture but not a musician, did not know the term, so it and anything not better known have been annotated. We have also assumed that the reader needs no introduction to such literary figures as Gertrude Stein, John Steinbeck, and Thornton Wilder.

We have identified Copland's own pieces on first appearance unless they are utterly clear in context; after that they are identified only when the reader might be unsure of what piece is being referred to. When Copland mentions a composition by another composer but does not give a title ("Piston's latest"), we have tried to identify the piece. Though we could refer to Copland's two-volume autobiography, co-authored with Vivian Perlis, in nearly every note, references have been kept to the bare minimum. Readers interested in a narrative account of Copland's life and music are advised to consult that excellent work as well as Howard Pollack's biography, *Aaron Copland: The Life and Work of an Uncommon Man* (New York: Henry Holt, 1999). The hope has been to strike a balance between fussy overannotation and the assumption that our readership knows everything.

Copland often mentions that he is enclosing something (clippings, a photograph, a letter to Copland himself) with his letter. In no case in the correspondence published here is this enclosure still with the letter. We have therefore dispensed with the standard note "no longer with letter." In some cases, the materials may exist elsewhere in the Aaron Copland Collection in the Music

Division at the Library of Congress. The photographs that Copland sends his parents, for example, are now among the photographs in the Copland Collection, and we have used two of these as illustrations.

Copland did not make copies of his personal correspondence. Thus his letters, with the (admittedly considerable) exceptions below, are held not in the Copland Collection but rather among the papers of their recipients. Searching them out is an unending task, and we are conscious of the many people and places yet to contact. Because of the high volume and quality of materials we had already gathered, however, we decided to proceed with publishing a selection of what was at hand—already more material than could fit in a single volume. We were fortunate that the Library of Congress, where one of us worked through 2002, holds the papers of many of Copland's principal correspondents, while Yale University, where the other studied through 2000, holds those of several more. The New York Public Library for the Performing Arts was also a fertile source. The list of abbreviations on page xiii gives a complete list of collections that yielded material for this book; a complete list of collections consulted—even one limited to those containing Copland letters and omitting false leads—would be much longer. Three disappointments may be worth documenting here: the Martha Graham papers at the Library of Congress contain no significant correspondence; the Harold Clurman papers at the New York Public Library for the Performing Arts contain no correspondence; and the papers of Aaron Schaffer, to whom Copland wrote a series of letters during his early European years, seem not to have been preserved. The last is a particularly heavy loss, as Copland systematically avoided making any specific musical comments to his family, saving them for his letters to Schaffer.

A large amount of the material in this book is indeed from the Copland Collection. Copland inherited his letters to his parents, along with family photographs and other memorabilia. He kept drafts of some particularly important letters. And there are copies from the two times in his life when he had a secretary and preserved carbons—during his trip to South America in the fall of 1947 and his stay in London in the fall of 1958. He had secretaries on other occasions, especially during some of his stays in Hollywood, but preserved no carbons from these times. There are also copies of letters written for Copland late in his life.

While writing his memoirs, Copland asked friends for copies of his letters to them. Many responded generously, sending back either copies or, sometimes, the letters themselves. Thus from the Copland Collection there are letters, original or photocopied, from Arthur Berger, Nadia Boulanger, Paul Bowles, Henry Brant, Elliott Carter, Carlos Chávez, Israel Citkowitz, Mary Lescaze, Marcelle de Manziarly, Clifford Odets, and Roger Sessions. In some cases—notably Boulanger and Chávez—we have the body of Copland's correspondence; in other cases, only a few letters. These letters returned to Copland by the recipients or their heirs have been an invaluable resource for the present collection. The Copland Collection has also been a crucial resource for annotating letters found in other collections, for we were often able to clarify Copland's replies by referring back to what a correspondent had written to him.

Numerous libraries and librarians have assisted our work in assembling materials for this volume. Special thanks is due to our friends at the Music Division of the Library of Congress, who put up with hours of the elder editor's entering Copland letters on the circulation desk's computer and the younger's pulling endless boxes from the collection. In a staff where all are helpful and many are personal friends, it is hard to single out names, but we would be remiss not to mention Jon Newsom, Henry Grossi, Susan Clermont, Kevin LaVine, Stephanie Poxon, and Carl Cephas. We also received gracious assistance from the staff of the Rare Book and Manuscript Division of the Boston Public Library, Michael Dabrishius at the University of Arkansas Library Special Collections Division, George Boziwick and the staff of the Music Division of the New York Public Library for the Performing Arts, Suzanne Eggleston and Ken Crilly at the Irving S. Gilmore Music Library of Yale University, the staff of the Beinecke Rare Book and Manuscript Library of Yale University, and Helen Adair and Dell A. Hollingsworth at the Harry Ransom Center of the University of Texas at Austin.

Vivian Perlis provided the impetus for this project. When one of us said that he wanted to do an edition of the selected letters of either Charles Ives or Aaron Copland, she suggested the latter. When the second of us proposed this project independently, Vivian said simply, "What a wonderful idea," and suggested a collaboration. We are grateful for her wise counsel and abiding support as well as for the copies of Copland's letters in her possession that she graciously shared with us. Howard Pollack has likewise provided valuable advice and kind words. Ruth Ochs was a responsible and resourceful research assistant supported by a special research grant from the Office of the Vice President for Research at the University of Texas at Austin. Dean Robert Freeman and Senior Associate Dean Douglas Dempster provided funds from the College of Fine Arts at the University of Texas at Austin to cover the cost of photo reproductions. The University Cooperative Society subvention also provided generous financial support. All have our sincere thanks.

For permission to publish Copland's letters, we thank James M. Kendrick, John Harbison, and Vivian Perlis of the Aaron Copland Fund for Music; we are grateful to Laura Mankin and Alexis B. Hart as well for their assistance. Thanks also to composer Ronald Caltabiano for permission to publish his letter to Leonard Bernstein, a brief but touching note that closes this collection. Harry Haskell was unfailingly gracious, encouraging, and patient. At Yale University

Press, Lauren R. Shapiro, Mary Pasti, and Steve Colca expertly shepherded the project to completion and publication. Jessie Hunnicutt did an extraordinary job as copyeditor.

I wish to thank my wife, Mary, for proofreading, encouragement, and insight, and for understanding the concern with trivia that is both the delight and the torment of the editor of correspondence.—WS

I thank Wayne Shirley for his personal and professional generosity as well as for his eagle eye, having served not only as co-editor but also as a valued mentor and teacher; his correspondence was just as much fun to read as Copland's. Likewise, Robert P. Morgan offered sage advice at the early stages of this project, and I am grateful for his continuing support. As always, thanks are due my husband, Harris. As Wayne once wrote to me, upon the news of my marriage some years ago now, "life is better by two." Indeed.—EBC

Abbreviations

BIBLIOGRAPHICAL REFERENCES

C & P I   Aaron Copland and Vivian Perlis. *Copland: 1900 through 1942.* New York: St. Martin's/Marek, 1984.

C & P II   Aaron Copland and Vivian Perlis. *Copland since 1943.* New York: St. Martin's Press, 1989.

PHYSICAL DESCRIPTIONS

acs   autograph card, signed
als   autograph letter, signed
tls   typed letter, signed

ARCHIVAL SOURCES

AB/NYPL   Arthur Berger Collection, New York Public Library for the Performing Arts.

AC/LC   Aaron Copland Collection, Music Division, Library of Congress, Washington, D.C.

Adler/HRC   Papers of Stella Adler, Harry Ransom Humanities Research Center, University of Texas, Austin.

Army/LC   Papers of the Joint Army and Navy Committee on Welfare and Recreation, Subcommittee on Music, Music Division, Library of Congress, Washington, D.C.

AS/LC	Arnold Schoenberg Collection, Music Division, Library of Congress, Washington, D.C.
Burkat/Yale	MSS 25, Leonard Burkat Papers, Irving S. Gilmore Music Library, Yale University, New Haven, Connecticut.
ESC/LC	Elizabeth Sprague Coolidge Foundation Collection, Music Division, Library of Congress, Washington, D.C.
GA/Columbia	George Antheil Papers, Rare Book and Manuscript Library, Columbia University, New York.
GL/Yale	MSS 69, Goddard Lieberson Papers, Irving S. Gilmore Music Library, Yale University, New Haven, Connecticut.
IF/LC	Irving Fine Collection, Music Division, Library of Congress, Washington, D.C.
Ives/Yale	MSS 14, Charles Ives Papers, Irving S. Gilmore Music Library, Yale University, New Haven, Connecticut.
JM/Columbia	Jerome Moross Papers, Rare Book and Manuscript Library, Columbia University, New York.
LB/LC	Leonard Bernstein Collection, Music Division, Library of Congress, Washington, D.C.
LE/Yale	MSS 39, Lehman Engel Papers, Irving S. Gilmore Music Library, Yale University, New Haven, Connecticut.
Letter file/NYPL	Letter File, Music Division, New York Public Library for the Performing Arts.
LK/LC	Louis Kaufman Collection, Music Division, Library of Congress, Washington, D.C.
MMA/LC	*Modern Music* Archives, Music Division, Library of Congress, Washington, D.C.
NS/LC	Nicolas Slonimsky Collection, Music Division, Library of Congress, Washington, D.C.
Reis/NYPL	Claire Reis Collection, New York Public Library for the Performing Arts.
Riggs/Yale	Lynn Riggs Papers, Yale Collection of American Literature, Beinecke Rare Book and Manuscript Library, Yale University, New Haven, Connecticut.
Schuman/NYPL	William Schuman Papers, New York Public Library for the Performing Arts.
SK/LC	Serge Koussevitzky Collection, Music Division, Library of Congress, Washington, D.C.

Stein, Toklas/Yale	Gertrude Stein and Alice B. Toklas Collection, Yale Collection of American Literature, Beinecke Rare Book and Manuscript Library, Yale University, New Haven, Connecticut.
Taylor/AAA	Prentiss Taylor Papers, 1885–1991, Archives of American Art, Smithsonian Institution.
Thomson/Yale	MSS 29 and MSS 29A, Virgil Thomson Papers, Irving S. Gilmore Music Library, Yale University, New Haven, Connecticut.

CHAPTER ONE

Brooklyn and Paris,
1909–24

Born in 1900 to a family of Russian-Jewish descent, the young Aaron
Copland lived a comfortable, middle-class life in Brooklyn, New
York. His parents, Harris and Sarah, owned a successful dry-goods
store, and Aaron was the youngest of their five children. He was perhaps
closest to his eldest sister, Laurine, who encouraged Aaron's musical interests and introduced him to the piano. Aaron was a musical child, drawn
both to the piano and to composition; at age eleven he began writing an
opera—the plot was sketched completely, but the music never proceeded
past the seventh bar—and by his teens he was composing short piano
pieces. The earliest surviving letter in his hand provides evidence that he
was writing songs at age eight and a half, in this case as a thank-you to his
brother Ralph's friend (and later wife) Dorothy.

When as a teenager Copland decided to pursue a career in music, he
shared his decision first with Aaron Schaffer, a kindred spirit whom Copland had met in 1916 while on vacation in upstate New York. Schaffer was a
young literary scholar—a graduate student at the time—and eventually
became a distinguished faculty member at the University of Texas. Though
Copland's letters to his friend are lost, the surviving letters from Schaffer
suggest that the two discussed literature, art, aesthetics, religion, and politics. Copland even set some of Schaffer's poetry to music in three songs
from 1918. By this time, Copland had begun composition lessons with

Rubin Goldmark, a noted teacher in New York City who had been a student of Antonín Dvořák. The two worked together until June 1921, when Copland set sail for France with a scholarship to attend the Conservatoire Américain, a new school of music at Fontainebleau, for the summer.

Copland's letters to his parents document these exciting and decisive years, during which he immersed himself in the artistic life of Paris and also traveled to England, Germany, and Italy to explore the musical culture of Europe's major cities. His correspondence between 1921 and 1924 comprises some of the richest, most revealing, and most compelling letters that Copland ever wrote. His tales of life abroad are characterized by a mix of charming naïveté and increasing sophistication. At the end of his first long letter to his parents, Copland asked them to "save my letters as I have decided not to bother with a diary." And indeed his letters are a diary of the most delightful kind.

To Dorothy Levey

AC/LC. als.
[H. M. Copland stationery]

April 19, 1909

Dear Dorothy,

I received your pretty cherry this morning and thank you very much for thinking of me and also telephoning to me. I did not need three guesses I knew that it was from you, at the first guess. It certainly is great to have a sweetheart that is in the hat business, so they can send you cherries.[1]

Mother said I should tell you in this letter that you made me feel very happy this morning when I received your cherry. I even made up a song with your name in it. I will be very pleased to sing it for you the next time I come down, which I hope will be very soon.

With best love to everyone from all, I remain

Your sweetheart

Aaron

These for yourself.

x x x x x x x x x x x x x x x x x x x x x x x x x x x x^2

I am feeling very much better, and the doctor said he I will be able to be out very soon maybe Wednesday.

---

1. Perhaps an artificial cherry that might have been used as the ornament to a hat? In later life Copland himself seems to have been doubtful of the meaning of this phrase: when he reproduced the letter in the first volume of his autobiography (C & P I, 22), he started it at "Mother said I should tell you . . ."

2. A row of kisses.

To John Kober[1]

Courtesy of Vivian Perlis. als.
[H. M. Copland's Department Store stationery]

Oct 18 1917

Dear John,—

I was delighted to hear that you've bought a ticket for the concert.[2] Next time we ought to buy tickets next to each other. I will not be able to meet you at Nevins Street station as I take my music lessons Saturday morning and I shall remain in New York. However, I shall meet you at the <u>front</u> end of the 59th St. subway station. You take the subway at Nevins Street (no later than 2:05 P.M.) and go as far as 42nd St. (Grand Central). There, take a local and get off at 59th St. (Columbus Circle). <u>Walk</u> to the <u>front</u> of the station and wait for me if I am not there. I make the appointment <u>downstairs</u> as the streets are very confusing upstairs unless you know how to go. I'll be waiting for you at 2:45 P.M. [at] the latest, as the concert starts at 3.

I also have the program and in the musical literature that I have are included some of the numbers. These include Beethoven's Sonata Op. 110, the Brahms Intermezzo, the Chopin Valse, and the Ballade in G Minor. I also have the original song from which Liszt derived the "On the Wings of Song." It is a song by Mendelsohn[3] and I sing it often. I regret that we have no opportunity to meet before the concert, but Friday is my Military Training Day, so it is hardly possible.

If I do not hear from you I will consider the arrangements all right for you. I hope you understand them.

Yours,

Aaron

---

1. A classmate at Boys' High.
2. A recital by Leopold Godowsky at Carnegie Hall on Saturday, October 20.
3. Copland writes "Mendellsohn" but has crossed out the second *l*.

To John Kober

Courtesy of Vivian Perlis. als.
[H. M. Copland's Department Store stationery]

Dec 21, 1917

Dear John,—

Excuse the pencil, but I'm writing between a rush of business. Now that Christmas holyday is here, I'm very anxious to see you. The most convenient time I can think of is Teusday, Christmas afternoon (and maybe evening?). Will that suit you? Could you get the Tchaikovsky Pathetique Symphony No. 6 for four hands through your library. I heard the Philharmonic play it[1] and I am sure I can now show you some beauties in it that we missed. It is perfectly ravishing. Can I say more? If you write and let me know immediately whether you are coming (as I hope you are) I will get your card by Monday. Be over at about 2 P.M.

Yours,

Aaron

P.S. I have 4 piano pieces by my teacher (Goldmark) that I want you to hear. And this confidentially, I have just composed a song that I have not been able to sing to anyone yet, so you will be the first victim! The words, written by a Belgian poet are

> Sing, Belgians, sing,
> Although our wounds may burn
> Although our voices break
> Louder than the storm, louder than the guns,
> Sing the pride of our defeats,
> 'Neath the bright autumn sun,
> And sing the joy of courage
> When cowardice might be sweet.

They are, in my opinion, very stirring. Sir Edward Elgar has written music which is played as an obligato when the words are recited.[2] However, I have not seen the music.

Come, won't you?

---

1. Walter Damrosch and the New York Symphony Orchestra (not the Philharmonic) had performed the Tchaikovsky *Pathétique* at Carnegie Hall on December 1 and at the Brooklyn Academy of Music on December 8.

2. Elgar's *Carillon*, op. 75 (1914) for speaker and orchestra, sets this poem by Belgian poet Emile Cammaerts (translated by his daughter, Tita Brand-Cammaerts).

Copland left New York with plans not only to enroll at the summer school but also to study in Paris afterward—though with whom he did not yet know. At Fontainebleau Copland studied composition with Paul Vidal, took a few conducting lessons with Albert Wolff, and attempted to work with pianist Isidor Philipp. But undoubtedly his most important teacher was Nadia Boulanger, a young instructor in harmony. Copland seemed immediately entranced by her and, after the courses at Fontainebleau ended in September, traveled to Paris to begin composition study with Boulanger at her home on rue Ballu. Among his fellow students in Boulanger's studio were other young American composers, including Herbert Elwell, Melville Smith, and Virgil Thomson. But Copland was closest to

Harold Clurman, a young man about his age whom he had met through family before leaving for France. Clurman came to Paris in the fall of 1921 to study at the Sorbonne, and the two lived together until June 1924, when both returned to the United States.

To his parents

AC/LC. als.
[A Bord de "France" stationery]

Fri. June 10 1921, 9:05 a.m.

Dear Ma & Pa,—

I have decided to write you a little every day and so give you an idea of life on board this boat. After I left the deck for the first time, I looked over some of the numerous presents showered upon me. Harry Brin[1] gave me a fancy book about France, Arnold a swell wallet, and Charlie a brand new camera with plenty of films, so that you shall get plenty of pictures. I got on deck again just in time to wave good-bye to the Statue of Liberty. By that time, dinner was ready. It was very nice and I ate my share. Then I started looking for my deck chair, but I havn't found it yet. We just sit down in any chair until someone puts us out. It seems there arn't enough chairs to go around and I have been advised to get my money back. But, of course, you are anxious to know whether I am sea sick. Everyone agrees that they never saw the sea calmer, but nevertheless, I feel none too sure of myself. You know how it feels to be in the dentist's chair when he is drilling your teeth for 8 minutes. Well, the throbbing of the ship does the same to my stomach, only this is for 8 days! However, I have had no spills or mishaps, and so I feel the worst is yet to come. I feel fairly perfect when I stay on deck; it is only when I go below that the foolish feeling comes on me. You can well believe that I fly down those stairs and up again as fast as my long legs can carry me. To my great surprise, I slept quite well last night.

It seems that the fourth fellow missed the boat. So we have a little spare room in that dinky little place. But even if it were a palace, you couldn't get me to stay down there! I have met the other two fellows, and some more of the students going to Fontainebleau, but I haven't felt the need for company yet, and so have been rather by myself, looking out at the sea and resting. The piano is also below deck and so out of the question. I have begun reading my French book, but feel that I can learn more by listening in on some french conversations. There are a great many Frenchmen on board, and I make it a point to speak French to the stewards and waiters, even tho they don't understand me.

Saturday: noon

Today I feel fine. The sea is like a lake and so I am just beginning to enjoy the trip. Lets hope it stays this way. This morning I and a violinist got a pass to get into the first class and played there for an hour. It certainly was a relief to get something to do. Until now the time draged terribly, but now that I can eat and move off the deck I think things will go better. There is to be a dance this evening to help break up the monotony and then, of course, I read a great deal.—I am continuing now, after having eaten my dinner. We had some soup, some omelettes with potatoes inside, some mutton chops and french fried potatoes and coffee. I also ate the whole business for the first time since Thursday noon. They also serve white and red wine at meals. I don't like the white stuff, but the red wine tastes like poor port wine. I am getting used to it. I am very lucky in being seated next to three French people, who always converse in French. One is an old priest, another a painter, and a young woman who has attended college in America.[2] They are very nice to me and always encourage me when I try to splash some French.

Sunday: 6 p.m.

One more day gone, and still nothing but water, water everywhere. On board ship Sunday is exactly like every other day. Last night there was a very dense fog and the fog horn kept on blowing every 2 minutes. It was quite dangerous since we were right in the iceberg zone, but by to-night we shall be out of the way of those unecessary [sic] affairs, they tell me. I have gotten thoroughly accustomed to the movement of the ship and have not been at all sick since Friday, nor do I expect to be in the future. You can just imagine how glad I am. I also sleep and eat well. Tell Lil[3] they serve everything in a peculiar manner. Breakfast is opposite—first coffee, then eggs, and finish with oatmeal! At dinner if we have, say, green peas, they always serve them separately, and never with the meat. And then there is always the wine which everyone drinks like water, and it is little more than that. But best of all at meals are the three French people who have taken me under their care and teach me French while eating. They roar at my funny mistakes, and I learn by leaps and jumps. I spend a great deal of time with one of them, the painter, who is a man of about 30 and has been giving me the most valuable information about Paris, a fellow who reminds me of Aaron Schaffer sometimes.

Monday. 6 p.m.

I dont expect to add much to-day. Everything is about the same. Altho the sea is rougher to-day than it has ever been, I feel just as if I were at 628 [Washington Avenue].[4] To kill some time I took a bath to-day and so spent my first franc for soap! After putting 3 cakes in my trunk, I find that they do not supply any soap on the ship. Also, I forgot to tell you that there were handkerchiefs in my valise.

Wednesday—9 a.m.

Well, to-day is our last day on the water, thank Heavens! It was all very nice, but—! Yesterday, the sea was at its roughest, and after having decided I would never be sea sick again, I felt it worse than ever. The worst part of it was that I had promised to play a solo, and also accompany a fiddler at a concert in the first class. In spite of feeling punk, I played the solo,[5] 'tho I was the only one in a room of 400 people that had no dress clothes on. Even if I had had them, I would not have been well enough to change into them. I am enclosing the program. Ask Ralph to tell you who Irene Bordoni is (she was on the programme).[6] I had the exquisite honor of being congratulated on my playing by the captain of the ship, who is like a king here. So much for that.

We expect to arrive at Havre sometime during the night, and leave for Paris about 7 A.M. to-morrow morning. I expect, then, to go to a hotel that my friend the painter has assured me is fine.

I'll mail this letter to-day in order that it may go off as soon as we land and write you again from Paris. You may write to me as soon as you get this letter in care of the school at Fontainebleau (Viola has the address), since by the time it gets there, I will be there also. At any rate, I may send you a cablegram from Paris, as I imagine you must be anxious to hear from me by now. Well, you need never worry. If anything extraordinary should happen (like my giving a concert in Paris) why, I will cablegram to you immediately.

It is impossible ["useless" crossed out] for me to name everyone to whom I send my love, but spread it around generally, to yourselves, the folks, Lil and Eva and the girls in the store.

Yours for Paris,

Aaron

P.S. Give my special thanks to La[7] & Charlie who lavished on me book, candy, shirts and camera. To-day I expect to drop Arnold and Uncle Sam a card, tip the waiter and steward. Now that the trip is almost over I can say that altho France may not be a Paradise, it is H--- to get there anyway (at times)! (Save my letters as I have decided not to bother with a diary.)

---

1. Harry Brin and Arnold Mittenthal are Copland's cousins; Charles Marcus, his friend and later brother-in-law.

2. The painter was Marcel Duchamp.

3. Lillian Coombs, the Copland family's Barbadian maid.

4. Copland's home address in Brooklyn.

5. According to a program in one of Copland's scrapbooks, he played the first movement of Beethoven's Sonata in E minor, op. 90.

6. Irene Bordoni was an actress and singer well known in both Paris and New York.

7. Copland's favorite sister, Laurine Copland Marcus.

To his parents

AC/LC. als.

Hotel Savoy
30 Rue de Vaugirard
Paris, France
June 18 (Saturday) [1921]

Dear Ma & Pa,—

I have just finished my dejeuner (dinner), and have come up to my room to write you this letter. I suppose by this time you must have received my cablegram and therefore know that everything went smoothly. The last night on the boat was very beautiful. We arrived at Havre at about 9 A.M. and took the train for Paris at 10. I had dinner on the train for 12 francs (about $1.00) and in giving me my change the man tried to cheat me, but I caught him, by gosh! Ever since then I count my money over skeenteen times. On my arrival in Paris I took a taxi to a hotel recommended to me by my friend the painter, but as they had no rooms vacant, I took another taxi to the hotel I am now at, where Aaron Schaffer stayed. It is a nice place, comfortable bed, big window, but no running water. And yet they have electric lights in my room! For lodging without meals they charge 8 francs ($.70) a day! Its cheap enough and quite good. After washing up, on the day I arrived, I took a bus to the center of the town. Then I began walking to see what I could see. Well, I walked and walked and walked. I noticed that the main avenues are very pretty, with trees and wide sidewalks, but the side streets are very narrow compared to ours. All the main streets are a little like Hester Street because of the great number of taxis which run around the city like cockroaches. The taxis are very cheap. You can get anywhere in the city for 50¢ including the tip to the driver, which is of the highest importance. I finally landed at a Swedish Ballet performance, which I enjoyed immensely.[1] Of course, I had to eat supper, and I went to a restaurant. They all have tables on the street, and when the waiter brought me the menu, I couldn't understand a blessed thing except omelette (which happens to be spelt the same as in English) and so I had to order that, altho I had omelette on the boat for breakfast and omelette on the train for dinner! Don't forget for one moment that I was talking French all the time as I found no one who could speak English. Before going to the ballet I had found out from a cop how to get home by carline, but after the ballet, I found he had told me the wrong directions. I then proceeded to get lost and ended up by being forced to take a taxi home! Thus ended my first day in Paris. I was quite alone as I had always been with the painter on the boat and not with the pupils of the school. The painter, by the way, is not coming to Paris until to-morrow and he has promised to call me up then. He has been very good to me and is exactly the sort of person I wanted to meet.

On my second day (Friday) I started out by going first to the bank where I got my check book without the slightest trouble, they did not even bother taking my signature. From there I went to the American Women's Club, where you can secure information about Paris[,] and played on their piano a while. I also found that Mrs Tuttle[2] was in Paris and had invited all the pupils to tea in the afternoon. I came back in the afternoon and met her and all the pupils again. Mrs. Tuttle was particularly nice to me it seemed. We are all going to Fontainebleau one week from to-day (June 25th), so that by the time you get this letter I shall be there. I have been obliged to leave my trunk at the station until I go to Fontainebleau. At night I attended an opera performance and got in for 4 fr. 50 centimes (about 40¢).[3] Another pupil of the school was with me, and we stopped in for an ice cream soda (they charge 30¢ for one). By the time we decided to go it was 12:30 and I found that all trains, cars and buses stop at twelve! There was nothing left to do but take a taxi! Well, I'll know better next time. Today I shall look around for more sights.

I am beginning to itch for mail from you already so don't fail to write if you have not done so already. I am feeling fine. Love to all.

Aaron

Have you sold the piano? How is Sally Joyce[4]?

---

1. At various times Copland recalled the ballet he saw that night as Milhaud's *L'Homme et son désir* and as the collaborative ballet *Les Mariés de la Tour Eiffel*. Both are listed as works he saw at the Ballets Suedoises during his first days in Paris in 1921 in his "trip abroad" diary (AC/LC). The generally accepted date for the premiere of *Les Mariés* is June 19, 1921, one day after Copland's letter. It would therefore seem that it was *L'Homme et son désir* that Copland saw on his first day in Paris.

2. Mrs. George Montgomery Tuttle, member of the American Friends of Musicians in France and president of the American committee sponsoring the music school at Fontainebleau.

3. Probably Debussy's *Pelléas et Mélisande*, the only opera Copland listed in his diary as having been seen before the fall of 1921.

4. Sally Joyce Copland, infant daughter of Ralph and Dorothy Copland; the "intellectual niece" in Copland's letter of August 16, 1921.

To his parents

AC/LC. als.

Hotel Savoy
Friday—11 P.M.
June 24th, 1921

Dear Ma & Pa,—

I have just finished packing my valise, after spending a quiet evening at the library. I am going to Fontainebleau to-morrow by the 9 a.m. train. The hotel proprieter has promised to wake me at 7 so that I shall have plenty of time. Paris is getting rather hot, so that I am not so sorry to get away.

Yesterday I went to see about my trunk. I found it at the station and the custom[s] officer had to go thru it. It took him exactly 15 minutes to get all the rope off. During that time I was warned that all new articles were taxable. You can imagine how I shivered, thinking of the socks without the labels torn off and the shoes that were plainly new. But altho he went thru each drawer of the trunk, he didn't notice anything. Talk about luck! Then I was forced to take the trunk in a taxi to the station where we leave for Fontainebleau, at the other end of Paris. It is there now, and all I have to do is to check it to Fontainebleau when I buy my ticket to-morrow. I also took 200 francs from the bank to-day, as I thought it was wise to have plenty ready money with me, besides my check book. It seems that including all expenses here and on the boat, for tips, taxis, board and meals, I have spent somewhere between $30 & $40 dollars of the original fifty odd dollars that I started with.

Today, my friend the painter from the boat, treated me to dinner and we spent the afternoon to-gether. I am gradually getting more accustomed to their way of doing things here. Think of it, I have never even seen a glass of milk since I left New York. They don't serve it anywheres. But they have the most marvellous bakery shops, where for a few pennys you can get the most delicious cakes and pastries. It seems to take the place of our candy stores. Then, you have no idea how silly Prohibition seems from here, when all the saloons are wide open, with women standing at the bar like the men. And, don't forget this,—I have never yet seen anyone drunk in Paris! Everytime I take a glass of beer here, I think of you, altho they never serve it cold enough for your taste, since ice is also very scarce in Paris. And so, I could go on writing forever, but I must get to bed, so that I can get up in time, to-morrow. It seems strange to think that when I am getting in bed here at 12 o'clock, you are having supper in New York at 7 o'clock. Its a funny world, anyway. Love to all. I'll write you from Fontainebleau,

Affectionately,

Aaron

Regards to Lil, Eva & the girls in the Store.

To his parents

AC/LC. als.

Fontainebleau—
June 25th, 1921

Dear Ma & Pa,—

At last I am in Fontainebleau! Everything has turned out splendidly. There was an autobus at the station to meet us, and we had dinner at the Palace. It certainly is a marvellous place, all surrounded by forests and woods, which are open to the public during the day. The conservatory rooms are on the ground floor, the girls live upstairs, and the boys live with French families around the town. I am living in a room for myself which I like very much. It is as big as our parlor, with 3 windows bigger than ours, is nicely furnished, has running water, and the nicest old lady to take care of me, who speaks French only, so that I am forced to learn by talking to her. I have already hired a piano (at about $5.00 a month). The house is on a very quiet street, about a 10 minute walk from the Palace, where we all eat our meals. The dinner was very good, so I don't think we'll have any trouble on that point. My trunk is going to be sent here to-night. You have no idea how good it is to feel that I am settled at last.

To-morrow, a great all day affair is being prepared as the formal opening of the school. All the high muck-a-mucks will be here, there are to be concerts, speeches and fireworks. I really can't see why they make so much fuss. The school is really to begin on Monday. All the pupils are not here yet, as one of the boats are late.

I have been playing on one of the baby grands at the Palace all afternoon, and enjoyed myself immensely, after not having any piano for over 2 weeks. I have decided to study piano here also, for 220 francs (about $20.) a month extra. If I don't think I'm getting my money's worth, I'll quit after a month. The piano teacher, Isador Phillip,[1] is very famous, and known all over Europe and America, and I think it is certainly worth the money.

The town of Fontainebleau itself is very sleepy, but tries very hard to be up-to-date. They have one or two movies even. And by the way, in the Paris moving picture houses, I noticed that they advertized only American pictures, with Charles Ray and Norma Talmadge and Charlie Chaplin. I already noticed that there are a great many tourists who come here daily, to see the Palace and the Forest. And I must say, they are worth coming to see. Some day soon, I shall take my camera and get some pictures to send you.

Now I must get back to the Palace to eat supper. In the mornings I must be up at seven, so it will be a case of early to bed, early to rise. There is nothing to do here at night, anyway.

Well, I'm sure you'll be glad to hear I am so nicely settled. Love to all.

Affectionately,

Aaron

---

1. Pianist Isidor Philipp.

To his parents

AC/LC. als.

June 28, 1921 (Teusday)

Dear Ma & Pa,—

Well, I have been here now for three days, and am very well satisfied with everything. My room here particularly pleases me. And Mrs Mousset, my landlady, takes very good care of me. She wakes me up in the morning, takes the spread off my bed for me every night just like you used to do. The meals at the palace are also satisfactory, altho here we drink more tea and water, and less wine and beer.

On Sunday they had a big celebration. All the town was decorated with American and French flags, there was a concert in the afternoon in that ballroom whose picture I once showed you, and there was another concert and fireworks at night. Damrosch[1] and Mrs. Tuttle and a great many of the biggest musicians in France were here, all in honor of the opening of the school. On Monday work really began. There are, for the present, only 4 composition students, altho more are expected to arrive. However, we had a class, and I was quite pleased with our professor, Paul Vidal. He is a man with Mr. Goldmark's tastes,[2] and was therefore, quite satisfied with the stuff I showed him and played for him. However, he is not the sort of man I shall want to study with, when I get to Paris in the winter. As regards piano, I learned just in time, that Isadore Phillip, the piano professor, was to come here only once every few weeks, and as there are about 60 piano students, he certainly won't have much time for each separate one. I therefore decided it was not worth while studying with some assistant of his, and prefer to work by myself during the summer and go to someone in the winter. The piano that I hired won't be here until next Friday, and I am anxiously waiting for it, since the pianos at the palace are so near one another, that when they all start going at once, it sounds like a crazy house to me! I have made a trip thru the other rooms and parts of the palace to see Napoleon's various bedchambers, libraries, art galeries and so forth. It certainly is a great sight.

My trunk arrived safely and you can just bet I breathed again, once I had it open and saw that everything was safe and sound. The suits were hardly creased, and I am wearing for every day, the brown suit that I discovered in the closet at the last moment. Do you remember? Tell Louise I'll choke her, because she gave me pajamas about six times too big! Then you must remember that I had my blue suit pressed just before we packed the trunk. Well, the tailor must have given Louise the wrong vest, because it is much too big for me and doesn't seem to match the rest of the suit. But I don't suppose there is any way of correcting the mistake now. Maybe, for the winter, I shall get it cut down to fit me. I still have some of those chocolates you gave me and they sure do taste nice now, since there is very little decent candy in France.

Of course, I haven't heard a word from you yet, and hope everything is all right. You must have received my boat letter, by now.

After this, instead of sending my letters to the school, you can send them right to my home. I will give you the address on a separate sheet of paper. Now, that I am settled and will have less news to write, don't be surprised if I write a little less often. Love to all.

Affectionately

Aaron

---

1. Conductor Walter Damrosch, who co-founded the American Conservatory at Fontaine-bleau with French composer and conductor Francis Casadesus.

2. Copland considered Rubin Goldmark, his private composition teacher in New York, to have very conservative musical taste.

To his parents

AC/LC. als.
[Hotels St. James and D'Albany stationery]¹

chez Mme. Mousset
195 Rue St. Merry
Fontainebleau
July 11th 1921

Dear Ma & Pa,—

I have just received your letter about the robbery and the selling out, and must say it was exciting enough. I don't suppose there's much hope of recovering the goods. I still don't understand what you will do with the store if you do sell out, because the lease doesn't expire till May. However, I hope that anything you want to happen, does happen.

It certainly was good to hear that you got my cablegram and letter. It also makes me feel good to think that by this time you must have received still more letters that I wrote you from Paris and here. Of course, now that I am being so well-taken care of, you need have no worries whatever. I'm simply in love with this quiet, little town, and everything connected with it. I'm very friendly with all the pupils, and they all call me George, in honor of George Copeland,² the famous pianist, so that I've almost forgotten my real name. But George suits me. Theres nothing new of any great importance. I'm working very well, consider[ing] its summer, but its not so very warm here. I've had my first lesson in Conducting from Albert Wolff of the Metropolitan and enjoy it immensely. If ever the opportunity to conduct presents itself, I won't be so green at it. The composition teacher has taken a liking to one or two songs I wrote in Brooklyn, and promises to have them sung here sometime. Altho, as you already know, I am not studying piano here, I am, nevertheless, allowed to attend the classes whenever I like, and listen to all the instruction. All I need do, is apply the instruction to myself. So you see, everything is running as smooth as pie. The meals are fine, everything they give you is very tasty and home-like.

Our favorite sport here is to go bycicleing. We ride on the country roads, thru the marvellous forest for hours without meeting a soul. Finally we arrive at a small village, very ancient and very quaint. By now, I am an expert cyclist. We hire the bikes, they charge 10¢ an hour.

I am enclosing the statement that the bank sent for the first month, and added the translation of whatever words I thought you would not understand. I hope to do this every month so that you can see for yourselves where I stand on money matters. Tell everyone it would make me poor to write to each one separately. But give them all my love.

Affectionately,

Aaron

---

1. The letterhead is crossed out, with the note "(Just borrowed this paper)."
2. American pianist best known for his performances of contemporary French music.

To his parents

AC/LC. als.

August 3, 1921

Dear Ma & Pa,—

To-day your letter (dated July 15th) arrived with a letter from Aaron Schaffer, and [one from] Bob Gordon and a card from Miss Rutenberg[1] from Cleveland where she is spending her vacation with some friends. So you see I am being kept supplied with mail. I suppose you understand by now, that I have received all your letters up to date, tho they were slow in coming.

I am enclosing some photos I took which I hope will give you a little better idea of just what Fontainebleau is like. Also a clipping about a concert given at the school at which I played a composition of my own. Sad to say, it made quite a hit; I say it is sad, because I can't get over the idea that if a thing is popular it can't be good!

I can't help smiling when I see that you seem to think it is much cooler here than in New York. We have had weather here, hotter than I've ever been thru anywheres, but its been rather cool for the last few days.

Perhaps you'd like me to sketch out a day for you as I live it here. In the morning I hear a knock on the door and the following scene takes place:

ME: Oui, madame (Yes, madame)
MADAME MOUSSET: Sept heure et demi, monsieur
(Half-past seven, monsieur)
ME: Merci, madame (Thanks, madame)

Copland on bicycle, with harpist Djina Ostrowska, Fountainebleau, 1921.
Provided courtesy of the Aaron Copland Collection at the
Library of Congress.

Then, of course, I turn over and snooze for 5 minutes more and finally get up. I hustle down to school for breakfast, and then practice there on a baby grand for a few hours. I then return home, and read and play some more. After dinner, we take a short walk and then genearlly work thru the afternoon until 5 p.m. Often there is a concert at the school at that hour. After supper, we often take a long walk or go to the cake and ice cream store (no sodas) where they have tables on the side-walk, and we sit and talk. Thats generally the plan for week days. On Sunday, I lay off work, and sometimes go for a bike ride to nearby towns.

Madame Mousset has just brought me a second letter from you, which tho written 10 days later than the one I got this morning, they both have come on the same day. So if ever you don't get mail from me, blame it on the boats. I expect to write on an average of once a week. You ask how many pupils there are here. I should say about 85, and when they all begin to practice at the same time, you can just imagine what it sounds like. Sometimes I run away from the Palace as if it were a crazy house, and get back to my own room where it is nice and quiet.

I advise you to send my letters in care of the school again, as you are the only one who knows this address and I never get all my mail together. So here it is again:

> c/o Ecole de Musique
> Palais de Fontainebleau
> Fontainebleau, France

You won't have to bother sending my musical magazines much longer because my subscription runs out in September.

Well, theres no more news for the present. Give everyone my love. Tell Eva I hope she played well the evening of the concert.

Affectionately
Aaron

---

1. Minne Ruttenberg, a pianist with whom Copland had played summer jobs in the Catskills.

To his parents

AC/LC. als.

Aug. 16, 1921

Dear Ma & Pa,—

A few days after I wrote my last letter, yours arrived. More recently Dorothy's letter came, and it was all the more appreciated, since it was hardly expected. I would have thought that taking care of that lovely little brat on the enclosed picture might prevent one from thinking of such trivialities as France and brothers-in-law. (In France they call a sister-in-law a "beau-soeur," which literally translated means "beautiful sister." So you see the French are polite, at all costs.) Tell Dorothy that I hate to deprive her of an answer for her thoughtfulness, but if I did write her, it would start a precedent, and then everyone would expect one. I think its just as good that everybody who wants to, should read the stuff I send you. But I'm only too tickled to receive mail. Also don't let Dot forget to thank Estelle for the nice letter she sent me.

Talking about letters reminds me that I received one from Harold Clurman recently. He is sailing for France on Sept. 14th and I am quite sure we shall be bosom friends as we have a great deal in common. I have invited him to come to Fontainebleau for a day or two just before I leave for good. He can stay at my house as I have a big double bed. He has already accepted and I am looking forward to the time of his arrival.

I expect to go into Paris about the first of next month to look for a room for the winter. I have addresses of people who know of such rooms. I hope to get a nice room with some family and take meals at a restarant. The Latin Quarter (the name of the part of Paris where I shall surely live, since all the students are there) is simply filled with restaurants[1] where you can get regular meals of the best kind for 75¢. At any rate, I expect to try that plan and see how it works out. After I get settled I shall certainly look up Alma's relations and the man Adler gave me a letter to.[2] I have found he is quite well-known over here as a pianist, and I may get him to help suggest a teacher for the winter, as I am still undecided who I wish to study with.

Quite a few students expect to leave after the end of the second month, some because of jobs and others for various reasons. To-day I got permission to borrow books from the library of 40,000 volumes in the Palace. It sure does give me a thrill to walk into that marvellous room (its a block long and all decorated in gold like a ball room). They have all sorts of old, old books in English and French, and if it wasn't for the fact that we can only go in once a week, I would never get out of there.

The weather here has certainly taken a remarkable turn. After being scorching and rainless all summer, it has suddenly become cold and wet. That sweater you gave me at the last minute comes in very handy. And for my bed at night my landlady has given me the lightest of light feather beds that would keep one warm even at the North Pole.

Did I tell you that I wrote a long letter to Mr. Goldmark and told him, finally and at last, that I was here for good? He's too clever not to have guessed it by this time, tho. What Dot said about the post card I sent her at 8 years old is very amusing.[3] I was quite sure I had never thought of music until I was 11. She mustn't forget to save it for me to see some day.

Tell Lil to hurry up and write that letter (if she hasn't done so already). Now I think I've told you all the news. Give my love to everybody and a special kiss for Sally Joyce, my intellectual niece.

Affectionately,

Aaron

P.S.—Hurrah for the Maxwell, say I! Tell Lou the Frenchmen still think Carpentier is a gentleman and Dempsey a brute.[4]

---

1. Corrected in ink from "restarants."

2. Alma Harwood, New York patroness of music, and Clarence Adler, Copland's piano teacher in New York City.

3. This "post card" is the first letter in this collection.

4. The Maxwell is presumably the Copland family's new car. In July 1921 the American boxer Jack Dempsey defeated Georges Carpentier of France for the heavyweight title.

To his parents

AC/LC. als.

Sept. 19, 1921

Dear Ma & Pa,—

I've been itching to write you this letter for the last two days, but never got the opportunity. Just think, I have an appartment!! With a little luck, a few lies and lots of bribes, I finally landed one. You have no idea how overjoyed I am. It is big enough for Harold and I, and I have wirelessed him the good news to the Paris boat. But, let me catch my breath and tell you the full story.

I went to Paris Saturday as I had intended and looked all over until 3 p.m. but found nothing. Finally, in a window on one of the boulevards I saw a little announcement of a small, furnished place to let. I immediately went to the address given, feeling it was too good to be true. I found it was only an agency, in a private house, and no signs. They promised me what I was looking for if I signed a paper promising to pay [them] 10 per cent of the rent for 3 months. I was, of course, willing to sign anything. They then gave me the address of a place, warning me not to mention the fact that I was sent by an agency. I went to the place in question and found a little 3 room "suite" on the top (4th) floor—bedroom, dining room and kitchen—in the Latin Quarter, just what I wanted. The rent was 300 francs a month (about $25.00)—for Harold and I making $12.50 each. I grabbed it, swore I was from a friend, gave the janitor (they call them "concierge" here) 100 frcs. deposit, and prepared to jump for joy. But I had forgotten the concierge. He (or rather his wife) calmly asked me for a tip, saying ten percent of the rent for one month, was the usual thing. I plunked down 10 frcs. and promised to pay the other 20 later. But most painful of all, was when I got outside, and had a wild desire to run up to every stranger

I met and howl at him the marvellous news. We will be able to make our own breakfasts and an occasional lunch. But I've forgotten to give you the most important thing—the address. We are to begin living there Oct 1st. It is at

207 Boulevard Raspail, (Paris)

a big wide street with subways and busses a half a block away. (Please don't pronounce Raspail like Raspale, but like this—Raspighy to rhyme with skiey. Ask Ralph to explain [to] you this puzzle.) Now you need never worry. I shall take care of Harold and he shall take care of me. I have been invited by the director of the school to stay with him and his family at the Palace until Oct. 1st. He will keep a piano for me, so I have accepted with thanks. So I move to the Palace on the 25th and stay there for 5 days. He made me promise not to tell this to any other student. So you see I am in good with the big muck-a-mucks.

All the excitement about the appartment happened on Saturday. I went to the Opera that night (M. Wolff, the conductor, gave me a pass) and on the next day went to visit the battlefields. By the way, for my last lesson with M. Wolff in conducting, we had a private lesson, and all unsolicited, he said some very nice things to me, 'tho he has never heard any of my compositions. He told me to come to him any time when I wanted advice or letters to anyone. In October he sails for America to conduct at the Metropolitan. You ought to see me conducting an imaginary orchestra, waving my arms wildly in the air, making faces at emty chairs. And just imagine, I have never had to pay for any conducting lessons!

But I have wandered from telling you of the battlefields. I could write a young book about everything I saw, but it would be too disgusting. We were conducted on a tour by the government, understand, and after a 2 hour train ride to Rheims, a big city in ruins, we were taken by autos to the actual war grounds. Before that we were given an elaborate dinner (or should I say banquet) and had a long speech and toast to America to which I responded, if you please! During the auto trip we were shown trenches, forts, barbed-wire entanglements, absolutely destroyed towns, and German cemitaries with black crosses. To think that men can be such beasts. One thing is sure,—I am absolutely inoculated against war fever, for all time to come, and not if everybody stood on their heads, would I fight in any army for any cause. I'd go to prison first. If everyone did the same there would be no war, and I'll be the first to start. However, if you saw those ruined cities, you'd say the world had had enough war for a little while, so you needn't worry about your son, yet!

I mustn't close this letter without telling you how marvellously my French is getting on. The proof is, I hired an appartment all in French. Next time I have to hire one, I'll get married, and let my wife find one. But she won't drag me with her, like I know some wives drag some husbands!

Just now the talk is all about the Concert.[1] I shall send you, I hope, a copy of the posters being put all over Paris, on which your darling son is HEAD-LINED. It surprises me that my hat still fits me. I just bought a new one (hat) in Paris for 25 frcs. Its very French and makes me look quite like the giraffe I am. But, I must close some time, so why not now? Love to all,

Affectionately,

Aaron

---

1. A concert in Paris celebrating the end of the summer music school was given at Fontainebleau on September 21 and repeated in Paris on September 23. Copland's "scherzo humoristique," *The Cat and the Mouse*, was played on the first half. See C & P I, 51.

To his parents

AC/LC. als.

Palais de Fontainebleau
Sept. 27, 1921

Dear Ma & Pa,—

Well, here I am back in Fontainebleau with all the concerts and excitement finished. But I must admit it was wildly exciting while it lasted. Under separate cover I have sent you a few of the preliminary announcements of the concerts here and at Paris, and one criticism of my compositions played that appeared in the Herald. I have a few others from French papers that I shall send you with a translation, later. But I must tell you the most interesting news of all. At the Fontainebleau concert the theatre, with its 3 balconies[,] was packed full. During the first part of the program I played one of my pieces for piano called "The Cat and the Mouse," which I had written in Brooklyn over a year ago. It had an immense success. During the intermission M. Durand, the music publisher, came to me and asked me if that piece was published. When I told him no, he said he would publish it!!! Let me try to calmly explain you what this means. In the first place Durand and Son is the biggest music publishing firm in Paris, which means the world. To finally see my music printed means more to me than any debut in Carnegie Hall ever could. Of course, it will all take time. Mr. Durand returns to Paris October 6th and I am to go to see him about the 10th. It is impossible to say how many weeks, months or years it will take before the piece finally comes out. But even if it never was printed, I would have the thought of the promise, at least. But be sure of one thing. Don't expect me to make any fortunes out of my compositions. Composing is not a business, but a luxury, which you are so good as to allow me to afford, for a little time anyhow. All we can do now, is to hope and pray for the fates to be kind, and hurry up with my piece. I received a long letter from Mr. Goldmark. What would he have to say to all this!

Well, Harold Clurman has arrived—safe and sound. I met him in Paris two days after his arrival on the evening of the concert in Paris and we went there to-gether. The next morning we both went to Fontainebleau and he spent a day and a half here with me, being thoroughly delighted with the place. He is a very, very nice boy, with some real intelligence and I am sure we shall get on immensely together in our apartment. By the way, thanks very much for the candy you were so good as to send. Between the two of us we shall make short work of it.

By the time you get this letter, we shall be all settled on 207 Boulevard Raspail, our winter mansion. Just now I am living in the Palace, quite lost among the hundreds of empty rooms. I only have to pay for meals. Mr. Casa-desus has been very nice to me, he has given me a piano in my room, where I work all day with delightful walks in the park between times. On Sat. Oct 1st I return to Paris for good. It will be like going out of the lime-light into darkness. But even I am beginning to get tired reading my name in the papers.

I haven't time to tell you of the closing reception in Paris on the afternoon of the concert, with the real champagne.

But don't think I've forgotten Washington Ave. I shall certainly think of you all eating those enormous dinners on Rosh-ha-shona and groan at the thought of missing the marvellous cakes on Yom-kippur. One needn't be religious to appreciate those things. Love to all.

Aaron

WARNING! Don't frame that stupid diploma I sent you!!—with the clippings

To his parents

AC/LC. als.

Oct 11, 1921
207 Bd. Raspail
Paris

Dear Ma & Pa,—

I really ought to be sending you a cablegram with this wonderful news, but I was afraid it would scare you. Just think, I have just sold my first composition. Let me catch my breadth [sic] and tell you the whole story. I wrote you that M. Durand, the biggest publisher in Paris, had promised to publish a piece of mine called "The Cat and the Mouse" after he had heard me play it at Fontainebleau. Well, I have just been to see him at his office here and have sold him the piece outright for 500 francs. I signed a contract with him and he has promised to have the piece ready in about 2 or 3 weeks, at which time I will send you a copy. Try to remember that in pre-war times, 500 francs was equal to $100. which is an extraordinary price to pay a young, unknown composer for a little piece of 5 pages. Then Durand is a very well-known publisher all over the world, so it gives one a reputation merely to be published by him. A great deal of the credit is due to Fontainebleau and the school as I could never have accomplished so much in so short a time without all that influence helping me. What will Goldmark and Adler have to say when I send them copies? Its too bad I am not able to play the piece for you, but you'll have to wait until I get home, unless some one plays it in N.Y. by some wild chance. Of course, this is only a beginning. One doesn't get exactly famous simply because he has written <u>one</u> piece which is printed. But it <u>is</u> a start. And the 500 francs tickles me silly, even tho it isn't a fortune.

I sent the letter of introduction that Alma Harwood gave me to her aunt and got an immediate reply inviting me to meet her in a box at the Opera. So your darling son calmly put on his very exciting tuxedo and marched gaily to the opera. Miss Florance (the aunt's name) is about 45 I judge, and was very nice to me. She is the sort of person one must know in order to meet other really interesting people. She has invited me to her house this Sunday and I have promised to play for her. Thats the least I can do for anyone who gives me the best seat I've ever had at any opera performance.

I read in the papers that you've already had snow in New York. Just think, here we are having beautiful summer weather. Harold and I always eat at restaurants which all have tables out in the street in real European style. There is one place here where you can get a meal for 6 francs which is exactly like the meal I remember having at Lorber's when it was on Grand Street. Tell Lil French cooking is delicious, particularly when you know how to order something besides omelettes.

So, we have a composer in the Copland family, it seems. Who says there are no more miracles.

Lovingly,

Aaron

To his parents

AC/LC. als.

Nov. 3, 1921

Dear Ma & Pa,—

I have put off answering your letter of October 19th until today, because of one sentence. You said "don't forget what I wrote you in my last letter about your birthday." It seems as if I haven't received the letter you mean, and I waited for it a few days. But, it doesn't matter. Whatever you told me to do on my birthday, of course, I shall do.

I am getting very well settled now, going to shows and concerts almost every day. We never need pay more that [sic] 5 francs (35¢) for a seat anywhere, so it is quite cheap, you see. Also I have finally found a composition teacher and have already had my first lesson. Now be prepared for a surprise. My teacher is not as you suppose—a man, but a woman of about 40, one of the very best known musicians in France, a teacher of Harmony at the Paris Conservatoire. Her name is Nadia Boulanger, and I met her first at Fontainebleau, where she also taught Harmony. I heard her conduct some lessons there, and realized she understands the kind of modern music I like to write, so that she was the teacher I was looking for. It has been all arranged and I have a lesson on Saturday morning of each week. She charges 60 frcs. (about $4.20) a lesson, which compared to the $6.00 I paid Goldmark is not so expensive. I am also very glad to see that you and pop urge me to continue with my piano lessons, as I have finally decided to do so. I am in the process of fishing around for a teacher and will let you know more later.

There is a Society here which is formed to give concerts of pieces not published by unknown composers. Mlle. Boulanger told me about it, and I submitted some compositions. They have selected two of my songs which will be performed, no doubt, sometime in December. So you see I am not being at all neglected.

The proofs of my piano piece have still not arrived, being about a week late, now; but to-day I got an invitation from Monsieur Durand, the publisher[,] to be present at a private musicale at his residence next Thursday. Lil would say I am "swinging in the right circles"!

About the first of December, I intend to begin taking some special courses at the College of France, which are free to the public. It will be very convenient as the college is within walking distance from here. The subjects will be poetry, history etc., not music.

I have received the Times newspapers and thank you. Also you won't forget what I wrote you about my "Musical America" in my last letter.[1] You ask what happened to my friend, the painter, whom I met on the boat? Well, like all boat acquaintances I lost track of him. I think he intended to return to the U.S. by October anyway.

The changes on Washington Avenue are quite thrilling. It always used to disappoint me when I came home from the country to find everything the same. This time, when I get back, things will be different!

The weather in Paris has been very poor. Not cold as yet, but we haven't seen the sun for weeks; it is always grey and rains a little now and then. I have, tho, put on my winter underwear, and received an extra blanket from the concierge. I receive quite some mail from all my friends in America, and even some Parisian letters, which rather tickles me. Tell Lou I wish him luck in the sweater establishment. My love to everybody and kisses for the kids—Felice, Shirley, Sally and Ralph on my 21st birthday.

Aaron

---

1. Copland had asked his parents to renew his subscription to the magazine *Musical America*.

To his parents

AC/LC. als.

[National Hotel, London, stationery]

Dec 23, 1921

Dear Ma & Pa,—

Here I am on the 3rd day of my stay in London writing the letter I promised. I have been on the go continually, trying to see all the town at once.

I begin to feel like a real cosmopolitanite, knowing already Paris, London and New York. If you asked me which city I preferred between Paris and London I should say Paris! The trouble I find with London is that it is much too like New York (only without skyscrapers). At any rate, it is very expensive to live here, perhaps even more so than at home. When I had to change some francs into pounds and shillings at the bank in Paris, I first realized how little the franc is worth outside Paris.

The hotel I am staying in here is a very nice, middle-class one, where you pay 8 and 6 (as they say here), or translated into American, 8 shillings sixpence a day (about $1.70). This, as in all London hotels, includes a very elaborate breakfast, which I am not used to anymore, as in Paris, noone has more than coffee and rolls. My other meals are taken in small restaurants around the town. I have found that no matter what price you pay, English cooking is awful! Compared to our (or any) restaurant in Paris, the food served here is tasteless, the sort of Yokel cooking you get at that hotel in Lake Carey.[1] However, they have some dishes here, which I have had for the first time since leaving home— for instance—oatmeal, a glass of cold milk, apple fritters etc. Of course all this doesn't bother me, since I am here for so short a time, but I wonder what the poor English people do!

With the help of a guide book I can find my way around town easily. Whenever in doubt I ask a bobbie (cop) the way, because I like to hear them talk. They are just barely understandable with their funny English accent. To tell the truth, sometimes I feel I can understand a Frenchman speaking French better than an Englishman speaking English! Just as during my first few days in Paris I walked my feet off, I find myself doing the same thing here. When I got my first glimpse of the Bank of England I thought of one of pop's favorite expressions—"strong as the Bank of England." Do you remember that movie "Deception" about the king Henry VIII who got rid of a few wives. Well, I've been to the tower of London and saw the spot where one was beheaded. Also here, they keep the Jewels of the present king and queen on view, a sight that would have made Lil's eyes do some funny stunts. I've seen the Parliament buildings, Westminster Abbey, Soho, Chelsea, Leicester Square, Picadilly Circus (what we would call Picadilly Square) and a million other sights.

Because of Christmas the concert season is rather quiet now, but I go to a lot of shows such as the Russian Ballet, and the Beggar's Opera. I have seen my friend [composer Herbert] Elwell twice already and expect to see him again to-morrow. I am keeping in touch with Harold in Paris, who is taking care of our apartment. Before leaving I received your parcel of music (the Bloch songs) and it was just right.[2] In my short postal to you I had no time to tell you of the "lovely" trip I had across the English Channel (a trip of 3 hours). To put it quite frankly I was 10 times more sea sick on that little ride than the whole 7 days across the Atlantic. It was the ordinary, small channel steamboat which jumped around like a cork, making me leave my entire dinner all over the boat! O it was beautiful while it lasted, I can tell you. But like all sea sickness, when the boat stopped, it stopped.

I'll write again some time next week. Did Lil and Eva get their packages yet? Love to all the folks.

Aaron

---

1. During the summers from 1910 through 1913, Copland attended summer camp on Lake Carey near Wilkes-Barre, Pennsylvania.

2. In a letter of November 20, 1921, Copland had asked his parents to send some music from home, including unspecified songs by Ernest Bloch.

To Ralph Copland

AC/LC. Photocopy of als.

207 Bl. Raspail
Jan. 19, 1922

Cher frère Ralph,—

Altho it may surprise you to hear it, I must make you understand that you're not the simplest person to write a letter to. I am capable of writing two sorts of epistle—one like I write home, having as its main type of interest what I had for supper last night and the other like I write to Schaffer, for instance, telling of the marvels of the "Group of Six."[1] Now the trouble is I have a funny feeling that to tell you of the supper or the "Six" would equally bore you. As a result, I put off the thought of writing at all till this impossibly late date. And now, all I can do is try to strike some sort of happy medium.

Perhaps you would be interested to hear a more detailed account of Goldmark's successor—Mademoiselle Boulanger. She is a woman of 40, I should judge, and is without any doubt the exception which proves the rule that there can be no great female musicians. This intellectual Amazon is not only professor at the Conservatoire, is not only familiar with all music from Bach to Stravinski, but is prepared for anything worse in the way of dissonance that I may choose fit to hammer out. But don't make the mistake of imagining her some sort of she-male, of formidable appearance and baritone voice. Thats just what she isn't! A more charming womanly woman never lived. But I'd better stop this raving or you'll end up imagining I'm in the throes of my first attack of calf-love. I therefore turn to Ricard Viñes, my Spanish piano teacher. He was the first to play Debussy and Ravel in Paris when they were both considered revolutionaries twenty years ago. To-day he devotes himself to the new men—and is helping me to play their music too. He is, in the last analysis, not a teacher, but a concert pianist (he played twice last week here)—yet I feel that no one could give me the sort of thing I want better. (Perhaps you could tell the folks about Boulanger and Viñes now, in less technical language.)

The concerts and operas here have been distinctly disappointing. One has the same number of mediocre programs and performers as at home,—only in greater quantity. Yet I never miss the occasional performances of stuff by Satie, or Honnegger or Fauré and others of the "discoveries" I've made since coming to France.

I haven't the slightest doubt that the family has a most phantastic idea of the excellence of my French. And I admit that there are days when I imagine I can understand anything said anywhere. But that delightful feeling seldom lasts long. Try to break the news as gently as possible to anyone concerned that 7 months is not 7 years and that there are still a few things I have to learn about the adorable language.

I seldom pass a real Parisian "boutique" without thinking of the wild shopping expeditions Dorothy would undertake, were she here. And what news on the Rialto of my intelligent niece Sally? With love to your better half and the chere petite.

Aaron

---

1. The group of young French composers known as Les Six included Francis Poulenc, Darius Milhaud, Arthur Honegger, Georges Auric, Germaine Tailleferre, and Louis Durey. Their music generally represented the "new spirit" (a phrase coined by poet Guillaume Apollinaire) of French modernism, its embrace of simplicity and insouciance.

To his family

AC/LC. als.

Jan. 27, 1922

Dear Ma & Pa,—

Since last I wrote you I have received two letters from you. The news about your intentions to sell out both businesses was very thrilling but you don't give many details. What are your plans afterwards? How long do you intend to live on Washington Ave. after May 31st. How about your trip to Texas and California. What does Pop intend to occupy himself with (since one can't play pinochle all day long). And what does Leon think of doing? I suppose its a little early for you to answer most of these questions, but let me know all about your plans as soon as you finish them.

And incidentally I might tell you of the things I am planning for the future and hear what you think of them. We have never talked very definitely about the length of my stay here, but I have always thought of about 2 years being necessary to round out my studies. I have now been in France 8 months and this is the way I have thought of spending the remaining 15 months. (I know this must sound like a very long time to you, but you know how time flies[.]) Here are my plans:—around Easter time I would like to spend about 3 weeks in Italy (visiting Rome, Milan, Venice etc.) a trip which would cost about 400 francs ($30.00) more than if I stayed at Paris. Then on about June 1st I would like to go to Germany (perhaps Berlin or Munich or Vienna) and stay in Germany for the entire summer, even up till Nov. 1st, in order to get about five months of German music and customs. Those five months would be very cheap. Because of the rate of exchange being so ridiculously low, you can live in Berlin or Vienna for $5.00 a week (all expenses included)—and live like a lord. Then on Nov. 1st I would return to Paris, continue my studies with Mlle. Boulanger and finally come home some time in the Spring of 1923. How does all that sound to you? I wish you would think it over and tell me just what your opinion may be. Perhaps you can offer suggestions or improvements.

Theres nothing new of any importance to tell you. Just now, the man is in the next room tuning my piano. They charge 10 francs here ($0.80 compared to the $4.00 of Steinways)[.] This morning I received another letter from John Kober, who is still on my trail. I suppose Lil will be glad to hear I have finally decided to answer him. I also received a letter from Mrs. Tuttle who wants to know if I am coming back to Fontainebleau this summer. Isn't that funny?

Give my love to all the folks and keep plenty for yourselves.

Aaron

To his parents

AC/LC. als.

Feb. 22, 1922

Dear Ma & Pa,—

Yesterday came your letter dated Feb. 8th. Also the music Shirmer's sent arrived safely, for which many thanks.[1] I'm sorry to say that there was nothing wrong with the price ($3.42). One cannot get any Shirmer's music in France simply because the French cannot afford to pay so much. Its very lucky I seldom need music from N.Y. isn't it? I intend having my "pitcher took" to-morrow and hope it will turn out satisfactorily.

I was glad to see that the letter I sent telling of my plans did not surprise you too much. Also that you are willing to let me decide for myself how to dispose of my time, and last, but not least, that there is no particular rush about my coming home. Your suggestion that I go back to Fontainebleau came as a sort of shock. You must remember that altho the school did a great deal for me in the way of free advertiseing and getting me next to Durand, I learned practically nothing from the composition teacher there (Mr. Vidal). To go back again, would only mean 3 months gone to waste, because I came to Europe, not to have my picture in the papers, and not to get my piece published, but to learn more about composition. That is the important thing, and there is plenty of time for the advertiseing and publishing later. I could give a dozen other reasons for not going back, but it is not necessary, as the one I have given will make you understand.

You also wondered in your letter whether 3 weeks in Italy and 5 months in Germany was long enough. I think 3 weeks in Italy will be sufficient because from a musical standpoint it is not very important, and it would be dull to stay much longer since I know no Italian naturally and could not talk to any one or go to shows. At any rate I would not be willing to leave Paris for longer than 3 weeks just now, because I don't want to interrupt my lessons with Mlle. Boulanger, and one can't go to Italy after June 1st because it is very hot and unhealthy there. Three weeks therefore around March 26th will be just right in which I can see all the sights. My plans are still rather vague, but I think I shall go first to Milan, then Rome and then Venice, spending about a week in each city. As for 5 months in Germany, I am not sure myself whether it will be long enough. One thing drags me back to Paris—that is Mlle. Boulanger's marvellous teaching. Yet, if I should happen to find a decent teacher in Germany—who knows?—I may not come back to Paris at all. With the help of my Yiddish (?) I hope to learn German quickly and will soon feel at home. Then the fact that it is so much less expensive than Paris may influence me to stay there. At any rate, for the present, we will leave it an open question as to how long I stay in Germany, but I plan to go there on June 1st. Before going I intend to write to Goldmark and Adler for letters of introduction to people. In the mean time I shall continue thinking it over very carefully, and any suggestions you may make will be highly appreciated.

I have just been wondering when the contract for the store runs out—is it May 1st or May 31st? Do you know how long you will continue living at 630 after you get out of the store?

Shortly after we give up our appartment on June 1st Harold is going to sail for home for the summer months. You must arrange with Elsie to see him at her house and he will be able to answer the million questions you must have to ask about our winter here.

I wrote Lil a letter not so long ago and hope she won't forget I expect an answer some day!

So long for the present. Love to all.

Aaron

---

1. The publisher G. Schirmer's. In a letter from January 21, Copland had requested that his parents send some music from Schirmer's publishing house and music store. Among the pieces he had asked for was the Suite for Viola and Piano by Bloch.

To his family

AC/LC. als.

March 15, 1922

Dear Ma & Pa,—

Two days after I sent my last letter, your's came with the exciting news about selling the store. It was hard for me to realize I had not been dreaming. Even now I can hardly picture you to myself as being anywhere except behind the yard goods counter or up at the desk. But with time I suppose I'll get used to the idea. What has happened to Louise, and Miss C. and the rest of the gang. And how long do you think you will continue living on Washington Avenue. (I suppose that last question is sensible enough, but to me it sounds crazy.) I shall look forward with great interest to your future letters to hear how things are planing out [sic]. Tell Charlie he has my everlasting blessings for offering to take care of my books. The music in Pop's closet can be thrown out, but all the other music is very valuable and I hope you will take good care of it somehow.

As for myself, I have no very thrilling news to tell you. Monsieur Senart the publisher has not written to me yet and tho I do not understand the delay, I am taking it as a good sign since he still has my manuscripts.[1]

I have just received my photographs to-day and will send them to you to-morrow, without fail. I hope you will think them worth all the fuss and waiting I have been forced to make you do. To say that the pictures flatter me, is to put it mildly, but the pictures ought to approximately recall to you what my features were like. Anyway, let me hear what you think of them.

The main thing occupying my mind just now is, of course, Italy. I have been making the necessary inquiries and have found, to my regret, that the trip will cost more than I first thought. The railroad fare for a round trip, allowing me to stop off at Milan, Rome and Venice[,] is 586 francs. Boarding (without meals) and extras for concerts and so forth will be about 400 frcs. more. I therefore figure that the trip must cost me about 1,000 francs extra—that is—1,000 francs added on to the usual 1200 I would spend if I stayed in Paris. At first the outlay

seemed so much that I considered calling off the trip altogether. But on thinking it over, I have decided that in Germany I will be able to make up the extra
thousand francs (about $90.) because of the very low cost of living. Also I hope
to save something because of the fact that the Italian lira, which at par value is
worth 20¢, is now only worth about five cents. So all in all, I thought you would
agree it is wisest to go now, since the opportunity doesn't come every day.
Therefore I am planning to leave Paris on the night of March 26th at 9 P.M.
The train runs thru southern France and Switzerland and arrives at Milan the
next day at 6 P.M. So you see it is almost a whole days trip in the train.
(However that pleases me better than 2 hours on the English Channel!) Now I
plan to stay in Milan 6 days, but it all depends on how interesting I find the
opera and concerts there. My next stop, at any rate, will be Rome. It takes 12
hours on the train to get there from Milan. After a week in Rome I shall go to
Venice (another trip of 12 hours), and finally end up in Paris on the 16th of
April. Besides seeing Italy, I have no doubt I won't want to look at a train after
its all over, but if you want to travel, I suppose you must sit in trains. Of course
as soon as I get into a new city I will drop you a card and then a letter will
follow. Whenever I want to talk Italian all I need do is use my hands! When one
is a pianist thats not so hard, is it?

Harold is going home for summer only and will come back in October to
finish his second year in college. I have written Sidney to buy me some music
and have told him to send you the bill.

Your suggestion about buying a new Spring overcoat makes me smile. If you
saw some of the things people around here wear and call Spring overcoats, you
would have to call mine brand new.

Next Sunday I am invited for the third time to a musicale at Durand's, one of
those horribly swell affairs. I wish Lil could see the men with full dress suits
and white silk gloves serving champagne.

Love to all

Aaron

---

1. Boulanger had contacted music publisher Maurice Senart on Copland's behalf. Copland
visited the publisher's offices on March 7 and performed his *Passacaglia* as well as three songs.

To his family

AC/LC. als.

[American University Union in Europe stationery]

[Paris] March 21, 1922

Dear Ma & Pa,—

I have decided not to wait for your letter, but to write right away in order to
tell you the great news. I have signed a contract with Monsieur Senart, the
publisher, who is going to bring out 2 of my compositions!!! First a piano piece

Copland in Paris, early 1920s. On the back of the photo,
Copland wrote, "On a breezy day in March on my way to a
concert, the River Seine in the background."
Provided courtesy of the Aaron Copland Collection at the
Library of Congress.

(longer than the "Cat and Mouse") called a "Passacaglia" and then a song for voice and piano entitled "An Old Poem." This, you must agree is a most gorgeous piece of luck which fell out of a clear sky.

This time, instead of selling the compositions outright, I have sold them on a royalty basis of 10% on each copy for the first thousand sold, and 15% on the second thousand. Of course that doesn't mean any money in my pocket as there is very little chance of selling more than 2 copies, I suppose. But who cares, I am published once more, thats the all important point. The fact is, I shall probably pay out more than I ever make on the song, because I have been forced to pay the poet, whose words I used, one guinea ($5.00), for the rights of using his poem for a song setting. (That is the usual price.) I will let you know later on, what firm in New York handles the Senart Publications, should any-body want a copy. Of course, you understand it is my teacher, Nadia Boulanger, who I must thank for this. Without her influence, this would never have come about. It is impossible for me to tell just when the pieces will be ready to send home to you, but you can bet it will be a long time. Anyway, its something to look forward to.

In the midst of the excitement I shall be off to Italy next Sunday. My plans have been slightly changed. Instead of going to Venice I shall visit Florance, which will not necessitate so much travelling. My first stop is to be Milan in any case. Most likely I shall spend most of my time at Rome. Luckily, I shall not have to make the trip alone, as another young American fellow,[1] also a pupil of Boulanger's, is going with me. As he can talk a little Italian, I won't have to work my hands so much. Then Mlle. Boulanger has promised to give me letters to some people in Rome, so you see, everything is planning out beautifully. I expect to drop you a card as soon as we arrive in Milan.

Last week I carefully wrapt my photographs and mailed them. I hope they arrive safely and in good shape. Today I am enclosing 4 snapshots that I hope will interest you.

I am waiting with as much patience as possible to hear what effects the selling of the store has had on everyone.

The next mail you get from me should bear an Italian stamp.

Love to all.

Aaron

P.S. Yesterday I received a letter from Martha Dreiblatt.[2] She says she may be in Berlin during the summer. Aaron Schaffer also writes the same.

---

1. Melville Smith.

2. Copland had met Martha Dreiblatt at the Fairmont Hotel in Tannersville, New York. Dreiblatt was related to the original owner of the Catskills resort.

To his parents

AC/LC. als.
[Grand Hôtel Métropole, Milan, stationery]

March 28, 1922

Dear Ma & Pa,—

I am writing you my first letter from Italy. I, and my American friend [Melville] Smith, started out from Paris as we had planned on Sunday. As we travelled 2nd class, and there are no sleeping cars except in 1st class, we did our best to doze off, now and then during the night. At 7 A.M. on Monday morning we arrived at the Swiss border line and had breakfast after having our suit cases examined by the custom[s] officers. At two in the afternoon we had to go thru the same rigamarole with the Italian authorities. At 6:30 in the evening we were in Milano, our first stop. We have gotten settled in an excellent hotel, where they charge 60 lire ($3.00 about) a day for room and 3 meals a day. Everyone talks French or English in the hotel, at least, so it is very simple to get around. Already I have done a great deal of walking around town and find it very fascinating. The main points of interest are the marvellous cathedral and the Opera House, called La Scala. We have already climbed to the top of the cathedral from where one can see for miles and miles around. To-night we have seats for the opera. We shall probably go there once again tomorrow night, and on Thursday, leave for Rome, where I intend to spend most of my time in Italy. One realizes very quickly here that the great majority of Italians are very different from the Wops we are used to at home. I forgot to mention that on our trip here, I got my first glimpse of the Alps and the Italian Lakes. They were both sights I shall never forget.

Before leaving Paris I received your letter and the corn plasters. Tell Pop not to buy any more copies of my piece[1] at Shirmers at that outrageous price, as I can buy them at Durands for 45¢, any day. In my last letter I told you I had sold two more of my compositions. I am sorry to say it will be a longer while than I had hoped before you will see them in print as I am not to get the proofs before the summer. There is one advantage, however. The publisher writes to me that the pieces will probably first be printed in a musical magazine which comes out once a year in November.[2] But since anything printed in that magazine must never have been previously published, we shall probably have to wait till next November to see them in print. After being put in the magazine (which means more royalties), they will be printed separately.

About one week after you receive this letter I shall be back in Paris with about 500 francs in the bank. As I should hate to be stranded for money, I am letting you know well in advance the state of my financial affairs.

As it is a very beautiful day and I am anxious to see more of Milan, I will close with love to all.

Aaron

P.S. I shall write again when I get to Rome.

1. *The Cat and the Mouse.*

2. Perhaps the *Revue musicale,* though it did not "come out once a year in November," and no Copland piece was published in the magazine.

To his parents

AC/LC. als.

[Hotel Lugano Pension Fleurie, Rome, stationery]

Apr. 7th, 1922

Dear Ma & Pa,—

I have now been in Rome 8 days and like the town very much. I shall stay here until the 12th, which will mean that I will have spent 1 day less than 2 weeks in Rome. On the 12th I take the train at 8:30 A.M. and arrive at Florance at about 2 in the afternoon. I shall have only 3 days in Florance and on the 15th start for "home" (Paris) at 5 p.m. We get to Paris the next day at 8 p.m.! So now you have my routine which I shall have accomplished, I suppose, before you get this letter.

Altho I have been flying around Rome all week, trying to see the sights, I don't know how I can fill 4 pages this week. I can't very well describe all I've seen, as that wouldn't be very interisting for you. I have, tho, attended the opera twice and also heard several concerts. We have presented some of the letters Mlle. Boulanger gave us and have been treated very kindly. The Hotel-Pension I have chosen has proved very satisfactory. They feed one a great deal of sphaghetti, rice, cheese and fruit, besides the usual dishes.

Harold has sent me the clipping I am enclosing. Of course, it was he who gave the reporter the information as to my present and future whereabouts.

I also got a letter from Herbert Elwell, the friend I visited in London. He is coming to Paris soon and will look me up. I have just received a letter from Aaron Schaffer. I had sent him a copy of my piece,[1] and he got one of the students at the university to study it and play it for him. The letter was so nice I was almost tempted to enclose it. It seems I'm getting famous in Austin. By the way, he intends to come to Europe this summer and I may see him in Berlin about August 1st as he goes to Paris first, in July.

Rather than hold this letter off for more news to write, I am going to send it off to let you know I am in the best of health and enjoying myself immensely. Love to all.

Affectionately,

Aaron

P.S. Of course, I'll let you know as soon as I arrive at Florance.

---

1. *The Cat and the Mouse.*

To his parents

AC/LC. als.
[Albergo-Pensione Nardini, Firenze, stationery]
(The Italian word for Florance)[1]

6 p.m. Teus. Apr. 11, 1922

Dear Ma & Pa,—

This morning at 9 P.M. [*sic*] I left Rome, one day earlier than I had intended, as everyone told me so much about the beauties of Florance, that I thought I ought to have 4 days here at least. We arrived at 2:30 P.M., after having a delicious dinner on the train. Then I began searching for a room in a hotel, which just now, is like looking for a pin in a haystack. Finally, after going into 10 places (with no exaggeration), I struck this one an hour ago by some miracle. Already I have bought a ticket for the opera to-night and now I am resting and writing to you at the same time.

Yesterday, before leaving Rome, I received your letter of the 26th which Harold forwarded to me. I was very sorry to hear Grandma had been so sick and hope she is well now.

Once more, you say you are thinking very seriously about coming to Europe. Of course, I wrote two letters ago, what I thought of the idea.[2] The only circumstance which has changed is that you say it is your only chance of coming as pop will go into buisiness next winter. I also see that it is not a question of Texas or Europe, but of a summer in the mountains or Europe. Yet, in spite of everything, if you ask me where you will get most rest and enjoyment I should say in the mountains. This applies particularly to Pop, whom I imagine, would have a better time in a decent Yiddisher hotel with plenty of pinochle than in the swellest dumps in Europe. Then don't forget that July and August are two very hot months in all the big cities here, and one has no energy for sight seeing. And yet, after all is said and done, I may be all wrong. You may enjoy some good Pilsner Beer in a good old German beer garden very much. So, in the end I leave it for you to decide what to do, and you can easily imagine how anxiously I shall await your final decision. I was thinking that you might even put off the trip till next spring (the ideal time to come) if Pop wasn't very anxious to go, and come here with Laurine or Dorothy or someone else in the family, and then we might all come home together. But if you decide to come in July let me know very soon as I shall have lots of advice to give you about traveling and so forth. It seems quite wonderful that there should even be a slight chance that I may see you in less than three months.

Now, to come to less important matters, I am very glad to hear of the good news you have to tell in each letter about my first published piece. The incident with the salesman at Shirmer's was very amusing indeed. You seem to be selling so many copies that I almost regret not having it published on a royalty basis. Don't be discouraged if no one seems able to play it for you, as its not nearly so difficult as they make it, which point I hope to illustrate some day. (Let me say right here that that famous critic of music, Mr. Charles Marcus,[3] is not going to like it!)

So there has been a great fuss about a name for the new baby. Well, that is as it should be. I, as a member of the family, have a right to put in my two cents, have I not? Therefore, as a connoisseur of names, I hereby suggest a name which I think is neither too common nor too fancy, too Jewish nor too Goyish, in short,—just right. Here we have it,—GINA (pronounce the G soft); or you can say it just that way and spell it like this—DJINA.[4] Of course, I know every-one's opinion of this marvellous suggestion of mine,—Lou will think it too stuck-up, Dorothy will think it too stagey, La will think it too odd and so forth,—but Lils will agree with me! Anyway, now that I've had my say, you can name the kid anything you like.

I will let you know when I arrive in Paris next Sunday. I leave Florance Sat. at 5:30 P.M. and arrive next day at 8 P.M.

Love to all.

Aaron

---

1. Explaining the word "Firenze" on the letterhead.

2. Copland had written to his parents on April 1: "And I was quite astounded to hear you asking my advice as to a trip to Europe. I am sure you understand it is very difficult for me to say whether you should come or not, because many of the things here which interest me immensely would not concern you at all. If you are deciding to either go to Texas and California or Europe, I most certainly would advise Texas, where you know many people and the language. Traveling for 2 or 3 months in Europe is an extremely tiresome affair, not to mention the expense which would be considerable since you would always have to travel 1st class. If you were coming to live for 6 months or a year it would be an entirely different matter. In any case, you ought really go to Texas and California first, as you have so long planned doing. I have a faint suspicion that the idea of coming to Europe would not have entered your head if I had not been here. But as much as I should like to see you, I do not think it a sufficient reason for so long a trip."

3. Copland's friend and, later, brother-in-law.

4. Not coincidentally, Copland had met harpist Djina Ostrowska at Fontainebleau, and she first encouraged him to visit Boulanger's harmony classes. See C & P I, 48.

The following 1922 letter was not originally the last in the series of remarkable diary-letters: when the Copland Collection reached the Library of Congress, the letters to his parents were in an envelope labeled "A.C. Letters from Paris to his parents / 1921–1924." Despite this title, the series as received by the library ended with the following letter. What has happened to the later letters is not known.

To his family

AC/LC. als.

Apr. 24, 1922

Dear Ma & Pa,—

It is needless for me to tell you how very deeply moved I was to hear of Grandma's death. I well remember the time I went to the Bronx to say good-bye to her, and something seemed to tell me then that I was seeing her for the last time. I was sorry that the card I sent Uncle Sam from Italy must have arrived at such an inopportune time.

A few days ago I received a card from Harold from Berlin. He will be back with me at the end of the week. Of course, I miss him very much, as you can easily understand that living together for so long has made us inseparable friends. But his trip to Berlin will help me a great deal in the way of practical knowledge of the city such as where to stay, where the good restaurants, bookshops etc. are, and all about the theatres and concerts.

During his absence from Paris, I have been leading a very secluded life, given up entirely to music and books. I wonder if you ever realize what a large part the reading of books on all imaginable subjects plays in my existence. I read, not to learn anything, but from the pure love of it. Had I gone to college, I should be graduating this year, but I never regret not having done so. Of course, there are plenty of people, who must see you with a college diploma to make them believe you are educated, but I feel my extensive reading has done a great deal to make up for any Geometry or Chemistry they teach one there. I often think, in planning ahead, that rather than teach or concertize to make a living, I should greatly prefer to write on musical subjects. I intend to make an attempt at writing some short articles this summer and sending them to musi-cal papers at home and see what happens.

To-morrow I recommence work with Mademoiselle Boulanger and still have about 5 lessons before the finish. I am not bothering to begin again with my piano teacher for so short a time. He was, in many ways, a very satisfactory teacher, but not, I am sorry to say, an entire success, at least, not a success in the sense that Nadia Boulanger is.

Already I am wondering what to do with all the books and music I have, and which will weigh down my trunk so badly. Then, I must leave lots of room to get more in, in Germany (particularly music) where things will be so cheap. There are two solutions, either I shall make a package and send it to you, or I shall put it in care of some reliable person in Paris, to keep for me.

I am still waiting as patiently as can be expected to hear of your decision about the European trip. Why must there be so many miles and miles of unnecessary water between us? Hope you are all in good health. My love to everybody.

Aaron

P.S. I received Jenny's Easter card and thank her for me.

During the summers of 1922 and 1923 Copland traveled for the first time to Germanic countries: Germany in 1922 and Austria in 1923. The following letter, describing his trip to Germany, is the first of his surviving letters to Nadia Boulanger.

To Nadia Boulanger

AC/LC. als.

Bei F. Jürges—
Brückenallee 17, Berlin
Aug. 15, 1922

Dear Mademoiselle Boulanger,—

If I have not written to you since the first card I sent, it is simply because there is so very little to write about. Even now, my main purpose in writing is to let you know that I intend to be back in Paris towards the beginning of October and hope you will remember to save me an hour. It is needless to tell you how anxiously I look forward to recommencing work with you again, n'est ce pas?

I have been in Berlin ever since I left Paris in June, but I haven't any very nice things to say of the city. D'abord c'est beaucoup trop bourgeois ici! Et puis, they drink too much beer here. I'm afraid that in my year spent in France, my view point has become so Gallic that I can't understand the Germans. Certainly they are not "très sympathique." The one good thing there is to say centers around money matters. One can live here twice as well as at Paris for half the money. Because of this, I expect to bring much music back with me, some of which I think you will be interested to see. (Incidentally, if you care to have me buy some music for you, just let me know what you wish, and I will be only too glad to send it to you.)

Naturally, since it is now the summer season, there is no serious music being performed. Before the opera closed I heard Max Schillings['s] "Mona Lisa," Hans Pfitzner's "Palestrina," and Busoni's one act "Arlecchino." None of these were very interesting. Most German musical activity seems to be centered in Vienna around Schoenberg and his pupils such as Egon Wellesz and Anton Webern. Whatever happens of any importance in Berlin seems to emanate from Schrecker[1] and his pupils.

As for myself, I have had ideal conditions for working,—a quiet room, an excellent piano and very few distractions as I know practically no one here. I have read over a great deal of new music; have gone thru the orchestral scores of "Pelleas," "Till Eulenspiegel" and [Scriabin's] "Le Poeme de l'Extase" note for note, to mention only a few. As for actual composition, my Ballet[2] is progressing very slowly but surely. I still can't find a satisfactory story to go with it, but I continue to develop the separate dances. Perhaps—peut être—we may orchestrate them together this winter.

I have not yet received the proofs of my "Passacaglia" or the "Old Poem" from Monsieur Senart, but as he said they would come "au courant de l'été" there is still time.

Please give my very best regards to Smiss[3] and also [to] Herbert Elwell if he is still at Paris. I hope your class at Fontainebleau is not too "ennuyeux"! Is it too much for me to hope that you may find time to send "un petit mot"?

Sincerely yours,

Aaron Copland

---

1. Franz Schreker, whose operas *Die Gezeichneten* (1918) and *Dear Schatzgräber* (1920) had been particularly successful.

2. This piece became the ballet *Grohg* (1925).

3. Fellow American and Boulanger student Melville Smith, with a teasing reference to Boulanger's French accent.

To Nadia Boulanger

AC/LC. als.

Bei Frau Steinhof
IX Hörlgasse 9, Vienne
July 25, 1923

Dear Mademoiselle Boulanger,—

Nothing of very great importance has happened to me since I left Paris. But I want to write you at least a few words so that you may have no cause for thinking that I have forgotten you. No! I most certainly haven't forgotten you. In fact, if I liked, I might get really sentimental about the Rue Ballu and all that it has meant and still means to me. Mais, après tout, vous le savez aussi bien que moi, et puis—n'est-ce pas, c'est vous qui a dit—'Copland n'est pas romantique du tout'!? [But, after all, you know it as well as I, and moreover—it is you who said—'Copland is not at all romantic,' right!?] Not being romantic, I mustn't get 'sentimental' about anything, must I? But I am sure you will understand what I feel I owe you after two years of work, just as you understood the emotion in my apparently cold Passacaglia. (Est-ce que, vraiment, vous comprenez quelque chose dans cet anglais un peu 'tordu'?) [Can you understand something of this slightly convoluted English?]

Next week I am going to Salzburg with my friend M. Clurman. Six successive evenings of modern music[1] should prove a big enough feast for even so insatiable a gourmand as myself. I suppose you have seen the programmes, but to be sure, I am enclosing a copy. I am particularly interested in hearing Miaskowsky's work,[2] because Boris de Schloezer, whose opinions are generally reliable, has spoken very well of him. Bartok's second violin sonata—(the first is already published);—Hindemith's Clarinet quintette and the works by Bliss, Prokofieff, & Krenek[3] should be especially worth while. Then there are the unknown names of Janacek, Shoeck, Jarnach etc. which sound tempt-ing.[4] All in all, the programmes are satisfying, but I wonder why they thought it necessary to give Roussel's 'Divertimento' or Szymanowski's early 'Hafis-lieder' or Lord Berners' rather silly 'Valses bourgeoises.' Et Sem Dresden—je me demande ce que ça peut être! [And Sem Dresden[5]—who's that!] (I have noticed with regret that Mlle. de Manziarly's 'Trio' is not included on the list.) I shall write you an account of the Festival and we shall hear what we shall hear.

After spending five weeks in Vienna, I can only say that it is 'pas mal,'—beaucoup plus sympathique que Berlin, mais loin d'être Paris ['not bad'—much more sympathetic than Berlin but far from being Paris]. It lacks, per-haps due to the war, a certain care-free atmosphere—[']la joie de vivre.' But of course, these are first impressions, and I will be able to judge it better when I am here longer.

I have found excellent surroundings in which to work and spend most of my time on composition and learning German. Thru an abonnement [subscrip-tion] I am enabled to read over lots of new music and I am specializing in Bruckner, Reger and Mahler! (Vous savez que Reger est pour les Allemands ce que Fauré est pour les Francais!) [You know that Reger is for the Germans what Fauré is for the French!] I have played a Violin Sonata by Reger (op 72) which is surprisingly good and encourages me to get more familiar with his work. On the other hand, for me, Bruckner is 'carrément mauvais' [just plain bad]!

Pour le ballet, il n'y a q'une chose à dire: je fais mon possible—qui est quelque fois cinq heures par jour. [As for the ballet, I can say only: I do my best—which is sometimes 5 hours a day.] So even if I don't accomplish any-thing I have the satisfaction of knowing that I worked hard!

Et Gargenville?[6] et Fontainebleau? Et Madame Boulanger et Hesselberg et Mary Sanders et tout le monde va bien j'espere [and everyone is well, I hope].

Sincerely,

A. Copland

P.S. Is there any music you should like me to send you?

---

1. The first of the annual festivals of the International Society for Contemporary Music.

2. The piece was not played.

3. These are Arthur Bliss's *Rhapsody* for mezzo, tenor, and chamber ensemble; Sergey Pro-kofiev's *Overture on Hebrew Themes*, and Ernst Krenek's Third String Quartet.

4. Leoš Janáček's Third Sonata for Violin and Piano, Othmar Schoeck's *Hafislieder*, and Phi-lipp Jarnach's Sonatina for flute and piano were performed.

5. Sem Dresden, a conservative Dutch composer, whose Sonata for Flute and Harp was performed at the Salzburg ISCM Festival. Dresden was the co-founder in 1922 of the Dutch chapter of the ISCM.

6. Nadia Boulanger's home near Fontainebleau.

Copland returned to Paris in the fall of 1923 and resumed his composi-
tion lessons with Boulanger for one more year. He then set sail for New
York City in June 1924 with a commission to write a work for organ and
orchestra, with Nadia Boulanger as the soloist, to be performed by both the
New York Symphony Orchestra, conducted by Walter Damrosch, and the
Boston Symphony Orchestra, led by Serge Koussevitzky.

To Nadia Boulanger

AC/LC. als.
[Paquebot "France" stationery]

12 Juin [1924]

Chère Mademoiselle,—

Demain soir nous y serons. Tant mieux! Nous avons eu un traversée misér-
able, surtout quand on pense que c'est la belle saison. Comme marin je suis
raté—vous pouvez deviner le reste. Enfin, aujourd'hui tout ça est bien fini—il
fait très beau, la mer est calme, et je vous ecrit.

Mais ce n'est pas la lettre que j'avais l'intention de vous écrire. Après vendredi soir, je me suis dit qu'il faut tout de même écrire quelque chose pour être
bien sûr qu'elle comprenne. Comprendre quoi? Mais c'est justement ça que je
ne peux pas vous dire maintenant, six jours après. (Voilà ce que c'est d'être
américain!) Mais vendredi soir, je vous assure, j'étais assez ému pour vous dire
tout—how grateful I am for everything you did for me in those three years as
teacher, advisor and friend—seulement, il y avait trop de monde. Aujourd'hui,
avec mon bon sens habituel, je suis sûr que vous comprenez, et je n'ai plus
besoin de vous rien dire.

Et Clurman et moi, nous sommes bien curieux de voir quel effet New York
va nous faire. En attendant, nous envoyons à Madame et à vous nos meillieures
amitiés and our very best regards to all the 'gang.'

A. Copland
P.S.: Clurman m'a dit qu'il va vous écrire de New York.

[Dear Mademoiselle,—

Tomorrow evening we will be there. Thank God! We have had a terrible
crossing, especially when one thinks that this is the good season. As a sailor, I'm
a failure—you can guess the rest. Anyway, today all that is quite over—it's a
beautiful day, the sea is calm, and I write to you.

But this is not the letter I intended to write you. After Friday evening, I told
myself that I had to write something to be sure she understands. Understands
what? But it is exactly this which I cannot tell you now, six days later. (This is
what being American is like!) But Friday evening, I assure you, I was moved

enough to tell you everything . . . only, there were too many people around. Now, with my usual good sense, I am sure you understand, and I don't need to tell you anything.

And Clurman and I, we are quite curious to see what effect New York will have on us. In the meantime, we send to Madame and you our warmest regards. . . .

P.S. Clurman told me he would write you from New York.]

CHAPTER TWO

The World of Modern Music, 1924–31

A fter his return from Paris, Copland concentrated on writing a work for organ and orchestra to be performed by Nadia Boulanger during her visit to the United States. Thanks to her connections with conductors Walter Damrosch, of the New York Symphony Orchestra, and Serge Koussevitzky, newly appointed to the Boston Symphony Orchestra, she had arranged a commission and two performances of Copland's piece, guaranteeing his auspicious introduction to the American public. Koussevitzky in particular proved a valuable supporter; after presenting the *Symphony for Organ and Orchestra* in February 1925, he eagerly premiered Copland's next big work, *Music for the Theatre* (1925), in a concert sponsored by the League of Composers, an organization devoted to contemporary music.

Copland quickly settled into the New York music scene, coming to know a group of young American composers centered around the League of Composers and assuming a position of some respect among his colleagues. He became involved with both the league and its journal, *Modern Music,* as well as the redoubtable women behind those two institutions: Claire Reis, executive director of the league, and Minna Lederman, editor of the journal. In 1925 Copland published the first of his many articles in *Modern Music,* at that time known as the *League of Composers' Review.* As a critic, Copland strove to be tactful, honest, and helpful. He was genuinely eager to promote the work of young composers, and to this end he and fellow American Roger Sessions created their own concert series in 1928, producing two or three programs of contemporary chamber music each year. Both Copland and Sessions spent a fair amount of time abroad during the four years of the concert series, and as a result much of their organizational work is documented in correspondence. The two composers argued frequently, however, and their collaboration ended in 1931. Their friendship eventually diminished to collegial amiability.

Also during this period, two of Copland's most important musical relationships were formed when he met Israel Citkowitz and Carlos Chávez in New York City around 1926. Citkowitz, who was nine years younger than Copland, was at first a protégé, whom Copland willingly nurtured. He sent Citkowitz to study with Boulanger, and in the summer of 1929 the two men lived together, though the experience seems not to have been a happy one. Chávez and Copland were peers, united in the quest to bring recognition to modern American composers. Letters to Citkowitz are unusually revealing of Copland's personal life and feelings, while those to Chávez frequently muse on professional as well as musical matters.

To Nadia Boulanger

AC/LC. als.

Aug. 26, 1924

Dear Mademoiselle Boulanger,

Thank you so much for the program. I can very easily imagine all the work it must have been to prepare five of my things to be played at Fontainebleau and I am extremely grateful to you for having taken so much trouble upon yourself.

I have been a little reluctant to write to you this time because I have nothing very glorious to tell about myself. Two weeks ago I politely resigned my position as jazz pianist at Milford.[1] I found it impossible to work on the organ sinfonietta[2] because I could get no piano in a quiet place. As the time was getting short, I thought I best to leave. During the six weeks I was there I got very fat (dites-le, au moins, à Marion Sarles!) [tell that, at least, to Marion Sarles!] and I made an ink copy of the 'Cortège Macabre.'[3]

Just now, I am in Brooklyn, living at my sister's house—but by the middle of September I hope to find a room for myself where I can work. I spend all my time now, working on the organ composition. Let me tell you how far it is advanced.—For several reasons I have decided to make it in three movements instead of four. The first movement will be a short andante (the andante I wrote in May), then the scherzo, and lastly will come the most important movement with which I originally thought I would begin the work. It will take about twenty minutes altogether. (Honneger's first violin sonata has three movements arranged something like that.)

So far I have completely finished only the first movement, which is also orchestrated. But the other two movements are, pour ainsi dire [so to speak], finished—that is, they are clear in my mind, but I must still write them down and orchestrate them and fill in the details. If I send it to you by October 1st, you will still have two full months to prepare it. It goes without saying that any corrections you make, I approve of, a priori. I am so glad Smiss is coming here,—as soon as I have shown him the first movement, I will send it to you before the other two movements. If you have anything to suggest, please, by all means, write me immediately.

Now that my score is ready for Koussevitski I have been wondering just what to do about having the parts copied. It is terribly expensive here, but I suppose it must be done, and I shall manage to get the necessary money somehow.

Forgive me for making this a 'business letter.' I should have preferred telling you about other things—our jazz-bands, for instance, or Gide's 'Corydon,' but I'll leave it for another letter.

Now that Smith has gone, Gargenville must be very quiet. Clurman and I expect to make him talk for hours and hours about everything that has happened since our departure. (By the way, did you receive Clurman's letter?)

I hope Madame Boulanger is in the best of health and hasn't completely forgotten me as yet. Remember me to everyone else I know in France! With best regards from Clurman.

Your devoted friend

A. Copland

Please address me:

Chez Mrs. C. Marcus

557 E. 12th St.

Brooklyn, N.Y.

---

1. Copland played as part of a jazz trio at the Hotel Colonial in Milford, Pennsylvania.
2. The *Symphony for Organ and Orchestra*.
3. A piece taken from Copland's unperformed ballet *Grohg*.

Boulanger came to the United States in the winter of 1924–25 to perform Copland's *Symphony for Organ and Orchestra* in New York and Boston. The piece was premiered by Walter Damrosch and the New York Symphony Orchestra on January 11, 1925, and heard in Boston that February. At that time Copland began a correspondence with conductor Serge Koussevitzky that lasted until the conductor's death in 1951. (It took Copland some time to notice the proper spelling of Koussevitzky's last name.)

To Serge Koussevitzky

SK/LC. als.

135 W. 74th St
New York City
Jan. 25th, 1925

My dear Mr. Koussevitsky,—

Mademoiselle Nadia Boulanger has told me that she intends to play my 'Symphony' for Organ and Orchestra with the Boston Symphony Orchestra on February 20th and 21st.

If you can spare half an hour when you are in New York this week I should be delighted to play my work for you on the piano. If you will telephone me (Trafalgar 0185) when you get here I can arrange to see you whenever it will be most convenient for you.

Trusting to hear from you, I am,
Sincerely yours,
Aaron Copland

After performing Copland's *Symphony for Organ and Orchestra* in New York and Boston, Boulanger returned to France in the spring of 1925.

To Nadia Boulanger

AC/LC. als.

135 W. 74 St.
April 3, 1925

Dear Mademoiselle,—

It was a great relief to know you were back safe. From the silence, I take it for granted you are never coming back here.[1] I suspected as much. Is there time yet to change your mind?

I have many little things to write you about. First, the Guggenheim Foundation. This was organized recently to give scholarships to young men like myself. Mr. Surrette[2] is on the Board of Trustees and has asked me for letters from my teachers. Must I bother you with this stupid business? I'm afraid I must. Please send me a letter of recommendation as soon as you can find time. Mr. Damrosh has already sent me one. The scholarship is for 2,500, is to begin in October, and can be used anywhere.

I suppose Miss Wolff told you about Rochester. It will be a good opportunity to hear the 'Cortège.'[3] I shall write you my impressions later. I had a rendez-vous with Koussevitzky here in New York. It came about in this manner. The League of Composers have asked me to compose a work for small chamber-orchestra, which they will have performed next season. Because Stokowski conducts 2 concerts of the other Guild,[4] they wanted to get Koussevitsky for 2 concerts for their League. I was chosen to see Koussevitsky about it. He is delighted and has accepted. (But it is still a secret so do not mention it too much. Dieu sait pourquoi! [God knows why!]) At first, I thought of setting part of Rimbaud's 'Saison en Enfer,' but I have changed my mind and now I think I will write a series of pieces to be called 'Incidental Music for an Imaginary Drama.'[5] I think that is a better idea. I even have a few themes already. While talking to Koussevitsky, he said that he was willing to play anything I gave him next season, and had even announced over the radio that he would repeat my 'Symphony [for Organ and Orchestra]' at the end of this season on an all-American program. But since time is too short, the all-American program will not be given until next winter. (Who will play the organ part, I wonder?)

Puisqu'il est si emballé que ça [Since he is so enthusiastic], it occurred to me only today that perhaps I can get him to perform the entire ballet, divided into three movements like this:

I Cortège Macabre

II Three Danses

III Fourth Danse and Finale.

It is all no longer than an ordinary symphony and I believe is well contrasted. Of course, if this is too much for him to swallow I shall give him only the 'Three Dances.'

So much for possible performances, for all of which I have only you to thank.

I have written letters to Bloch and to Sokoloff.[6] I received two lovely ones from Marcelle and from Hesselberg.[7] They gave the flute and clarinet song here and G. Laurent wants to give it in Boston in April.[8] The performance here was quite bad—I think I shall add two more songs to Elizabethan words and make a group as you suggested long ago.[9]

Mengelberg gave the Second Symphony with chorus of Mahler. How very modern the orchestration is! Thirty years ahead of its time. How I wish I could hear all the others, especially the 'Seventh.' The music critics treat Mahler badly in New York. I shall write an article 'In defense of Mahler.'[10] Once more I have you to thank for discovering Mahler for me!

Yours

A.C.

P.S. Please don't forget the Guggenheim letter. And the score of the Symphony? Is it being copied? I have 'un peu d'argent' [a little bit of money] now so give it to a copyist and send me the bill. Also please have a second copy made of the organ part and send the bill also.

---

1. Boulanger first returned to the United States for an extended visit during World War II. She visited several times in later years, once to conduct the premiere of Copland's Nonet.

2. Thomas Whitney Surette, music educator, 1861–1941.

3. *Cortège macabre* was premiered by Howard Hanson and the Rochester Symphony Orchestra on May 2, 1925.

4. The International Composers' Guild, chaired by Edgar Varèse, was the predecessor and rival of the League of Composers.

5. The final title would be *Music for the Theatre.*

6. Nicolai Sokoloff, conductor of the Cleveland Orchestra. At the time Ernest Bloch was director of the Cleveland Institute of Music (he would resign one month later).

7. Marcelle de Manziarly, fellow student of Nadia Boulanger. She would be the dedicatee of Copland's "Heart, We Will Forget Him" from the song-cycle *Twelve Poems of Emily Dickinson.* Eyvind Hesselberg was also a Boulanger student.

8. "As It Fell upon a Day." Georges Laurent was principal flutist of the Boston Symphony Orchestra.

9. These were never written.

10. "Defends the Music of Mahler," letter to the editor, *New York Times,* April 5, 1925.

In 1925, Copland published a brief article on George Antheil in the *League of Composers' Review* (soon to be retitled *Modern Music*). Antheil was furious at the article (which seems generally kind and only slightly patronizing today) and sent editor Minna Lederman a two-page, single-spaced letter that he demanded be published in response. ("My concerts in Europe have not 'resembled' riots . . . they were riots"; "[Copland's] twaddle about 'structure' and 'a sense of climax' betray his fundamental Faure and Ravel nature.") Copland's letter to Antheil was probably written at the request of Lederman in an attempt to defuse the situation. Copland and Antheil maintained a slightly bristly friendship until Antheil's death.

To George Antheil

GA/Columbia. als.

14 April [1925]

My dear Antheil,

I have meant to write you for some time past. I take it for granted that you have seen the article I wrote about you and which was published in the January number of the League of Composers Review.[1]

The idea of writing that article came to me as a result of the reception given your Jazz Sonata at a concert earlier in the season.[2] All the music critics took the stupid attitude that you were a mere bluff, trying to scandalize the musical public. I decided to do what little I could to offset that prevalent notion, knowing as I did from our personal contact, how very sincere and very talented you are.

In writing the article I decided not to do mere propaganda, but to give my candid and purely personal opinion of as much of your work as I had heard—an opinion which I felt no hesitation in writing for print since I had already made it clear during our afternoons of musical discussion.

I am writing all this simply because I know how sensitive you are as a rule, to all that is said or published about you or your music,—and I want to urge you to take my article in the spirit in which I wrote it.

I hope this letter is entirely unnecessary. I had rather not written the article at all, if it is to cause any strained feelings on your part.

Write to me, won't you? I should like to hear more about the 'Ballet Mechanique'[3] and what other interesting things you are doing. Are you thinking of coming back to America soon? I hope so, we need a little excitement around these parts.

Give my best regards to Miss Beach.[4]

Sincerely,

Aaron

---

1. Aaron Copland, "George Antheil," *League of Composers' Review* 2 (January 1925): 26–28.

2. Antheil's *Jazz Sonata* for piano (1922).

3. Antheil's *Ballet mécanique* (1924).

4. Sylvia Beach, owner of the Parisian bookstore Shakespeare and Company, over which Antheil lived.

To Serge Koussevitzky

AC/LC. als.

Oct. 6, 1925
135 W. 74th St.
New York City, N.Y.

My dear Mr. Koussevitsky:

Mrs. Reis has asked me to inform you that the League of Composers has accepted my new work for chamber orchestra ("Music for the Theatre") for performance on the 28th of November. I should like to send you the score immediately, but with your permission, I shall first have the parts copied, which will take a few weeks. I hope you will have no objections if I come to Boston to hear the rehearsels, and perhaps, a day or two before they begin, you will allow me to give you an idea of the work at the piano, as we did last winter with the 'Symphony.'

Since I have mentioned the 'Symphony,' I shall take the liberty of pointing out that if you intend to repeat that work, it will be necessary to find another organist, as Mademoiselle Boulanger will not be in America this season. I should be glad to send the organ part to whomever you may select.

Also, I want you to know that I have a new score for large orchestra ("Three Dances") that I am keeping for you and the Boston Symphony. The parts are almost ready, I only await your pleasure in the matter.

I sincerely trust that my new works may not be unworthy to have expended on them the genius of your baton.

With kindest regards to Madame Koussevitsky, I am,

Yours devotedly,

Aaron Copland

In 1926, Copland once again set sail for Europe, where he spent the summer with Harold Clurman.

To Israel Citkowitz

AC/LC. als.

Villa Cendrillon
Guéthary, Basses Pyrénées
France—July 12 [1926]

Dear Israel,—

I could write you a young book. So very many things have taken place since my last letter, that merely to mention them would fill a page. Since you last heard from me, I've taken my little turn around Europe: Zurich, Munich, Strassburg and Paris; and then off again here to this ideal séjour on the south-west coast of France—GUÉTHARY. Not bad for a quiet boy like myself.

But to really treat you properly, I should begin even further back,—on a certain Saturday afternoon in the middle of June.[1] The scene is a beautiful theatre off the Champs-Elysées, filled to the last strapontin, with an audience of more than 2,000 people among whom one can distinguish James Joyce, Serge Koussevitsky, Ezra Pound, Darius Milhaud, Nadia Boulanger, Marcel Duchamp, Alfred Knopf, Boris de Schloezer etc. etc., each and everyone buzzing with the excitement and expectation of hearing for the first time anywhere a program which contained—oh marvel of marvels—two new works from the pen of that young genius, your only true rival—George Antheil! Must I say more? To say more is to spoil all. The proud possessor of this very extraordinary audience fed it on Hashed Potpourri of almost every 19th-century composer mentioned in the music histories (Symphony in F) and then proceeded to out-sack the 'Sacre' with the aid of a Pleyela and amplifiers, ventilators, buzzers and other what-nots (Ballet Mecanique).[2] No ordinary concert as you can see. The Symphony was a disappointment even to such Antheilians as myself, but the Ballet Mecanique brought forth the usual near-riot so everyone went home content. Though it give you your usual attack of apoplexy, I am in all honesty bound to repeat my unshakeable conviction—the boy is a genius. Need I add that he has yet to write a work which shows it. If he keeps on exactly as he has started, the sum total of all his genius will be exactly nothing. Voilà!

The following day we left for Zurich[3] and spent three pleasant days there, hob-nobbing with the musical celebrities of Europe, Asia and Africa. There was only one composition that you should have heard (and that you will probably not hear soon) Anton Webern's Five Orchestral Pieces. The orchestral sonorities he manages to get are magical, nothing less. There was nothing insufferable at the festival, but on the other hand, nothing except Webern's pieces seemed strikingly original, and they were written in 1913.[4]

While in Zurich, I was able to play some of my stuff for the Universal Edition people and something may come of it. Which reminds me to tell you that only to-day I have received the proofs of the 'House on the Hill' and the 'Immorality' from 'my' Boston publishers, E. C. Shirmer, who now possess the signal honor of being the first gentlemen to print my music in America.[5] We poor American composers—(you ought to hear Louis Gruenberg elaborate on that subject)—no conductors and no publishers and no nothing.

Damrosch is going to repeat the Music for the Theatre! I wonder why. He wrote me a letter asking me to come with the score—I came—he glanced at it casually—we exchanged politenesses—and thats all there was to it. Simple, n'est ce pas? Who said it was difficult to get played in N.Y.

I was back from Germany before I received your letter, so the books you asked me to send must wait. But you can borrow my [copy of Arnold Schoenberg's] 'Harmonielehre' for as long as you like. Think twice before you write a 'Socrate.'[6] Satie's work is highly serious and its genius lies in its discreetness: he simply makes the music a frame in which to fit a literary masterpiece. It seems the only setting possible for literary masterpieces.

Its nice to hear you are working so well. So am I. But it would be a crime not to work, given the ideal conditions I have. We have settled for the summer in a little villa all our own, which is exactly what we needed. Guéthary is in the Basque country, a small village built on the hills which rise up from the sea. On our right, half an hour away, we have Biarritz, the hang-out of Michael Arlen[7] and his crowd and on the left nothing less than Spain. (Before the summer is out we have promised ourselves a bull-fight!) I am working steadily on the piano and orchestra affair,[8] which is now only a matter of time. For relaxation, a duck in the sea. We intend staying here till Sept. 1st[.] (Harold sails Aug 18 and will probably see you before I do.)

You wrote some sort of mish-mash in your letter about being neglected or something. May I be allowed to point out that I have received 3 letters from you and I am now sending my third? I know I should have answered sooner and I wanted to answer sooner, but um Gottes willen [for God's sake], when one is a promising young composer, can one do what one wants? Certainly not. You'll see!

Yours

Aaron

Virgil Thomson, Walter Piston, Herbert Elwell, and Aaron Copland at Nadia
Boulanger's, 1925. Provided courtesy of the Aaron Copland Collection at
the Library of Congress.

1. June 19, 1926.

2. *Le Sacre du printemps* (1913) by Igor Stravinsky. The Pleyela is a type of player piano.

3. Where the fourth festival of the International Society of Contemporary Music (ISCM) took place June 18–23.

4. Copland had in fact missed the opening concerts of the Zurich festival, which conflicted with Antheil's concert: thus he had not heard Zoltán Kodály's *Psalmus Hungaricus,* Arthur Honegger's *King David,* or Arnold Schoenberg's Wind Quintet. He did, however, hear Paul Hindemith's *Concerto for Orchestra* and Kurt Weill's Concerto for Violin and Winds.

5. *The House on the Hill* (text by E. A. Robinson) and *An Immorality* (text by Ezra Pound) are both works for women's choir. Often known as *Two Choruses,* the pieces were written in 1925 for the Women's University Glee Club of New York.

6. Citkowitz had written that he was contemplating setting Plato's *Phaedo.* Erik Satie had set sections of the *Phaedo* as *Socrate* in 1918.

7. British novelist whose best-known work is *The Green Hat* (1924).

8. The Piano Concerto (1926).

Copland returned from Europe in the fall of 1926, settled into a studio on the Upper West Side of New York City, and set about completing his Piano Concerto.

To Roger Sessions

AC/LC. Photocopy of als.

223 West 78th St.
New York—March 18 [1927]

Dear Roger,—

I was delighted with your letter, the idea of your being in America[1] and the thought that we shall see each other soon (which, incidentally, will save me from writing at great length now). And how delightfully silly of you to have imagined that there was any shadow of a misunderstanding between us when my not writing to you is quite simply explained by the Concerto, that is finishing it and playing it. That was in February,[2] and then of course I thought it was too late to write, since Teddy[3] had been announcing your arrival for the last month and a half.

It goes without saying that I am very keen to see the Symphony.[4] As far as I know Koussie expects to do it in April—he even told me he might do an All-American program, though he didn't say whether or not he thought of doing the Symphony then. Anyway I know he is favorably disposed towards you and that an eventual performance is certain. I would even say it was certain for April if one could say that any conductor's plans are certain. Lets hope that Fate wills me in Boston at that time; otherwise I will have to be satisfied with a muddled version over the radio.

You are apparently not aware of the fact that I am returning to Europe this

Spring due to the fact that they are doing the 'Music for the Theatre' at the Festival in Frankfort. Wouldn't it be nice if we could sail together? I am thinking of going on the Homeric, April 30th but have made no reservations yet. If you know the boat you are taking, do let me know it. (I travel 2nd class as a rule, but am considering 3rd tourist . . . and you?) I shall be in Paris until the end of June—then to Frankfort—and then somewhere for the summer in Germany or Italy.

I'm glad you liked the Jazz article.[5] It has helped considerably to get the whole business out of my system. You will find me a young man admirably stripped of all theories now. Lets hope it lasts.

Heres to seeing you soon

Yours,

Aaron

P.S. My telephone no. is Susquehanna 0528

---

1. Sessions had written (February 25, 1927) that he would be in the United States from March 15 to April 30.

2. Actually, Copland's Concerto was first performed January 28, 1927.

3. Composer Theodore Chanler, a friend of Copland's and fellow student of Boulanger's.

4. Sessions's First Symphony (1926–27).

5. Aaron Copland, "Jazz Structure and Influence," *Modern Music* 4 (January–February 1927): 9–14.

Copland indeed returned to Europe in the spring of 1927, spending the majority of the summer in Germany.

To Nicolas Slonimsky[1]

NS/LC. als.

Königstein i. Taunus
July 14, 1927

Dear Kolya,—

I'm a pig! I'm a pig and a sinner and a wretch. But apparently I'd rather be all those things than write a letter. I detest writing letters and it is my great ambition in this world to find a friend who'll love me so that he'll be willing to write me letters without ever expecting an answer. (Did ever selfishness go further?) But even a pig has a conscience and my conscience has been giving me no rest for the past week saying 'Aaron my boy, you simply got to write to your old friend Kolya.' Whereupon, here I am.

For the summer I am tucked away all by my lonesome in this little German country resort, one hour outside of Frankfurt. I drink large quantities of 'pier'

[beer] for the sake of my inspiration. For two months its an ideal life, particularly since I know that on Sept 10th I set sail once more for the crowds and excitements of New York.

The Festival in Frankfurt[2] was more notable for its banquets and lunches than for the music presented. My own piece[3] came last in a three hour program which finished the Fest and the poor fagged-out public could only be roused from its lethargy by the pin-pricks of a jazz mute. But the infamous viola solo put everyone to sleep;[4] that is, everyone except Hertzka[5] who seemed to like the piece and stayed awake. So much for Frankfurt. Undismayed, I am going to Baden-Baden to-morrow to more Festivals—chamber operas by our fat friend Darius [Milhaud], Hindemith, Toch, Kurt Weill.[6]

In Paris, I visited Tansman[7] convalescent at a Roman Catholic hospital. The talk turns invariably to the American tour with its wonders and marvels. Sascha [that is, Alexandre Tansman] is doing much better than Ravel it seems, with contracts pouring in from all sides. I also saw Sanroma[8] chez K— [Koussevitzky]. Why is he always so gay? We spoke of you and bemoaned the fact that you were so far away. Oh yes, and once K—himself spoke of you—not exactly in the same tone I admit—but still he did speak of you, your name passed his lips, which fact alone I find distinctly encouraging.[9]

Did I tell you I got a job as lecturer next season at the New School for Social Research in N.Y.? Twelve lectures, once a week, beginning Sept 30.

I hope to come home with a Trio on Jewish Themes and have a piece for large orchestra under way.[10] Unfortunately the chamber orchestra ideas seem to have gone up in smoke.[11] (Perhaps I am suffering under an inhibition in that direction . . . !)

Where are you in the world? Breaking the hearts of what young ladies at what summer hotel? (I wish you could have seen Dukelsky's[12] outfit when his Sonate pour orchestre was played. The boy has missed his vocation. He really should be editing a fashion sheet for the well-dressed man.)

If I don't like to write letters, I adore receiving them especially when I'm all alone in Germany . . .

As ever,

Aaron

P.S. For your Eagle Eye and the clippings may Heaven reward you.

---

1. Copland knew musical polymath Nicolas Slonimsky principally as Serge Koussevitzky's musical secretary through 1927 and as the organizer of chamber orchestras specializing in new music.

2. The fifth festival of the ISCM.

3. *Music for the Theatre* was performed on July 4.

4. The "infamous viola solo" is the slow, pensive solo in the Epilogue of *Music for the Theatre.*

5. Emil Hertzka, head of the music publishing firm Universal Edition.

6. At the festival of chamber opera held in Baden-Baden, Copland heard Milhaud's brief opera *L'Enlèvement d'Europe,* the premieres of Hindemith's *Hin und Zurück,* and Ernst Toch's *Die Prinzessin auf der Erbse.* Copland also caught a performance of the early, one-act version of Weill's *Mahagonny* (later known as *Mahagonny-Songspiel* to distinguish it from the full-length *Aufstieg und Fall der Stadt Mahagonny*). Copland's comments on the festival can be found in *Copland on Music* (New York: W. W. Norton, 1960), 183–88.

7. Composer and pianist Alexandre Tansman.

8. Jesús María Sanromá, official pianist of the Boston Symphony Orchestra and noted performer of contemporary music.

9. Slonimsky had been fired by Koussevitzky earlier in 1927, supposedly on account of a newspaper article that ran under the title "My Musical Secretary Knows More than I Do." See Nicolas Slonimsky, *Perfect Pitch: A Life Story* (New York: Oxford University Press, 1988), 104–5.

10. *Vitebsk* and the *Symphonic Ode.*

11. Slonimsky had apparently asked Copland to write a piece for his projected Chamber Orchestra of Boston, which gave its first concert on December 20, 1927.

12. Composer Vladimir Dukelsky, later known as Vernon Duke.

To Roger and Barbara Sessions

AC/LC. Photocopy of als.

> Haus Leopoldine
> Am Hainenberg[?]
> Königstein l./T.
> Aug 18 [1927]

Dear Barbara & Roger,—

I meant to write weeks ago to bless both of you for the leniency with which my deplorable conduct was overlooked. (Barbara's coals of fire particularly were a balm.) But, as you have probably discovered by now, I am a most efficient creature in everything except letter-writing. I remember your letters arrived just before I left for the festival at Baden-Baden—which, by the way, was much more interesting than the one at Frankfurt.

The decision of the Sessions family to return to America has caused much excitement in France if I can judge by the letters coming from Juziers. Both Israel [Citkowitz] and Roy Harris devoted a paragraph to the subject. I, for one, am DElighted and shall do everything in my power to make America seem so nice that you'll want to stay for good. (The first thing being to start our Young Composers Society . . . !)

My own days in Europe are numbered. I sail the 10th. Königstein has been very nice indeed, but the summer has seemed so frightfully short. I have been able to do little more than get a half dozen new things under way: a Trio on Jewish Themes, a string quartet movement, a new orchestral piece,[1] some E. E. Cummings songs,[2] some piano pieces. And now, back to America, to fight for every half hour I can devote to composition—besides the enormous amount of time to be wasted on 'lectures' on modern music. These are mere details—what I mustn't neglect to tell you is that Königstein hasn't been at all warm—nor so very lovely at that!

I am to hear [Richard Strauss's] Electra on Teusday. Roger, mon cher, you had better be satisfied with your thrills of 10 years ago and not take a chance hearing a real performance in 1927 if I can judge by playing over the score. How naive and sympathetic the banality in Mahler is, compared to the empty, heartless banality of Strauss. Though I must admit Strauss's harmonic sense is extremely acute and he never fails one at the most dramatic moments. I have been spending much time over [Stravinsky's] Oedipus Rex—a very different story indeed and I look forward to the discussions we are to have concerning it.

I hope all has been going well with both of you—that Barbara is completely restored to health and Roger has his Violin Concerto almost finished. Let me know when you expect to sail.

Faithfully, as ever,

Aaron

P.S. The Irony of Fate. Now that I am done with jazz an article by I. Goldberg is to appear in the Sept. 'Mercury' on 'A.C. and his Jazz.'[3]

---

1. *Symphonic Ode.*

2. In fact only one song, "Poet's Song," is known.

3. Isaac Goldberg, "Aaron Copland and His Jazz," *American Mercury* (September 1927): 63–65.

That September, Copland returned to New York and began teaching at the New School for Social Research.

To Nadia Boulanger

AC/LC. als.

223 West 78 St
New York
Dec. 19, 1927

Dear Mademoiselle,—

It seems like years since I wrote you last. I have nothing of any real importance to write you—I've written no new works hèlas!—but I have an irresistible desire to speak with you again after this long silence.

First let me list the various trajedies. (1) I have word from the Universal Edition from Vienna that they never did receive the 'As it fell upon a day' you sent to them. I suspected as much. Would there be any way of your tracing it at this late date? (I have a copy here of course.) (2) I am mystified by the fact that

I have never heard a word from Strecker about the violin pieces.[1] Do you know anything about it? I wrote as you told me to do, but have received no answer whatsoever so far. What should be done? (3) I sent your letter to Mengelberg 3 weeks ago. No reply yet. This looks ominous! To balance these evil tidings perhaps you should know that I have (1) a request from M. Hettich[2] for a vocalize-etude which I shall be glad to do if I can discover a model to go by, i.e., the books already published as a guide to what is wanted. (2) I have news from the Universal that the 'Music for the Theatre' is now transformed into 'Tragödie im Süden,' ein Ballet im Fünf Sätze. The ballet story is appallingly melodramatic, but the action has been well put to the music, and I have no doubt that the good German opera public will be delighted. The Universal assures me that a production is certain; even possibly this season yet. For once, it is pleasant to sit back and watch a formidable organization like the Universal do the unpleasant business of finding performances.[3]

Roy [Harris] is here making the winter more lively. I am astounded by his business-like efficiency—I never realized he had it in him. Imagine, he has seen and played his music to everyone of any importance in New York from Varèse to dieu sait qui [God knows whom]. And his activities in behalf of a good performance of his Sextet are amazing.[4] But seriously, when I think of him as I first knew him, and think now of the choruses,[5] I can't help but marvel at the progress he has made—and marvel at you too, who made it possible. He plans to return in February and he seems truly anxious to get back.

I have only one more lecture to give in my course. They offered me a second series of 12, but I refused because I wish to have all my time for composition after Jan 1. When I think that 1927 is coming to a close and that I have produced no work signed 1927, I assure you I have a sinking feeling of the heart.[6] It is as if the entire year were wasted. This won't happen again if I can help it! Nevertheless I have agreed to give a second course next October. We are ending the season with a concert—I am enclosing a program to amuse you. I am extremely impatient to get back to work once again.

Mrs. Wertheim[7] gave me $160. for Israel [Citkowitz]. Is he behaving himself? I often have bad visions of him causing you untold trouble and annoyance. Reassure me, please!

The seasons greetings to you and Madame.

Devotedly

A.C.

---

1. Copland's *Two Pieces* for violin and piano, "Nocturne" and "Ukelele Serenade," both composed in 1926. Willy Strecker was the director of the music publishing company B. Schotts Söhne.

2. A. L. Hettich, a professor of voice at the Paris Conservatoire, published a series of "vocalises-études" for voice and piano between 1907 and 1935. Many distinguished composers contributed wordless vocal solos to this series, including Gabriel Fauré, Vincent D'Indy, Darius

Milhaud, Francis Poulenc, and Maurice Ravel (whose *Vocalise-étude en forme d'un habanera* is the one work in the series to have entered the general repertoire). American composers who wrote vocalises-études for Hettich include Copland, Frederick Jacobi, Henry Hadley, Lazare Saminsky, and Blair Fairchild.

3. *Tragödie im Süden* was never produced.

4. The "Sextet" is actually Harris's Concerto for piano, clarinet, and string quartet (1927). This piece influenced Copland's Sextet (1937), an arrangement of his *Short Symphony* (1933).

5. Probably student works composed for Boulanger, like Copland's *Four Motets.* No known work by Harris from before 1928 fits in this context.

6. In fact, "Poet's Song," to the words of E. E. Cummings, is dated 1927. Copland had hoped this would be part of a cycle; thus he did not see it at the time as a completed work.

7. Alma Wertheim was a well-known patron of the arts who had given Copland $1,000 soon after he returned from Paris in 1924. She also supported the Cos Cob Press, a small music publishing firm founded in 1929 that focused on scores by young American composers.

To Roger Sessions

AC/LC. Photocopy of als.

Monday [March? 1928]

Dear Roger,—

Something has come up which needs your immediate advice. The International Society for Contemporary Music suggests that we give our concerts under their auspices. There are several pros and cons. We are given absolute freedom in every way. The I.S.C.M. will concern itself with the practical end— get the hall, print programs etc. We can probably get more publicity for the concerts because of their name and possibly make surer of having the critics also. The I.S.C.M. (Alfred Human is president) is what sends the music for the International Festivals in Europe as I suppose you know. They have never had any other activity, such as sponsoring concerts etc., but, as I had known, from earlier in the winter, are anxious to be more active. This offer came thru Mrs. Reis who is on the board of the I.S.C.M.! (I suppose she would get a certain satisfaction from dragging along in this precarious way with us rather than be left out altogether from the 'Youth Movement.') I don't think this matters if our purposes are better served, however. There are several other advantages— composers who are played will be probably more impressed by a long title than an anonymous society, etc. etc.

My idea would be to announce the concerts thus: R.S. and A.C. present so and so and so and so under the auspices of the I.S.C.M.

The principal objection seems [to be] that we don't start that way with as complete a sense of freedom. There is almost certain to be a little confusion in the beginning as to what society is what in the mind of the public. Second, God knows what complications may arise.

One reason and one reason only makes me consider this offer very seriously and that is the fact that you will probably be gone for 3 years. If we start now, I want absolutely to continue. But I don't feel able to swing such a thing all by myself, without at least your moral support in America. I think it would look presumptious on my part to want to run a Society entirely alone—and it would look thus in the eyes of the public.

Tell me what you think. If you decide it would be better to go it alone, I'm willing. Only write within 24 hours after getting this if you can.

Autre chose [another thing]. Have any overtures been made to [composer] Quincy Porter?

Have you asked Teddy [Chanler] to cable a reply? Perhaps we can do his violin sonata if he has nothing new. After all, its never been given in public in its entirety.

Will Barbara please ask the Warfield-Bonime[1] combination if they will help perform one or two violin sonatas for us?

With my very best to you both and in haste

Aaron

---

1. Ruth Warfield, violin, and Gertrude Bonime, piano. Sessions wrote Copland on March 15, 1928: "Bonine [sic] is in Europe, I believe, but R. Warfield is, I am sure, willing to play."

To Barbara and Roger Sessions

AC/LC. Photocopy of als.

Monday eve. [April 1928]

Dear Barbara and Roger,—

I'm too tired and too sleepy to give you an adequate report of our debut but I'm rather happy about how it all panned out. I'm really sorry you weren't with us—I should have liked you to have been there so that we could have discussed the music (particularly Chavez'),[1] so that you could have passed on the spirit of the concert which I didn't think quite satisfactory, so that you could have helped out at the party which was a dismal affair etc. etc. People asked for you both and the moral responsibility of the occasion was rather heavy on my slim shoulders. But I'm a man to accept the inevitable—and everything that happens in connection with the two of you I always place in that category! Margy Naumberg[2] tells me you won't sail until after the 6th so you will be at one concert anyhow and that evens matters up considerably. As it happens, the Sonata[3] will be an invaluable aid in bracing up the second program which had been weakish in its original form.

To me the most surprising thing that took place was the way the critics turned out. I think its an indication of what the concerts mean to the musical life here generally. Mary C.[4] is sending you all of the clippings. They all damned Chavez which I think is a sign of the real excellence of his music . . . Anyhow the critics were there and we seemed like a very important organization! (Mrs Reis was astounded but very pleasant about it.) The audience seemed more literary and theatrical than musical. I don't quite understand why it was so. The enthusiasm, which was greater than at similar functions of the League[,] did not quite reach my expectations—does that surprise you?

Ruth Warfield, looking marvellously, played Teddy [Chanler]'s Sonata rather badly which wasn't surprising considering her recent illness and the short time she had to prepare it. [Walter] Piston was here for his final rehearsal and the concert and bowed in response to much applause—the audience liked the Three Pieces[5] though they seemed to me to be little more than well written. I don't know what the Thomson sounded like because I played the percussion part to the astonishment of Henry Cowell.[6] I won't go into Chavez' stuff now. I have copies of his music to play for you as soon as I can get you near a piano and my article on him is appearing in the N[ew] R[epublic] this Friday.[7]

Mary has been extremely efficient throughout, tho new problems have arisen which seem almost insoluble. The only wrong thing she did was to lose your telegram before I saw it, but I heard it from memory and if I hadn't been such an excited ass I would have sent one in return.

Yours, 'tired but happy'

A—

---

1. The Sonata for Piano, played by Chávez himself, and a set of three Sonatinas.

2. Margaret Naumburg, educator and author of *The Child and the World* (1928).

3. Sessions's First Piano Sonata (1927–30) was in fact not finished in time for the second concert.

4. Mary Senior Churchill, a noted patron of contemporary music and dedicatee of Copland's orchestral work *Statements* (1935). She funded the Copland-Sessions concerts.

5. Three Pieces for flute, clarinet, and bassoon, written in 1926.

6. Virgil Thomson, *Five Phrases from the Song of Solomon* for singer and percussion. Copland was the single percussionist and played a tom-tom, gong (one stroke), cymbals, and "a high, clear wood-block."

7. Aaron Copland, "Carlos Chávez—Mexican Composer," *New Republic* 54 (May 2, 1928): 322–23.

To Roger Sessions

AC/LC. Photocopy of als.

Sunday [April? 1928]

Dear Roger,—

Last week, when no letter came saying the [Piano] 'Sonata' was finished, I naturally began to suspect trouble. Your letter therefore was reassuring. Don't worry, twice underlined, should satisfy anyone.[1] However, you most certainly have my sympathy. I think writing a work to order for a set date excellent—when one has finished it. But, of course, the situation you are now in is horrible and my feelings as a fellow-composer and as a concert-manager are at war with one another. As the former, I should like to say, dont you worry; after all its the Sonata which is important and not its being ready by a set date. But, as co-director of the C-S Concerts I should like to see the public get what it is promised. (As the other co-director, I know you feel the same.) O Hell,—I hope I don't sound as if I were worried. I refuse to be like the famous cook who blew out his brains because the fish didn't arrive in time for the king's dinner.

All things considered, it would seem highly desirable that the Sonata be finished, however. You have until five minutes before the concert—24 hours a day.

I was delighted to hear you are coming to Washington.

Thank heavens, you have at last found something of which you can disapprove.[2] Naturally, I agree with you. Putting the importance on 'modern' and 'novel' is stupid—it simply happened because of a series of events which I can explain when I see you. I think, in general, tho, the publicity hasn't been bad. We already have about 30 subscribers for both concerts. Mary C.[hurchill] calls me up in the greatest excitement every time a new subscription comes in. You're really missing half the fun.

Theres been talk of a party after the concert. My idea was to ask people we like and the participants to go to some place after the concert. Mary C. was willing to stand the costs but I prefer it to be à la Boulanger, everyone paying for themselves. This will be a real innovation in modern music societies.

By the way, I hear thru dark channels that the L[eague] of C[omposers] has decided to invite the two of us to join their board! Don't breathe a word of this, whatever you do.

Theres nothing else.

[Pianist Richard] Buhlig is playing at our second concert nine pieces by [Dane] Rudhyar (Three Paeans), Adolf Weiss, a pupil of Schoenberg's, and Ruth Crawford a girl who lives in Chicago.[3] He refused to do the [Herbert] Elwell and I can't blame him (that I believe is my first real error as to music) so John Kirkpatrick is doing them instead. (Keep this under your hat too.)

Affectionately

[dash instead of signature]

---

1. "Don't worry about the sonata," Sessions had written and twice underlined. Nevertheless, the sonata was not finished in time for the concert. Pianist John Duke played only the first two movements in the concert, which took place on May 8.

2. Sessions had written: "Don't worry or apologize about not including my sonata in the next announcement. As you know 'modern music' in that sense bores me to tears, & I am very happy that I escaped. When we meet I may even take mild exception to that form of publicity which I don't feel advances our cause & might even do it harm."

3. That is, nine pieces by these three composers. Ruth Crawford (later Ruth Crawford Seeger), three of whose works were performed, would become one of the abiding American modernist composers.

To Nadia Boulanger

AC/LC. als.

Santa Fe,
New Mexico
June 1 [1928]

Dear Nadia,—

I should have written you these past many months, but there were so many things to write about I became paralyzed at the mere thought of transcribing them all to paper. And it always seems useless to write you unless I can write you <u>everything</u>. Now that I am 2,000 miles away from New York and our musical season is over all these things that seemed so important to write you then do not seem so any longer. Anyway you must have heard many of them from Roy [Harris] when he came back and recently from Roger [Sessions], perhaps also from Israel [Citkowitz] to whom I write regularly knowing how much he needs my moral support.

When I look back at the winter it seems to me that the only real thing accomplished was the fact that I have finished my slow movement for string quartet.[1] I have just made a copy for you because I am most anxious to know what you think of it. Please show it to Roy and to Israel. (I dedicated it to Roy because it was his enthusiasm for the opening phrase which gave me the incentive to finish it.) The rest of the winter was spent in giving lectures and giving concerts. I should so much have liked to discuss both of these activities of mine with you, particularly the concerts. They went off surprisingly well— particularly from the standpoint of the press. The difficulty will always be to find good music by Americans. But we want also to play the young Europeans who are just beginning to be known in Europe like Conrad Beck or [Nikolai] Lopatnikoff. Thats where you can help us (not to mention the Americans!)[.] Please ask Beck to send us one or two of his recent chamber music works so we can introduce him to N.Y. next season. Also if you know of anyone else who is writing really worth while things, do let me know. We expect to give three concerts next season.

I am spending two months here in this old Spanish town of Santa Fé. I have a room and a piano and am hard at work[,] thus making the summer six weeks longer than usual. There will be an interruption of two weeks in July when I play my Concerto at the Hollywood Bowl under [Albert] Coates. (I don't look forward with much pleasure to this because the time for rehearsel—these being summer concerts—is necessarily too short to hope for a good perfor- mance[.]) In August and September I will be back at the MacDowell Colony[2] in Peterboro where conditions are ideal for work. I wish very much to turn out a large piece for orchestra this summer—and it is on this that I am working principally. Secondly, I should like to do a Trio—piano, violin, cello—for our concerts.[3] As I have the thematic material already it shouldn't be impossible. It becomes increasingly difficult to work during the winters in New York. I have stopped answering the telephone and see as few people as possible—but still it is difficult. But as long as I must give lectures to make money and as long as I feel that the concerts can become important in our musical life I don't see very well what can be done.

I was very much relieved by what you said about Israel's work in your letter of last January. I hope he has continued to improve. Your letter induced Frederick Jacobi to help again with financial aid so that Israel has enough money until the end of October. Just now I don't see who I can turn to for more money then, but I suppose someone will occur to me. Hasn't Israel met anyone at your house who might be induced to help him—even if only for a few months? Since I shall probably be in Paris next Spring I should certainly like to have him stay at least until the fall of '29.

It seems strange to be so far away from Paris at this time of the year. Still, I suppose, it is good for me to see America a little, and then of course, playing at the [Hollywood] Bowl is an excellent introduction to the Pacific Coast. Still, I do miss the rue Ballu very much. Now that Katherine[4] isn't there to write me all the little details about what is going on I feel very much out of it. Perhaps, during the summer you will be able to find a little time to write me. (Address: 223 W. 78 St. always.)

Give my best regards to Madame Boulanger. Tell her I miss her taquinage [teasing] as to how 'celebre' I have become. With deep affection, as ever

A.C.

---

1. The second of the Two Pieces for String Quartet.

2. Named for composer Edward MacDowell, the MacDowell Colony in Peterborough, New Hampshire, is the oldest artists' community in the United States. Copland first resided there in 1925, returning for a total of eight visits between 1925 and 1956; he later served as president of the colony from 1961 to 1968.

3. Copland was working on the *Symphonic Ode* (1927–29) and the piano trio *Vitebsk* (1928).

4. Katherine Wolff, student and confidante of Boulanger. She attended the Conservatoire américain at Fontainebleau in 1923, then stayed on to study with Boulanger in Paris (as had Copland before her).

On August 25, Carlos Chávez wrote to Copland (the first letter from Chávez preserved in the Copland Collection) with news of the reorganization of the Orquesta Sinfónica de México, newly under Chávez's direction. He wrote: "One of the features of the [1928–29] season is your being invited; I've talked a lot about it & the programs are already out and you in one of them. And here is the official invitation: will you come down to

Mexico City and play your Piano Concerto? I give you free choice about date: from September to February, on the first Sunday of such months. You will select the date that suits your convenience in the best way." Faced with this rather imperious summons, Copland replied in his politest and kindest tone.

To Carlos Chávez

AC/LC. Photocopy of als.

MacDowell Colony
Peterboro, N.H.
Sept 7, 1928

Dear Carlos,—

Your letter gave me much joy both as friend and as musician. I felt happy that you wanted me to come and grateful when I thought of how hard you must have had to work to get the truly surprising terms. My first impulse was to say 'I'm coming'! But when I thought of <u>when</u> it could be, I realized it wasn't so easy to arrange as I imagined at first.

These are my arrangements for the winter: from October until Christmas I lecture at the New School. In January I have already signed contracts for lectures in Boston (Jan 12th) and in Cleveland (Jan 29th); and a manager is trying to get more engagements for January (which I must have in order to eat!)[.] That leaves, as you can see, only the concert in February as a vague possibility, but even so, it would be a problem to get to Mexico City in time for sufficient rehearsels.

The more I think of it, the less I should like to make the trip in a great hurry and leave again in a great hurry. I wish to come to Mexico City for two months, not two weeks—and not only that, but two months while you are there. But you are coming back to New York in February, aren't you? And I must give at least two Copland-Sessions Concerts between February and April, mustn't I?

Don't you think it would be better to wait until the next season (1929–1930) when I could make all my arrangements long in advance. I admit that when you first suggested the idea in New York I thought of it as something quite fantastic, but now I assure you I am really very keen to come there and am asking you to postpone the visit with the greatest reluctance and only because I am so anxious to come when I can stay for a long time and under ideal conditions. From the standpoint of your public, the idea of playing the 'Concerto' is highly amusing to me, but they have not heard so much modern music that it can make a great difference whether they hear the 'Concerto' this year or next.

Carlos, my boy, I know how you are. I know that when you conceive an idea you are not at rest until it is accomplished. And so I am sorry to send this letter and not the immediate acceptance you hoped for, but please don't hold it against me. I hope you will still want me to come for the second season of your concerts because I can promise now that I will arrange my affairs so as to make it possible.

I am to be at the MacDowell Colony until Oct. 1st. I have been occupied on a new orchestral work which I hope to submit for the Victor Prize of $25,000 (this is a dead secret!) and have also made arrangements of my two string quartet pieces for string orchestra and my Organ Symphony for orchestra alone.[1]

Roger Sessions wrote me a letter from Paris in which he says, "I have talked to Nadia Boulanger about Carlos; she is enthusiastic and would like to have his sonata[2] played in Paris next year. So I'm letting her have my copy."

I too am practicing the 'Sonatina' because I am going to play it at my first lecture.

The greatest good luck with the Orquesta Sinfonica Mexicana!

Affectionately always

Aaron

P.S. Harold [Clurman] and Gerald [Sykes],[3] who are both in Peterboro, send their love and best wishes for the orchestra.

---

1. Copland had hoped to finish the *Symphonic Ode* and submit it for the RCA Victor Prize but did not complete the piece in time. Instead, he submitted the *Dance Symphony*, a work drawn from his early ballet *Grohg*.

2. The Sonatina for Violin and Piano, published in *New Music* 1, no. 4 (1928).

3. Writer Gerald Sykes was a close friend of Copland's; the two met in 1925 and lived together briefly in 1930. Copland dedicated the *Piano Variations* to Sykes.

To Carlos Chávez

AC/LC. Photocopy of als.

223 W. 78th St. New York
Oct 31 1928

Dear Carlos—

I waited several days since seeing Agea[1] before answering the letter he brought me from you, hoping against hope that something would turn up to save me from appearing like an altogether ungrateful wretch. But nothing has. I feel as if heaven and earth were being moved to bring me to Mexico City and I do nothing about it. In reality, this is not so. I really understand and appreciate how much you want me there and it makes me very sad not to be able to say: 'coming.' The reason is this: all my energies are at present directed to the winning of the Victor Prize of $25,000 and you understand how important such a sum of money is. But my orchestral work is no-where near being finished and

I cannot work on it until I am through with lectures, which is not until Jan. 27 as I wrote you. In order to finish it in time, I must devote at least three months of concentrated work on it which will have to be Feb, March, and April since the works must be submitted for the prize in May. (I am like a woman who is pregnant and dares not travel for fear it would endanger the life of her child!) What could be nicer than the offer you make me: to see Mexico City, to play my Concerto, to meet new people, to spend a week travelling back with you (which would be as great a joy as any of the others)—all this to cost me nothing; you must think me crazy to refuse. You can be sure I think myself crazy! But this craziness is one that any composer could understand: it consists in living with one desire—to finish a work which is incomplete. If I went to Mexico City in February it could not make me happy because the back of my mind would be saying to me always: you should be finishing your piece. This is as clear as I can make myself.

Instead of the Concerto I suggest that you give 'Music for the Theatre.' It is characteristic of me, is amusing for an audience, and the jazz parts are like an introduction to the 'Concerto' which I still hope I can play with you in your second season. I have my own original copy of the score, but the Universal Edition has the parts. Write to them immediately—if they do not answer, the simplest thing will be to have the parts copied in Mexico City and I will help pay the cost. It should not be expensive because it is only for small orchestra. Of course, only do this if the Universal refuses to send the parts. In any case I will send you my copy of the score—but don't tell Universal this.

I am so glad you are working on an orchestral piece also.[2] Is there any chance of showing it to Koussevitsky this season? If so, let me know, and I will mention it to him, or give it to him if you can send a copy.

Naturally we will give the 3 Mexican Pieces at the C[opland]-S[essions] concerts. My only regret is [that] they are so short.[3] I like the Fox very much— or as much as I can make out of it because as you must know it is terribly difficult to play. In fact, I can't wait until I hear you play it as only you can. Our first concert will be around Christmas, the second in February. Your pieces will be in February, unless we give a third concert in April. If we do, I'll save it until then so [as] to be sure that you are to be present at the concert. As works to play by Americans we have: 2nd String Quartet, Geo. Antheil; 'Paragraphs' for 2 violins & cello, Henry Cowell; Piano Sonata, Bernard Wagenaar, (and I hope one from Roy [Harris]); Songs, Blitzstein etc. From young Europeans: Sona-tina for piano, N. Lopatnikoff; Songs, Dukelsky; Sonata for violin & flute, Conrad Beck. Roger has nothing of his own, but I may perform my own song 'As it fell upon a day.' I need more music if we are to give three concerts.

Has Paul R[osenfeld] sent you his book? It contains an article on each of us, side by side.[4] I do not believe I like either article overmuch, but after all, they are both serious attempts to evaluate our music so we mustn't kick.

Why don't you write Mina Lederman to ask her to do the publicity you need? I doubt if she will refuse if you ask her personally. Or possibly, some-one like Miss Brenner could do the actual work and Mina could advise how, where and when to send it out. Or possibly, you could have all the mate-rial written and typed in Mexico City and Minna could send it out for you up here.

I am quite busy with my lectures now. But New York is pretty dull: no one is here—Roger, Roy, Henry [Brant], Varese, are all gone, so is Mrs. Wertheim and no parties chez Mrs. Walton.[5] Also no interesting music so far. Kousse-vitsky is to play "Appollo"[6] at his first concert—too bad you will miss it.

So you can be sure I miss you and wish you were coming back soon.

With best luck for the concerts

Most affectionately

Aaron

---

1. Mexican composer Francisco Agea.

2. Chávez had written to Copland on October 13: "In the last concert, February, I will give my last work, a sort of symphony I am now working on." There is, however, no Chávez orchestral work from this period.

3. Chávez's three pieces for piano have the titles "Solo," "Blues," and "Fox" (as in fox-trot). In fact no works by Chávez were performed on the February program.

4. Paul Rosenfeld, *By Way of Art: Criticisms of Music, Literature, Painting, Sculpture, and the Dance* (New York: Coward-McCann, 1928).

5. Blanche Wetherill Walton (1871–1963), patron of contemporary American music and host of many social events. See Carol J. Oja, "Women Patrons and Crusaders for Modernist Music," in *Cultivating Music in America: Women Patrons and Activists since 1860,* ed. Ralph P. Locke and Cyrilla Barr (Berkeley: University of California Press, 1997), 242–44; reproduced in this volume (fig. 29, pp. 264–65) is a document that Oja identifies as the guest list for a reception following the Copland-Sessions concert on April 13, 1930. (It is not, however, in Copland's hand.)

6. Igor Stravinsky's *Apollon musagète.*

Aaron Copland met painter/lithographer Prentiss Taylor (1907–91) at the MacDowell Colony, where they were both residents, in the summer of 1928. A correspondence between them, at first reticent, began the follow-ing November. The correspondence flowered particularly in early 1929, when Copland was hiding away weekdays at Mary Churchill's house in Briarcliff Manor, New York, in the hopes of finishing his *Symphonic Ode* in time to submit it for the RCA Victor Prize. Copland returned periodically to the city to rehearse for the American premiere of Stravinsky's *Les Noces* and to see Taylor. What might have been a long-term relationship was ended when Copland left for Europe in late spring 1929. (Copland was not good at saving letters received while abroad—whether "abroad" was Briar-cliff Manor or France—hence we have none of Taylor's letters to Copland from the 1920s.) In later years Taylor was a pioneer in the use of art in psychotherapy, but he is best known for his lithographs illustrating Langston Hughes's *Scottsboro Limited.*

To Prentiss Taylor

Taylor/AAA. als.

Sunday [November 25, 1928][1]

Dear P.T.—

I'd like to see more of you.

Wont you come to see me here at 9 Wednesday evening (I'd ask you for dinner but am dated up for the week)[.]

If you can come don't bother to answer this.

Yours

Aaron Copland

223 W. 78th St.

---

1. Date in later hand, perhaps from postmark.

To Prentiss Taylor

PT/AAA. als.

Wed. [January 30, 1929][1]

Dear Prentiss,—

Just when I was beginning to despair your nice note came. It was most flattering to read that you would be 'horribly disappointed' if you didn't hear from me. There needn't have been any fear of that. Writing you now reminds me of the first two notes I sent you—tho you are no longer the unknown quantity you were then. And in my anxiety to write you a specifically nice letter—to make you feel how much I like you, without any exaggeration that might make you think it unreal—I'll probably spoil everything!

I've been appreciating during your absence what a <u>very</u> pleasant time its been having you around. Also, what a mysterious creature you really are. In the midst of your chatter the real Prentiss quite escapes me. Without your help I'm sure I'll never ["really" crossed out] know you, and as far as I can see you give no signs of helping. You wont understand this; still, I keep on wondering, what is Prentiss like.

Instead of spending evenings with you I spend them with my trio.[2] The poor thing's still very constipated and worries me considerably. I look forward to the day when its done and wonder why I ever promised it. In the meantime it has me leading a hermit's life and I wish you were here to be my sole diversion.

On Sunday I was in Cleveland for 8 hours. Unfortunately my program was way ahead of the audience so that there was little connection between them.[3] Is this my fault?

I'm sending back your criticisms. They're absolutely classics of their kind.

I'm eager to hear about the ball—and even more, to have you here again. With love,

Aaron

---

1. Date in later hand, perhaps from postmark.

2. *Vitebsk.*

3. Copland had given a lecture-recital at the Cleveland Museum of Art, playing the second movement of Sessions's Symphony no. 1, two movements of Roy Harris's Piano Sonata, Chávez's Sonatina for Piano, one of Gershwin's Preludes, and an excerpt from his own Piano Concerto.

To Prentiss Taylor

PT/AAA. als.

Fri. [March 8, 1929][1]

Dear P——,

I sent my last letter with trepidation and received your reply today with even more trepidation.[2] After reading your letter several times and much consideration I've decided you're a darling! The main purpose of this note is to tell you so.

Its always a dangerous business to write the kind of letter I sent you. Now that I know how you took it, I don't regret having sent it, although I am sorry it should have upset you even a little. I don't expect you to change overnight—naturally its impossible—but I think you should get a technique for handling a consciousness of self or self-analysis; i.e. a technique that would consist of being as analytical as one pleased and still not let it interfere with ones daily actions—it should act on one subconsciously, one should be able to turn it on and off at will.

One more thing and I'm done. 'We must all take each other pretty much as we are' you say. Agreed. But I want to make certain that you give the real Prentiss to people every minute of the time, instead of only part of the time. It all comes under the chapter heading 'Being Real.'

(Also please don't forget that I might have written just as long a letter telling off your nice qualities if you hadn't started me on the other track.)

Anyway, it will be more than pleasant to see the very same Prentiss I left—is it only a week and a half ago—a few hours after you get this.

Love to you

Aaron

1. Date in later hand, perhaps from postmark.
2. This earlier correspondence apparently does not survive.

To Prentiss Taylor

PT/AAA. als.

Sunday [March 31, 1929]¹

Dear Prentiss—

I have an appalling letter to write you. The gist is: man proposes and God disposes. For reasons that have to do with the Churchills and too long to go into here, it will be impossible for you or H[arold Clurman] or G[erald Sykes] or anybody to come out here this week. I can't tell you how annoyed and sorry and disturbed I am. But this is what comes of not living in one's own house.

I'll write again when I have collected some piece of mind [*sic*].

I am most disappointed because it ruins the possibility of our being alone together for a goodly spell. Oh HELL [ink blot]

And love

Aaron

1. Date in later hand, perhaps from postmark. The same hand notes "special delivery."

Copland continued to work on his *Symphonic Ode* in the summer of 1929, which he spent in Juziers (near Boulanger's summer home in Gargenville). He returned to the United States in September.

To Prentiss Taylor

PT/AAA. als.
[Cunard RMS *Aquitania* stationery]

June 4 [1929]

Dear Prentiss,—

I can see the sea-gulls flying around the ship from the writing room window —so this seemed the right moment to begin a letter to you. I needed sea-gulls to brighten me up—these damn ocean voyages are dull with a particular brand of dullness that belongs especially to a ship. Said dullness ruins all my boat-letters—so don't expect much.

I opened the scroll and envelope as soon as we had passed the Statue of Liberty. The Bon Voyage was very cute—and sweet of you to take the trouble, and the swankly mounted photos will be to look at when I feel gay or low. They are both very much you.

The crowd on board is very mixed. Most of my time was spent in the smoking room and conversation was religiously plied with Greta Torpadie,[1] her husband, a Swiss divinity student from Hartford, a secretary of the New School, a novelist, etc. etc. The same things always happen on a boat. I exchange the usual pleasantries with fellow passengers, I carry a book around all day without looking into it, I note the blond but brainless collegiate with his female in tow, I decide after mature consideration to miss a meal, I escape the objectionable person who tries to rope me into playing at the ships concert, etc. etc. I feel as if I had made 70 trips instead of 7. You should have known me when I was newer at the game. Then I would have sent you a real boat-letter.

Anyhow, to-morrow we land—Israel [Citkowitz] will have to be up at 7 A.M. to meet me. I've had two radiograms, one signed MinnaMary,[2] the second, which read 'Hold Out,' signed IsraelEvaMarc.[3] So it seems I'm expected. Paris really should be grand, and now that I'm so near I cant wait till I get there.

I'll want to know all about Yaddo.[4]

You never did give me your Washington address. Send it along.

Someones just announced land.

Goodbye

Love

A

---

1. Soprano, dedicated performer of new music, and Speaker in the first American performance of Schoenberg's *Pierrot Lunaire*.

2. Minna Lederman and Mary Churchill.

3. Israel Citkowitz, Eva Goldbeck, and Marc Blitzstein.

4. Prentiss Taylor was spending the summer at Yaddo, the artists' colony near Saratoga Springs, New York. Copland would spend his first summer there in 1930; he was a major force behind the Yaddo Music Festivals that took place in 1932 and 1933.

To Prentiss Taylor

PT/AAA. als.

July 4 [1929]

Dear Prentiss—

I don't know what explanation you have given yourself for not hearing from me for so long a time, but whatever it was it was wrong. While in Paris it was impossible to write—since coming to Juziers it was inertia (too many things to write about) and also I was waiting to hear more than was contained in your first letter. The second one—the 12 page one—came 2 days ago with all its news about Yaddo, Gerald [Sykes] and the new friend. I think it about time someone wrote a chapter called 'P—— and his young men.' They should be catalogued according to the degree of affection: deep, deeper, deepest. This capacity of yours for being absorbed in three or four at the same time deserves emulation. Not to mention admiration. Don't gather from this that I was surprised at your finding someone at Yaddo. As you say, I expected it and wanted you to find it and was happy for your sake that you did find it. I'm sure it made Yaddo a much happier place for you. You were right when you guessed that I would 'understand'—not only understand, but approve. (My affection for you—whatever it is—has nothing exclusive in it now and demands nothing exclusive. I'm your very fond friend and hope to be always. But I cant in honesty put it any stronger than that.[)]

Its useless to try to give you a resumé of everything that's been happening. I was feeling 'intellectual' one night and wrote Gerald an account. Perhaps he showed it to you.

At the moment I am settled in Juziers with Israel [Citkowitz], and will probably stay the summer. It seemed the simplest thing to do. I felt I hadn't enough of Paris during the short, rushed two weeks I spent there and didn't want to go away as far as Switzerland. Israel offered his room for the summer and I accepted. Roy [Harris] and Nadia B. both live here besides 10 or 12 pupils of Nadia's. Even little Eva [Goldbeck] is coming out to join us for a few weeks so you gather that I don't lack company. I may take in Switzerland in September if the big piece[1] gets done in time.

I have a darling little room to live and work in. It has a lovely view across the valley with the Seine flowing peacefully through it and a garden under my window. A little French town you would find endlessly amusing. Its very primitive for one thing—I still don't know how to manage getting a bath. But there are no end of charming walks on by-roads that are very civilized-looking and yet as deserted as a Peterboro road. I like it here and feel I can work. The life we lead is so simple and healthy and for 'distraction' there is always Paris.

Talking of Paris reminds me to tell you that I caught a glimpse of the Bufanos[2] one night on the Terasse of the Select. Marc and Eva were both living in our neighborhood and so we saw a lot of them. Also Chard [Powers Smith], who promises to come out to Juziers to visit.

Our concert went off well.[3] I'm afraid Marc was extremely put out at not being included on the program. But I'm beginning to discover that when he feels most hurt he acts his sweetest. Anyhow we're still friends. We even went 'bumming' together one night—he took me to one place and I took him to another—though God knows we ended up as innocent as we started out. But it was amusing. Montparnasse has developed into one of the most demoralizing places I know. It has become the gathering place of all the queer boys of Europe. Especially the French hang out there. The terasse of the Dome on a Saturday night looks like a ball at 155 St.

You better not come to Paris.

Affectionately,

A.

P.S. Please tell me where to send you letters.

1. The *Symphonic Ode*.

2. Remo Bufano would create the puppets for which Copland wrote *From Sorcery to Science* in 1939.

3. A concert of American music presented in Paris. See C & P I, 159–60. The program included Copland's *Vitebsk* and his *Rondino* for string quartet.

To Nadia Boulanger

AC/LC. als.

[Cunard Line stationery]

Aquitania

Sept 26 [1929][1]

Dear Nadia—

What a surprise it was to find your letter here—and what a pleasure! And how proud it made me feel to receive such a letter from you, of all people.[2] It was doubly pleasurable because I know so well that the 'Ode' is the fruit of the past two years and that even now I feel in myself the power to do better. I have come to believe that the problem of writing music which is really important is a problem that is completely bound up with the possibilities of development that can be found in oneself as a person. I feel sure that if I can become more profound as a person my music will also become more profound. So that, for myself, in the future, my need is to become a greater man and the music will take care of itself. Your letter made me more determined than ever to devote all my time to composition from now on without any interruptions.

The trip has been much more pleasant than most. I found Mr. Goldmark[3] on the boat and several other friends. To-day I feel as if I could return to France to-morrow.

Remember me to Madame.

Affectionately

A.C.

1. Year in later hand, almost certainly Boulanger's.

2. Boulanger had previously written in an undated letter: "How happy & proud I would be if I could express what your Ode brought me as feeling of greatness, of power, as deepness—but you know my struggles with words & . . . I am quite miserable!"

3. Rubin Goldmark, Copland's former composition teacher.

To Israel Citkowitz

AC/LC. als.

Bedford—N.Y.

May 29 [1930]

Dear Israö—

The sight of your handwriting on an envelope becomes thank God less strange. After the long drought it is especially good to see it again. I'm sorry if you've ever worried about leaving me in the dark about your 'vie interieure.' Your long silence was almost self-explanatory—I guessed that important things were happening to you, too important to write about, and contented myself with waiting for that distant day when they belonged to the past and I should undoubtedly hear about them. I think of our relation as being in a state of equilibrium—we can always take it up whenever we please and go on from where we left off without any sense of a gap or a separation. At any rate, so it seems to me.

As a matter of fact its been a strange year in relation to friends. Theres been a general overhauling, a revaluation of values. It amuses me to think how imperceptibly these changes take place—and yet, one day there they are. For example, Gerald [Sykes] seems much closer now, due partly to our living together in Bedford for several months. Gerald understands me well ["now" inked over]—he makes up in perception what he lacks in sympathy (tho in relation to myself he has had sufficient on both scores). Harold [Clurman], on the other hand, has begun what might be termed almost a new life in which I play a much more modest rôle than in the old one. His love affair has made a man of him—he has developed a whole set of new friends who believe in him fervently and he has moments of real megalomania. And so he's on his way to being one of the really important critics in America. Of course the fact that he is also going to Yaddo this summer will bring us together again and will help to change our present relations.

Roy [Harris]'s stock is extremely low. I suspect he has me pretty much in the same class as N.[adia] B.[oulanger] now, a well-meaning but pernicious influence. That ruins everything because, as you know, I only thrive on sympathetic contacts. He attached himself while in N.Y. (he has gone to Cal. now) to a very impressionable young man by the name of Paul Rosenfeld[1] and together they went over the situation pretty thoroughly. We none of us came out very well— but we'll survive I hope. His Quartet[2] is his best piece so far and makes me wish I only knew him thru his music.

Something in me makes me welcome all such changes. Not, however, until they have happened. But when they have happened I embrace them.

My stay in Bedford will be over in another two weeks. I spend a month in town before going to Yaddo. Whether or not I go to Mexico this September is still a question. But I will almost certainly go to Europe next Spring for an extended stay of two years or so. I am seriously considering applying for a Prix de Rome. But principally I am interested in Germany, where I want to get some works played (I might also do a bit of propaganda there for American music). The wanderlust has me—I want to see Algiers, London for a longer stay, Marseilles, Capri, Constantinople . . .

Your own plans sound feasible enough. However much or little composing you do I advise you to finish the String quartet and W[ood] W[ind] Quintette you wrote about. They will prove great helps to your rep.[3] Also let me warn you that you will not be pleased with America unless you have a room & piano of your own. You're used to different things now and I feel sure it will be difficult to live at home for any extended period of time. Have you thought of that? To be quite truthful I only take your plans half seriously! As far as I can see your next five years are one big question mark—and if there have been upheavals in the past there will certainly be upheavals in the future to upset the best laid plans.

I finally heard the 'Ode.' I conducted it myself one morning at a rehearsel in Boston while K— [Koussevitzky] listened from the auditorium. I only really heard the slow parts, the fast parts were ruined by being played too slow. The end sounded gloriously. It was a revealing experience. The upshot was that I have for all time given up trying to make music look on paper what it actually sounds like. Applied to the Ode it means that I must completely rewrite the barring of the fast parts throughout. I'm working on it now and have discovered how much easier certain sections might have been written. For example, one part which originally had 13 changes of time—3/4, 7/8, 5/8 etc.—is now entirely 4/4. I never believed it could be done till I tried. So that not a note of the piece will be changed but it will look entirely different on paper. When I think of the loss of time and money (the parts must be completely recopied and re-corrected) I could weep. On top of this, I played it at the piano for Hertzka, head of Universal Ed[ition], who happened to be at Alma [Wertheim]'s one night and when he heard it was scored for a Mahlerian orchestra he advised her against publishing it. (Not that she'll take his advice.) 'Why you're crazy man,['] says he, [']there are not ten orchestras in all Europe that can supply 18 brass instruments.' This darling 'Ode' seems to be having a hard time in a cruel world.

I'm very pleased with the piano piece I am doing. It is a big work both in dimensions and meaning. For the moment its called 'Theme and Variations.'[4] Its a new form for me and lends itself beautifully to my particular kind of development from a single germ. But it needs time to fully flower and wont be done probably until the end of the Summer. Then if I can get Gieseking to play it I'll be satisfied.[5] He's the only one who can.

I've had two <u>very</u> sympathetic letters from Carl B.[6] I want you to write me your impressions of him as a person. He also sent me his Wylie songs which I find <u>not</u> so sympathetic. In a way its tragic that he should want to compose. Unless I am badly mistaken, his stuff is terribly old-fashioned and without a real spark. (Don't breathe a word of this to him, of course.) I've told him more or less the same thing already, but it does little good. How do you feel about it?

Now that the ice is broken—keep in touch, if and when, you can.

Affectionately

Aaron

P.S. Don't forget that from now on my address is Hotel Montclair 49 & Lex. Av. N.Y.C.

---

1. A joke: Paul Rosenfeld, a distinguished critic whose name would have been well known to Citkowitz, was ten years older than Copland.

2. Roy Harris's First String Quartet had been premiered at a Copland-Sessions Concert that April 13.

3. Either "reputation" or "repertoire."

4. Eventually, the *Piano Variations*.

5. German pianist Walter Gieseking, who had played in the first performance of Copland's trio *Vitebsk*, declined to perform the *Piano Variations*, writing Copland in unidiomatic English that "a work of such severity of style is not possible among the normal type of concert-goers."

6. Carl Buchman, American composer and editor.

To Carlos Chávez

AC/LC. Photocopy of als.

[Yaddo stationery]

Aug 15 '30

Dear Carlos—

I cant tell you how happy it made me to receive your very affectionate letter. Sometimes I could not help feeling that you had become so absorbed in your work in Mexico that you forgot me and all the friends you have here. But now I see it is not true—now I see you do miss me and the rest, which makes me very glad. Your letter made me feel very close to you, as if all the time we were separated was very little. Carlos, my boy, you really must try to come to New York in January. I have a great desire to see you again—and letters are such poor substitutes.

I have always had one principal concern for you—because of your half a dozen activities as director, conductor etc. you would stop composing. Now I see it begins to worry you also and—that is good! Is there no solution for this difficult problem? Is there no-one in Mexico who can help you run the school so that you have some time for your composition work? Before everything else, you are a <u>composer</u>. Which means you will never be happy until you have the time to compose. Of course, you know all this. But I want you to know that I know it too and that I am waiting impatiently for you to find the solution. So I was glad to hear that you had made a beginning with the two more 'Mexican Pieces' and the new orchestral work . . .

Its clear you are hungry for news so I will put you au courant of what has been doing.

As for myself, more and more I have been able to put aside every other consideration but composing. I have stopped writing articles, given as few lectures as possible, and lived in the country outside N.Y. from January to June so as to have time for myself. The only activity I have continued is the C— Sessions Concerts. The result has been not that I have written any more than usual, but that I have the necessary peace of mind for writing.

The work that I was writing for the Victor Prize (its called 'Symphonic Ode') is finished, but I finished it too late to send in for the prize. Instead, I sent in a work called 'A Dance Symphony' which I quickly put together from my early ballet. The prize has been decided recently (though not announced publicly yet)—the $25,000 was divided among 5 composers and I was one of them![1] So with $5,000 I feel rich. I dont know yet who the other 4 composers are, but there is a rumor that Bloch is one of them. This means that I am free for several years and do not have to lecture any more.

Koussevitsky was to perform the 'Ode' in March. Two weeks before the concert he told me the piece was so difficult rhythmically that he would need a summer to study it properly. So it was put off to this season and will probably be given in N.Y. in January. I am very anxious to hear it because I am sure it is by far the best thing I have done.

Just now I am working on a long piece for piano in the form of a Theme and Variations and am very pleased with the way it is going.

As for the others: Roy Harris is in California now, where he is married to a new wife. We performed his most recent work—a string quartet[—]at our concerts. Its probably his best work so far. He has a Symphony in 3 movements which you should see.[2] It is uneven I think, but has excellent things in it.

Sessions is to be in Rome one more year. He hasn't written much[,] but the Piano Sonata—you remember?—is now finished and the Symphony is published by the Cos Cob Press.

Paul Rosenfeld is spending the summer with Stieglitz at Lake George, only an hour from here. I will see him soon and bring him news of you.

I suppose you must be wondering what Yaddo is! I came here to spend the summer, but I like it so much that I will stay until November. It is a very large private estate which is given over to creative artists—something like the Mac-Dowell Colony. I have a wonderful studio in the woods—a Stone Tower which would make a perfect setting for an outdoor performance of the Tower Scene from Pelleas. Harold Clurman is here too.

If Yaddo had not turned out so perfectly, I should certainly have come to Mexico for Sept. and Oct. But with conditions so ideal for work (and costing nothing!) it would be a mistake to leave. You must not think that because the orchestra could not offer me a paid engagement I stay away. It would have been a pleasure to play for nothing, particularly now that I have the money for the trip. But the advantages of staying at Yaddo are so apparent that I must put the trip off for a while again. Don't despair, Carlos, it will surely happen some day.

Which reminds me to tell you—I played the 'Concerto' as recently as last week at the Stadium Concerts in N.Y. Coates conducted and did a good job. He speaks of arranging a performance in London in April. I expect to go to Berlin in March to see some of the new operas and to try to arrange some performances of my works in Germany—where they have never been given. If I like it well enough I may even stay a year.

This is news enough for one letter.

Affectionately

Aaron

---

1. Actually, the prize was split among four composers: Copland, Robert Russell Bennett, Ernest Bloch, and Louis Gruenberg.

2. Roy Harris's *Symphony—American Portrait 1929.*

To Serge Koussevitzky

SK/LC. als.

[Hotel Montclair stationery]

March 27 [1931]

Cher ami—

I was sorry to hear of the postponement, once more, of the 'Ode.' Nevertheless I understand perfectly the reasons for the postponement and I am convinced that you have my best interests at heart as always.

I should like to make a suggestion. Wouldn't it perhaps be wiser to put off the performance of the 'Ode' until next season. To give it now at the end of the season when you are tired and the orchestra and public is not fresh might be a mistake. Also, it makes the possibility of a performance in New York, which I naturally consider important, very unlikely. After all, I put two years of work into the 'Ode' and I should like to have it presented under the best possible circumstances. Since I have waited so long for a performance I am willing to wait another six months. Also, if you gave the work next season you would have time during the summer to study it carefully.

At the same time I realize that you may have reasons of your own which would make you want to perform it on the 17–18 April. In that case of course I have no objections to the performance now. But I thought it necessary to suggest the postponement until next season in case you too thought it desirable.[1]

Please let me know what you decide as soon as possible because the date of my sailing to Europe depends upon your decision.

Always faithfully

Aaron Copland

---

1. The *Symphonic Ode* received its first performance on February 19, 1932.

To Serge and Natalie Koussevitzky

SK/LC. als.

[The Benjamin Franklin Hotel, Philadelphia, stationery]

mercredi [Wednesday, 1931][1]

Chers amis—

Here is the promised letter. I have heard Stokowski conduct Oedipus Rex[2] and Le Pas d'Acier[3] and my 'Dance Symphony' and I have learned a great deal more about Stokowski as conductor. Of the three works I think he plays Le Pas d'Acier best. You will soon understand why. He has certain qualities which are undeniable—he can make the orchestra sound extremely brilliant, or very sensuous, or mystic. At the same time he has great personal energy and a very finished technique so that he commands respect. But as far as I can see he has no depth of feeling whatever and practically no sense of style. That makes almost everything he does imperfect from any artistic standpoint. At any moment you are liable to be shocked by his superficiality of feeling or some detail which is completely out of style with the rest. (The public of course doesn't understand this because everything he does sounds so effective—thus his Bach playing is absolutely false to the spirit of Bach but the public loves it because it makes Bach sound so sensuous and so brilliant.) This morning I heard him conduct Wagner and it seemed to me all wrong in spirit. This surprised me because I thought that Stokowski's sensuous touch would go well with Wagner's chromaticism but I realized when I heard it that it was the wrong kind of sensuousness—not full-blown enough, not rich enough, not German enough; too parfumée, too much of the boudoir. Then again, the spirit was wrong, because he seemed to be driving the music with a whip in a peculiarly modern and hectic way instead of allowing it to se deployer in all its fullness of emotion.

I've taken the trouble to make these general remarks because they apply to the three works I have heard here. For instance, Oedipus Rex was done in an 'effective' manner but the style was completely false. There is one quality you must have in order to give a good performance of Oedipus and that is le sens tragique de la vie. This Stokowski simply has not got,—instead he has le sens mystique de la vie which is something quite different. So that Oedipus as he does it turns out to be a mystic drama with dark green lights on the stage throughout. The sum total effect of this production is of an oratorio with incidental puppets rather than a stage work.[4] The puppets are not as objectionable as you might think because they are so big and even more because they hardly move, but they are practically negligible. The work is better as music than Stokowski makes it sound. In the first place he performs it entirely without any pause between the first and second acts—so that it becomes too long and tires the audience and the performers. Then he has a very bad habit of keeping the orchestra terribly subdued whenever a singer is singing. He is so very afraid of covering the singer[']s voice that he makes the orchestra sound emasculated. This happened almost continually. (He did the same thing in Wozzeck.) Matzenauer[5] did not seem to be in very good voice when I heard her, altho the interpretation she gave was pretty much the same as when she sang it with you. (I heard the story that she was very annoyed with Stokowski because he would not let her stand up when she sang her aria.) I have wondered what Stravinsky would say, also, if he knew that Stokowski doesn't begin Oedipus as he wrote it but adds a few trumpet measures (from the second act) before the speaker appears and thereby ruins that first wonderful impact of the work. I could go on with more details but this letter is getting long.

You can see from what I said that he would do justice to Prokofieff's work, as music that is. What goes on the stage is just silly.

He seems well pleased with the Dance Symphony and says he will repeat it at his regular concerts next season. It was very interesting for me to hear a work I had written so long ago. I like it very much in parts but not as a whole.

I am sailing on Friday and hope to see you in Paris.

Devotedly

A. C.

---

1. Year in later hand.

2. Igor Stravinsky's *Oedipus Rex*, which Koussevitzky had given its American premiere in 1928.

3. Sergey Prokofiev's ballet *Le Pas d'acier*. Stokowski conducted Copland's *Dance Symphony* on April 15, 1931.

4. In Stokowski's performance of *Oedipus Rex* the characters were represented by giant puppets made by Remo Bufano.

5. Contralto Margaret Matzenauer, who sang the role of Jocasta.

In the spring of 1931, Copland again traveled to Europe. In Paris he met Paul Bowles, a young composer who later became well known as a novelist (*The Sheltering Sky* [1949]; *Let It Come Down* [1952]), and the two traveled to Tangier, Morocco, together. Bowles also knew American expatriate writer Gertrude Stein, whom he and Copland visited at Bilignin, her estate in the south of France, where she often spent summers with her companion, Alice B. Toklas.

To Gertrude Stein

Stein, Toklas/Yale. als.

Tangier Maroc
August 25, 1931

Dear Miss Stein—

I ought to have written long ago to thank you for the delightful days I spent at Billignin. In a way of course, I didn't deserve them. I mean, my having come by way of P.[aul] B.[owles] made my invitation rather indirect, to say the least. But your hospitality reassured me, and made me doubly grateful.

Tangier is responsible for my not writing sooner. It wasn't easy getting settled. It took a week to find a house and furnish it. We have an African piano which looks like a piano but which sounds like hell! It would sound all right if we could only get a piano tuner who can tune. But they tell me he's not so easily found in Morocco. We tried one man who put it more out of tune than it was before he touched it. These are problems you are happily free of, but they make my stay somewhat precarious. Still, if I should have to leave to-morrow, I'd be glad you sent us, because it is lovely to see, and so I have to thank you on that score too.

I've written my friend Harold Clurman about the plays. I hope something comes of it. Remember me to Miss Toklas.

Sincerely,
Aaron Copland

To Henry Brant[1]

AC/LC. Photocopy of als.

c/o American Legation
Tangier
Morocco, North Africa
Sept 10 [1931]

Dear Henry—

You must admit you never expected to get a letter from Africa! But now that September is here ones thoughts travel to music and concerts even in Africa. And so very naturally to you. I've been carrying your letter about with me— your long and interesting letter—with all its list of grievances—wherever I've been—Berlin, Oxford, London, Paris, Bellay (to visit Gertrude Stein), Marseille, Oran (in Algeria), Ceuta (in Spanish Morocco) and finally here. And now finally I've overcome my natural laziness as correspondent. . . .

First let me tell you what will interest you most. I did meet Markevitch![2] It was in June in Paris at a soiree chez Mlle Boulanger. She was having a final reunion before vacation of all her pupils, so that Markevich was naturally there, as was [sic] Stravinsky's sons and Israel Citkowitz and many others[.] (I couldn't help but remark how naturally you would have fit in there.) You'll be amused to hear that M— reminded me of you. He has your build and the same peculiar way of holding his head forward and the same wide-open eyes. He struck me as being an extremely bright youth with a remarkably mature social manner. It is hard to imagine him in a situation which he would be unable to handle. I hear that he is much sought after in the choicest Paris salons and that the hostess who succeeds in getting him to attend her party is looked upon with envy. Not that he doesn't go out a great deal—but he has so many invitations that he cant attend them all. Of course his social talent has nothing to do with his musical talent which I wasn't able to judge as I haven't still seen a note of his music. If you have any curiosity on that score you can get most of them (the scores) as they are published by Schott and are listed in his catalogue.

I had a good time in Oxford and London at the Festival.[3] I met lots of English composers—a new breed for me. Vaughan Williams, [Gustav] Holst, Arthur Bliss, Frank Bridge, Constant Lambert etc. I've written up the Festival for Modern Music and you can read my impressions there.[4]

I didn't accomplish much in Berlin. You have to stay at least a year if you want to spread yourself about. At any rate the Berlin section of the I.S.C.M. is considering a concert of all American music for December which, if it comes off, may have made my stay worth while. While there I corrected proofs of my 'First Symphony' (so-called, but really the orchestral arrangement of my Organ and Orchestra Symph.) which is already out, and my 'Dance Symphony' which is to appear soon, both chez the Cos Cob Press of course. Among composers, I saw mostly Jerzy Fitelberg and Nicolai Lopatnikoff. The former I think is very talented indeed. I think you heard his String Quartet once at a League Concert and his Piano Sonata at one of our concerts. I also saw [American pianist Richard] Buhlig in Berlin, who threatened to play my Variations at the New School on Oct. 13. If he does let me know your impressions.

My plans for returning are still in a rather vague state. I expect to stay in Tangier until October and then probably return to Berlin for a while. At the latest I expect to be in N.Y. by Christmas. I look forward to starting some sort of a 'cercle' for composers such as we talked about once.[5]

What have you been composing during the Summer? (Those pieces you thought you left at my hotel were left there and are now reclining safely in

Brooklyn). Write me c/o Guaranty Trust Co. 4 Pl. de la Concorde Paris. I'm working on a new orchestral piece[6] and am very pleased with my thematic material. Its probably a Symphony.

One more thing—this very important. Next May I am going to run a Festival of American Chamber Music in Saratoga Springs at Yaddo. This is to be held before an invited audience including critics from N.Y. I am very anxious to have a new work of yours, one especially written for this occasion. It may be for strings, strings and soprano, possibly we may have an oboe and clarinet (piano goes without saying). This, I hope, will be a very important musical event, and I want you to do the very best you are capable of. Of course, you must come up to Yaddo to hear it. Write me what you think you'll do. (Personally I should like to have something for 1 string or more with piano, or possibly a string trio.)

If Stokowski does my Dance Symphony in N.Y. let me have your impressions. I'm not going to let Koussevitsky do the 'Ode' until I return. Keep me posted, wont you, about what goes on—one has a very lost feeling here.

With best regards for your family

Always

Aaron Copland

---

1. Henry Brant, American composer who served as Copland's amanuensis in the later 1930s: the final orchestral score of *The City* is in his hand (as is, presumably, the lost orchestral score of *From Sorcery to Science*).

2. Igor Markevich, Russian-born composer and conductor.

3. The ninth festival of the ISCM.

4. Aaron Copland, "Contemporaries at Oxford: 1931," *Modern Music* 9 (November–December 1931): 17–23; reprinted in *Copland on Music*, 193–99.

5. Copland started a "Young Composers' Group" in 1932.

6. The *Short Symphony*.

To Israel Citkowitz

AC/LC. als.

Tangier Maroc
Sept 22 [1931]

Dear Israö—

I was awfully glad to get your note. I was on the point of having very lugubrious thoughts on the subject of our relations, the kind of thoughts you had (apparently) last summer, and which I was now really feeling only for the first time. I was on the point of writing you, not to make playful reproaches, but to tell you seriously how sad it made me feel to think you were slipping away and that we were gradually losing all sense of contact the moment we were separated. I'm sure that this habit we've gotten into of not corresponding any longer is bad. I dont even mean the writing of honest-to-God letters because I know they need a certain amount of "inspiration" about which one can do nothing. But its the lack of any word at all which creates the vacuum and discourages the writing of any serious letters ever. N.[adia] B.[oulanger] and I never correspond but that is an entirely different matter, because our relationship is more or less static and will always remain what it is now. But our case is different and we cant go on for two years, as we just have, with impunity. I dont mean that its your fault that we haven't written each other; I suppose if I kept writing letters, you'd reply. Je constate, c'est tout. [I make note, that's all.] Its both our faults,—and here is a beginning, in a new direction . . .

Paris isn't on my itinerary, which is now practically settled. I'm leaving here on Oct 1st and gradually working my way back to Berlin by way of Fez, Algiers, Marseilles, Genoa, Innsbruck, Munich. That gets me to Berlin about the 10th. There are several reasons for my going back,—Roger & Barbara [Sessions] will be living there, and the I.S.C.M. is intending to give the all American orchestral concert I told you about. I plan to stay until about Dec 15, and then go directly to London and sail for home from there. There may be a chamber music concert to arrange in London if the English section of the I.S.C.M. will further the idea. (I wrote Edward Evans suggesting your songs as a part of the program.) Anyway, I want to be home by about Jan 1, in order to hear Koussie do the Ode (endlich!) [(finally!).]

If I stay at Strub's again, as I hope to do, and if the extra bed is still there, you must come to visit me for a week or so. All you'll need is carfare. We'll time your visit well, so that it comes at some special time, when some special event is being given. Though I imagine Germany will be special event enough all by itself. (I wonder if you know that Fred Jacobi's wife is giving a violin Sonata Recital there in Nov. with Ribaupierre.)

Tanger has been an experience. I cant say its been very good for my work; so that I'll be glad to get back to civilization and piano tuners, but I feel I've seen something. The Oriental part of the World, in short. For instance, Paul [Bowles] and I were invited to an Arab's home for lunch. The women disappear at the sound of a stranger and one eats with ones hands out of a common dish with the male members of the family. I mention this because I get much more of a kick out of seeing one interior than seeing the outsides of a dozen villages. Nevertheless, they say Tanger is too international, and that one must go further South to see the real Arabian cities—so I'm going to spend a few days at Fez on my way back. Fez, they say, hasn't been open to Europeans very long.

It gave me a 'coup' to see you at a Paris address. Have you actually moved from Juziers, bag and baggage? The paragraph about that miscreant Teddy Chanler made me think you are just like the Queen in 'Alice in Wonderland' who goes about crying 'Off with his head!' about everyone she sees or knows. It made me tremble for my own. Of course you're right, but what did poor Teddy do?

The only music I have with me is the volume of Mozart's Quartets and Quintets. I'm getting to know it well, all of it, and will leave Morocco understanding him 100% better.

My address is American Legation here until Oct 1—after that Am. Express in Berlin.

Always,

A—

Copland continued to recommend that young American composers, including Paul Bowles, study with Boulanger in Paris. Virgil Thomson was openly critical of Boulanger, however, and wrote to Copland on November 26, 1931, with his reservations. Here Copland defends Boulanger as a teacher.

To Virgil Thomson

Thomson/Yale. als.

[Undated 1931]

Sat

Dear V—

I can't answer your airmail[1] fully now since we are to meet in London soon. I'd rather discuss le cas Boulanger with you then. As far as you and I go there is no particular hurry. You certainly make the case against N.B. well enough and I'm not so blind as to be unaware that there is such a thing.

In relation to Paul [Bowles] this, briefly, is what I think. There is no matter where or how a pupil learns his stuff just so that he learns it. Therefore it makes no difference whether he studies with N.B. or Dukas. But I know absolutely nothing about Dukas as a teacher and I do know N.B. can teach counterpoint so I naturally send my friends to N.B. Secondly, it is useless to be a pupil if you are unwilling to enter into a pupil-teacher relationship. (Roy [Harris] was too old to do this and so were you in 1926.) I'm all for the teacher influencing the pupil—it doesn't matter what pet ideas the teacher happens to have or what means are employed to drive them home—the pupil should swallow them whole for a time and if he has any guts he'll throw them overboard soon enough. If not, it proves he's just a pupil and it doesn't matter whom he studies with. I know N.B.'s pet ideas and I know the maternal means she employs but I know nothing of Dukas' pet ideas etc. So it boils itself down to sending pupils to a known quantity. As soon as I feel the disadvantages outweigh the advantages to be gained from being N.B.'s pupil I'll stop sending pupils, but that time hasn't come yet.

Always

Aaron

P.S. If Paul is awaiting an answer please tell him I am sending him one c/o Bernad Faÿ. I have 4 different addresses and don't know which to write to.

---

1. Thomson's letter is published in *Selected Letters of Virgil Thomson,* ed. Tim Page and Vanessa Weeks Page (New York: Summit, 1988), 100–101.

To Carlos Chávez

AC/LC. Photocopy of als.
[The Allerton stationery]

Dec 26 [1931]

Dear Carlos—

I hope this letter reaches you before you leave Mexico for New York, because otherwise I would be ashamed to greet you because I have taken so long to answer your letter of last Sept. But at first, I waited for the Sonata for Horns and Unidad that you said you were sending. But they never came. I'm sorry, because we could have performed them in Berlin. Instead, I played the Sonatina in London.[1]

I have just returned from Europe, and as yet, have no permanent address. I cant tell you how much I look forward to seeing you soon again. All you wrote about music in America awoke a responsive echo in my heart.[2] I am through with Europe[,] Carlos, and I believe as you do, that our salvation must come from ourselves and that we must fight the foreign element in America which ignores American music. I am very anxious to see the music of Mexican and South American composers and I hope you will bring scores with you. And I have plans to go there myself in the fall to see how things are.

This year there are no Copland-Sessions Concerts. Instead, I am arranging a Festival of American chamber music in May at Saratoga Springs,[3] about 5 hours from N.Y. and Boston. I hope we can give the Horn Sonata there, tho the 4 horn players must come from N.Y. which makes it an expensive project. I wish you could be there too.

Let me know when you are coming. It cant be too soon for me.

With love

Aaron

---

1. The Sonata for Four Horns, *Unidad,* and Sonatina are all works by Chávez. Copland performed the Sonatina at a December 16 concert of American music sponsored by the British Section of the International Society for Contemporary Music.

2. In a letter dated September 7, 1931, Chávez complained bitterly about the dominance of European musicians and conductors in American musical institutions.

3. The first Festival of Contemporary American Music at Yaddo. Chávez's *Unidad* for piano was performed.

CHAPTER THREE

The Depression Years,
1932–37

In the summer of 1932, the First Festival of Contemporary American Music was held on April 30 and May 1, 1932, at the estate of Katrina and Spencer Trask, known as Yaddo, in Saratoga Springs, New York. Copland was principally responsible for selecting the programs and performers. The concerts featured pieces by members of the newly formed Young Composers' Group, students of Boulanger, and people Copland knew through the League of Composers, as well as chamber works by Mexican composers Carlos Chávez and Silvestre Revueltas. To provide some historical background for the more contemporary works on the program, Copland also included a selection of songs by Charles Ives, at that time a relatively obscure figure. The songs were enthusiastically received, and the performance (with Copland at the piano) stands as a landmark in the reception history of Ives's music. Another highlight of the Yaddo festival was the symposium on critics and composers, a wide-ranging discussion that addressed the touchy subject of the relationship between young composers and music journalists. Copland moderated the forum and offered some remarks of his own that sparked a controversy when subsequently quoted, and misquoted, in the press. It was widely reported that Copland had described newspaper critics as a "menace" to American music, whereas he had in fact impugned only a certain type of unsophisticated reportage. Copland quickly clarified his comments in a flurry of letters to the newspapers, explaining that of course the critic was "an absolute necessity" to the young composer.

At the end of the summer, Copland headed south for a five-month visit to Mexico City and its environs. Chávez had arranged an all-Copland concert at the National Conservatory, and Copland also spent a couple of months in the rural village of Tlalpam. In Mexico he completed the *Elegies for Violin and Viola* (later withdrawn from his catalog) and continued to work on both the *Short Symphony* and *Statements for Orchestra.* His visit to a Mexico City dance hall, the famed Salón México, inspired a new piece by that same name. *El Salón México,* completed in 1936, marked a new direction in Copland's music toward a melodic, accessible idiom that the composer himself described as "imposed simplicity."[1] This conscious adoption of an accessible style rooted in folk traditions eventually brought Copland his greatest successes with such works as *Billy the Kid* and *Appalachian Spring.*

This new approach was in part a reaction to the changed cultural circumstances of the Great Depression. Copland was motivated by the crisis to reach out to the broadest possible audience, and he was also no doubt inspired by Chávez's role as a clear leader in the Mexican musical scene. In terms of Copland's political alignment during the 1930s, a letter to Israel Citkowitz documents his sympathies with communism. Though never a member of the Communist Party, Copland found it in himself to make a public speech before a party function in Bemidji, Minnesota, during the summer of 1934.

While vacationing in Minnesota, he received a commission from the choreographer Ruth Page for a new ballet score. Copland composed the work, *Hear Ye! Hear Ye!* rather quickly, partly by reusing music from other pieces, and he seemed rather dismissive both of the project and of Page. But it was an important commission insofar as it provided the first opportunity for Copland to see one of his stage works produced. He was obviously drawn to the ballet as a form and genre, given that his first orchestral work had been a ballet; *Grohg* had never been performed, however, and Copland used some of its music for *Hear Ye! Hear Ye!* which premiered in 1934.

The 1930s were a remarkably productive era for Copland: he completed *Statements for Orchestra* and the *Short Symphony* early in the decade, composed *Hear Ye! Hear Ye!* in 1934, finished the orchestration of *El Salón*

México in 1936, and wrote an opera for high school performance, *The Second Hurricane,* that same year. This creatively fertile period would continue throughout the 1940s as Copland solidified his compositional voice, his professional friendships, his network of contacts, and his place in American musical life.

Copland organized the two days of concerts at the First Festival of Contemporary American Music at Yaddo; the programs included his own *Piano Variations,* the *Stabat Mater* for soprano and string quartet by Virgil Thomson, seven songs by Charles Ives, *Unidad* for piano by Carlos Chávez, the *Serenade* for string quartet by Marc Blitzstein, and the Suite for Flute and Piano by nineteen-year-old composer Henry Brant.

---

1. Aaron Copland, "Composer from Brooklyn," *Magazine of Art,* 1939 (reprinted in *Our New Music,* 1941; rev. and enlarged ed., *The New Music, 1900–1960,* New York: W. W. Norton, 1968), 160.

To Charles Ives

Ives/Yale. als.

March 7, 1932
52 E. 58 St.
New York City

My dear Mr. Ives,

I have programmed a group of 5 or 6 songs from your volume of '114 Songs' for performance at a Festival of Contemporary American Music at Saratoga Springs in May.[1] I should be extremely obliged if you would send me immediately two copies of the '114 Songs' so that I can begin work with our singer.

I very much regret to hear through Henry Cowell that you are not enjoying good health just now but I hope it will improve in the near future. If so, it would be a pleasure for me to meet you personally.

Yours sincerely,
Aaron Copland

---

1. The seven songs were "The Indians," "Walking," "Serenity," "Maple Leaves," "The See'r," "Evening," and "Charlie Rutlage."

On May 2, the Associated Press dispatched a story about the Yaddo festival, claiming that "the long-standing feud" between composers and critics had "flared into the open" at the conference. Copland was widely quoted as referring to critics as a "menace" and felt compelled to set the record straight.

Open letter to the *New York Times*, May 8, 1932

I cannot allow the attached syndicate dispatch to go uncommented upon, in spite of the fact that it is difficult for me to believe that any one could possible [*sic*] take at its face value this obvious attempt on the part of a young Associated Press reporter to turn me into the Representative Sirovich of composers.[1] It would be very naïve to imagine that a conference between critics and composers was arranged at the First Festival of Contemporary American Music at Yaddo for the childish purpose of giving composers an opportunity to tell the critics where "to get off at," as the saying goes. On the contrary, our purpose was the thoroughly serious one of considering the relation between the American composer and the music critic of the daily press and to discover what might be done to make that relation more vital and more important than it now is. The very premise on which the conference was based was that the composer needs the critic (just as much as the critic needs the composer). Far from being a "menace" to the composer, he is an absolute necessity, if only because he serves as middle man between the public and the creative artist.

I can assure you that no petty or antagonistic motives actuated what was said. Nevertheless, the general sentiment of the conference was that the music critics of the daily press will soon come to realize that the position of the American composer has changed, and that he is no longer satisfied with the merely tolerant and often apathetic attitude of the press toward American music in general (as exemplified by the absence of the press from a festival at which the work of nineteen representative Americans was presented), and that the casual attitude adopted by them toward our new American music is no longer apposite to the body of vital music which is being created—and what is more, performed.

AARON COPLAND

P.S. This letter may be published if you so desire. In justice to myself I am forced to add that the above remarks are made distinctly in relation to new American music as a whole and not to my personal creations, which have almost always been quite sufficiently noticed, due to the particular auspices under which they were presented.

---

1. Representative William Irving Sirovich (Democrat of New York) had recently made headlines by leading the U.S. House Patent Committee in complaining about harsh drama criticism ("Congressmen Assail the Drama's Critics: Sirovich Leads Attack," *New York Times*, March 1, 1932).

To Carlos Chávez

AC/LC. Photocopy of als.
[Yaddo stationery]

May 8 1932

Dear Carlos—

So glad to get your letter with dates etc. I am sending you the Trio[1] immediately. Please have it copied and sent back soon as I think I will need it and it is
the only copy I have.

I will see to it that I am in Mexico before Oct. 7 so that I can be there for the
concert. I would like to be there for the Ode on August 19 but I dont think I
can be there so soon.

The Yaddo Festival was a great success, even better than I had hoped. Sanroma played the Unidad[2] well—tho not the way you would have played it. I liked
the piece very much—it is pure Chavez. The Revueltas was very amusing.[3] It
seemed like a little Mexican drama and I could easily imagine it being danced.
To my great surprise the Lange Quartet were very enthusiastic about it and say
that they will play it again next season at Mr. Rossin's house. On the other hand,
some of the musician-listeners were confused because the form of the first two
parts seemed so broken up—but I wasn't. Congratulate him for me.

Now, at last, I am working. And thinking always of my trip to you and
Mexico.

Always

Aaron

---

1. *Vitebsk* (1928).
2. Chávez's piano piece.
3. Silvestre Revueltas's Second String Quartet.

To Virgil Thomson

Thomson/Yale. als.
[Yaddo stationery]

May 10 [1932]

Dear Virgil—

You may be happy! The Stabat went even better than I had hoped.[1] It had
the kind of success which blows every one over, whatever their tastes. I'm
delighted for you because I feel it's the first real success you've had in America.
I'll see to it that the League of Composers performs it in N.Y. next season
(which won't be difficult because Mrs. Reis heard it and was enthusiastic) and
that the Cos Cob Press publishes it (Mrs. Wertheim was also here & liked it
very much.)

The critics were conspicuous by their absence. I lit into them at a conference, an AP reporter got the story, and thereby stirred a hornets next. There is now a case going on of Copland vs. the Critics. Since they always treated me with kid gloves they consider it rank ingratitude—biting the hand that fed my rep[utation] etc.

The whole Festival went off very well—I can't tell you how sorry I am that you weren't here. It would have made an impression on you, I'm sure. Well, maybe next year.

Best luck with the Quartet in Paris.[2]

Always,

Aaron

---

1. Thomson's *Stabat Mater* for soprano and string quartet (1931).

2. In fact, Virgil Thomson's Second String Quartet had its premiere in New York City in 1933.

To Henry Brant

AC/LC. Photocopy of als.

[Yaddo stationery]

May 18 [1932]

Dear Henry—

Your long letter deserves a better reply than I can give it at the moment. (I'm not in a letter-writing frame of mind—I had to do too much of it before the Festival.) But I will allow myself the following observations of your impressions:

A. From my standpoint (as impresario) the Festival was a success, since everyone seemed to be really interested in what they were hearing. There wasn't the usual apathy that goes with listening to American music. In short, the right atmosphere was created.

B. The tiff with the critics is all to the good—. You're right in saying they shouldn't be scared, but nothing less will move them to think about the American composer at all. So.—

C. Your piece did not get the reception it deserved.[1] But then its probably not as easy to really hear as you and I imagine. I was near Citkowitz while it was being performed and I could see he was having the right reactions. But to ask [newspaper critic Irving] Kolodin for the same is asking too much. There is no tradition in America of the talented 18 year old composer. No one has ever seen one before so its hard to believe in it. An 18 year old = a student; which is natural enough when, up to now, a 50 year old is still a "young" composer in America.

D. Make it a rule: Never expect anything from newspaper critics. (There'll be one exception every 20 years.) You'll only get serious consideration from people who have actually studied the music under their own hands or eyes.

E. Some friendly advice: get a different bow [to the audience]. The one you have at present is not simple enough—too stiff and self-conscious to please me. It looks too much like Henry Brant the great composer coming to greet his public! Be a great composer but be natural and unaffected about it. Ponder this.

F. You are absolutely right about the Blitzstein work.[2] Very few people get past the sight of that triple Largo. Its really a very simple work with good form—but rather too 'voulu' [willed] as the French say.

G. If you are going to write that orchestral piece I advise you to study lots of scores from the standpoint of orchestration.

H. Are you improving your mind?

I'll be back in July.

Always,

Aaron

[OVER][3]

---

1. Brant's Suite for Flute and Piano, played by Georges Laurent and Jesús María Sanromá.
2. Blitzstein's *Serenade* for string quartet, all three movements of which are marked "Largo."
3. The photocopy does not contain a postscript.

To Carlos Chávez

AC/LC. Photocopy of als.

52 West 58 St.
New York
Aug 8, '32

Dear Carlos—

I was about to write to you when your telegram came. I have many things to tell you and to ask you.

First, about the 'Music for the Theatre' score. I will send it air-mail before a week has passed. I can't send it immediately because I am correcting the proofs which have just come from Vienna. There are several small changes (making it a little shorter) and even one in orchestration (of the Dance movement). But I'm sure it will reach you in time.

You say you need it for [your] Sept 2nd program. Does that mean that you will not do the Symphonic Ode on Sept. 2 as you originally thought of doing?

I have been thinking very much of you and Mexico and I would have written to you before but I still do not know the exact date of my arrival in Mexico City. All I can say is that it will be sometime between September 1 and Sept. 30. I hope it will be early so that I can hear the concert of Sept. 2. If I come by boat, it will be early, but if I come by automobile it cannot be until a little later. It is too long to explain why there are these complications, but the important thing is that I will be there—soon. As soon as I have finally made up my mind, I will let you know the exact date.

Can you tell me two things:

(1) Give me an address where I can have my mail sent, until I have a permanent address.

(2) Give me the name of a hotel where I will stay I suppose until I get definitely established in my own place.

You'll be glad to hear that I am studying Spanish and reading a great deal about Mexico, so that I think I can already find my way around the City without a guide!

I am spending a quiet summer in New York, working on the same new orchestral piece[,][1] which I hope to finish in Mexico.

And looking forward 'passionement' to my Mexican trip.

Always love

Aaron

---

1. The *Short Symphony.*

To Carlos Chávez

AC/LC. Photocopy of als.

Aug 18 [1932]
52 W. 58 St.
N.Y.

Dear Carlos—

I was so glad to get your letter with all the excellent programs and musical plans. I will try very seriously to be there for the 2nd of September program but you must help me if possible. I will tell you how. I am going to drive my car as far as Laredo and at Laredo take the train to Mexico City. I cannot leave N.Y. before Wednesday, Aug. 24. This leaves only nine days for the whole trip so that it would mean a terrific hurry (in hot weather) and even then it is not too certain that it can be done. But if I had one week extra it could surely be done. So I have thought that perhaps you would be able to and willing to exchange concerts, so that the Cuarteto del Conservatorio would give its concert announced for the 9th on the 2nd; and so the concert of my works could be given on the 9th and I could certainly be there by then. Is this idea possible? I hope you will do what you can to make it possible. Please send me a telegram in either case whether or not it is possible; and please send it not later than Monday, the 22nd.

I am bringing with me a young violinist who is a pupil, companion, secretary and friend! His name is Victor Kraftsov.[1] I'm sure you will like him.

I will send you a wire from Laredo to tell you the exact time of my arrival. Till soon, with much love

Aaron

---

1. Copland's companion, who later Americanized his name to Victor Kraft.

Copland in fact arrived in Mexico City on September 2. That night, Carlos Chávez and the Orquesta Sinfónica de México offered the first ever all-Copland program, featuring Copland's Two Pieces for String Quartet (1928), the *Piano Variations* (1930), two works for chorus and piano: "The House on the Hill" and "An Immorality" (1925), and *Music for the Theatre* (1925).

To his parents

AC/LC. als.

Mexico City
Sept. 3, 1932

Dear Ma & Pa[1]—

Here I am, at last in Mexico City. The trip from San Antonio took two nights and a day on the train and was absolutely uneventful. We just arrived in San Antonio in time to catch the train that would bring us here in time for the all-Copland program.

Well, we arrived on the morning of the concert and were met at the station and have been very well taken care of ever since. An apartment had already been found for me in a quiet but central part of the city. Not long after my arrival people from the newspapers came and I am sending you some of the results. The article is too long to translate and says mostly things that you already know.

The concert took place yesterday evening. There was a rumor that the American Ambassador would come, but he didn't show up. It was an interesting experience to hear a whole program made up of my own works. The newspaper criticisms will come out later.

In the morning, Chavez took me to meet one of the Cabinet ministers, so that I feel I'm already a friend of the Government! No one seems to mind the change of president which I suppose you read about in the papers.[2]

The City itself reminds me much more of Europe than of America. Its hard to believe I havent crossed any water to get here. Its a great help, having so

many friends here, tho I must say, the Mexicans I see in the streets seem to
have little relation to the Mexicans who are my friends. The city is a great
mixture of magnificence and of poverty. But it has great charm too.

I know you must have been disappointed that I didn't see the folks in Dallas[3]
but there just wasn't time if that concert was to be made.

Tell Leon that the car stood up under the strain so he can be proud of it.[4] We
had only two punctures in all, and one break in the gas line which occurred in
the mountains at night in Tennessee and might have forced us to spend the
night where we were stuck, if we weren't rescued by a farmer-mechanic who
happened along by chance.

Thats all for the moment. Write me at the address I gave you.

Love to all

Aaron

---

1. These two letters to his parents, on September 3 and September 10, are among the very few
later than 1922 to survive.

2. Pascual Ortiz Rubio resigned the presidency on September 2, 1932, and Abelardo Rodrí-
guez was chosen to complete his term.

3. Copland's mother, Sarah Mittenthal, was raised in Waxahachie, Texas, a town near Dallas,
and much of the Mittenthal family remained in that area.

4. Copland had borrowed a car from his brother Leon for the drive to Texas.

To Serge and Natalie Koussevitzky

SK/LC. als.

Moneda 16
Mexico D.F.
Mexico
Sept 5 1932

Dear friends—

I should have written you before, but a summer spent in New York does not
leave one with much to say. Still, I ought to have written if only to ask what kind
of a summer you have had and to ask after your health and the news, etc.

Well, Mexico is very different from New York! I have only been here a few
days, but I can already see that. I drove in my auto as far as San Antonio, where
I left my car, and then took the train. Chavez had arranged an all-Copland
program for the 2nd of Sept. (Two Pieces for String Quartet, Piano Variations,
Two Choruses for Womens Voices, and Music for the Theatre) and it was a very
interesting experience for me to listen to it. Later he is to play the 'Symphonic
Ode.' At last I have found a country where I am as famous as Gershwin!!

I have finished three separate movements for orchestra, but only two of
them belong in one piece and the third in another.[1] I will try to finish the piece

with the 2 movements by adding a third, and if I get it done by January, I hope you will still have a place for it on this year's programs. It is very different from the Ode and I hope you will like it.

If I can't finish in time, perhaps you will consider repeating the [First] Symphony in the new orchestral version,[2] or Music for the Theatre, or even the Dance Symphony[,] which would be new for Boston. But I don't have to give you ideas about this. I know you have plenty of your own.

You dont know how sorry I am not to be at the boat in New York to meet you when you arrive. I'll be there in spirit though. I plan to be back in the States by January 15. Try not to forget me until then. I shall follow your activities from here.

Always devotedly
Copland

---

1. Probably movements from the *Short Symphony* and *Statements for Orchestra*.
2. The First Symphony is a rescoring of the *Symphony for Organ and Orchestra* without the organ.

To his parents

AC/LC. als.

Mexico City
Sept 10, 1932

Dear Ma & Pa—

I received your first letter just two days after you sent it so you can see that aeroplanes have their uses.

I have been having a little more difficulty in getting settled than I had expected. Chávez got me a small apartment which is excellent and costs only $30 a month. But the rooms are small, and to bring a piano in here would disturb all the neighbors. So we have been looking for a small studio near the apartment and that isnt so easy to find. Everything is very cheap here: you can ride in a taxi from any part of the city to any other for a flat rate of 15¢, and you can eat a regular meal in the swellest <u>American</u> restaurant for two pesos (60¢). I only go to Mexican restaurants occasionally so as gradually to get used to the strange tasting food. Breakfast I have at home. There are plenty of movies in town, all showing American movies, but I haven't tried any yet. Last night I saw my first show. It was scheduled to begin at 9:30, but actually didn't get started until 11 P.M. Its a very Mexican habit to be always late, and nobody seems to mind. I manage to get around all right on the little Spanish that I have been able to pick up. But there aren't as many people who talk English or French or German as I thought there would be.

Gradually we are visiting the suburbs. Last Sunday we went to a place called

Xochimilco which is an Indian village in exactly the same state it was before Columbus discovered America. To-day we expect to visit Chapultepec (its hopeless to try to pronounce these Mexican-Indian names) where the President lives. The city itself is the strangest mixture of new and old. Its the first city I've ever been in where it seems quite the regular thing for the poorer classes to go around bare-footed, and this on the busiest streets where there are the most modern office buildings.

Chavez is to repeat some of the music given at the all-Copland program at a new series of concerts. The Ode will be given in November.

The weather is ideal, not too warm and not too cool. Each day it rains for an hour or two, but even that will stop in October when the rainy season comes to an end. Its hard to believe that we are 7,000 feet above sea level because I don't feel it in any way.

Love to all the folks

Aaron

P.S. Here are more newspaper clippings too long to translate.

To Henry Brant

AC/LC. Photocopy of als.

> Quinta Catipoto
> Av. Allende y Matamoros
> Tlalpam, D.F.
> Mexico
> Nov. 16 [1932]

Dear Henry—

Wasn't it odd—two hours after I sent you that program c/o Pan Americans at the New School your letter came. It was like an answer to a prayer! I was really quite starved for news for no one has been writing me. At such moments I always think of you because your letters are so complete and therefore satisfying.

What with [Jerome] Moross being performed, [Lehman] Engel published, yourself accomplishing the impossible in getting 11 flutes for a public performance, and the [Young Composers'] Group concert in Dec. I should say that we started something last year.[1] I'll be curious to see whether the crowd will have been able to keep up a spirit of camaraderie by the time I get back or whether the spirit of rivalry is too much for them. I hope they can stick together for there are many things to be done, as you know.

My Mexican trip has been all I could have hoped for and more. I cant rave too much about the country itself—nor the populace, for that matter. The first two months I spent in Mexico City—now I have a lovely house in the country where conditions for work are ideal. But dont think I've finished a whole batch of new works, as you would have done. No, I'm still turning out my 1932 opus and I'll consider myself lucky if I come home with it completely finished. At any rate I have two movements of it done and orchestrated and its the third I'm working on now.[2] I'm using an orchestra with no trombones or tuba and only 2 trumpets. It should be interesting to see what that gives. I still haven't a name for it, and I begin to despair of getting a really satisfactory one.

Music in Mexico is practically confined to Chavez and his activities. The entire musical destinies of a nation lie in his hands. The only other composer down here who seems of any consequence is Revueltas. I'm sorry you didn't say how you liked his 'Colorines.' Its been played here several times and goes over big with the audience. In general, the Mexican public receives Revueltas' music more enthusiastically than they do Chavez'.

So Ives is still cause for ructions eh. I begin to feel unfortunate in missing both the Theatre pieces and this last thing.[3] How is the Master—still among the living?

Your reaction to [Rubin] Goldmark doesnt surprise me. Fifteen years ago he may have had some excuse for his attitude, but now . . . You deserve someone better. The anti-Boulanger movement seems to be taking on alarming proportions. I'll have to look into it when I get back. That will be about Jan 20. I plan to take in New Orleans and the Deep South on the way back.

Ask Elie [Siegmeister] to write me—if you see him. And you write again too whenever the spirit moves you.

Always

Aaron

---

1. In 1932 Copland led an informal organization of composers known as the Young Composers' Group. Elie Siegmeister, Arthur Berger, Israel Citkowitz, Vivian Fine, Jerome Moross, and Henry Brant gathered in Copland's apartment to discuss each other's music.

2. The *Short Symphony.*

3. Brant's letter to Copland (to which this is an answer) talks of Ives only in terms of Brant's wish to edit "the seedy and uneven places," making Ives's music available for performance. The "Theatre pieces" are probably the *Set for Theatre Orchestra,* first performed on February 16, 1932, in New York; "this last thing" may be Slonimsky's set of performances in Europe of *The Fourth of July,* premiered in Paris on February 21 and in Berlin on March 5, 1932.

To Carlos Chávez

AC/LC. Photocopy of als.
[The Menger, San Antonio, Texas, stationery]

Jan 2 [1933]

Dear Carlos—

Just a few words so that you'll know we got here safely. Before leaving Catipoato I got your letter. It seemed strange to leave Mexico without seeing you again. We had a brilliant send-off at the train, but I missed you. But of course I'm glad you're resting at Jalapa and making firm resolves to carry out the inevitable that must some day come about.[1]

As soon as we crossed the border I regretted leaving Mexico with a sharp pang. It took me three years in France to get as close a feeling to [*sic*] the country as I was able to get in three months in Mexico. I can thank you for this, for without your many kindnesses, the opportunity for knowing it and loving it so well would never have come. I think always of my returning soon—

The Acapulco trip was marvellous. When I came back I saw Paul Strand, who has taken the house in Tlalpam, as you probably have heard.

To-morrow we start the big trip home. I'll let you know when we get to N.Y.

My best to you

Always

Aaron

Victor wants to be remembered to you.

---

1. In March 1933 Chávez became chief of the Department of Fine Arts in the Mexican Secretariat of Public Education.

To Mary Lescaze[1]

AC/LC. als.

[Hotel Whitney, Savannah, Georgia, stationery]

Jan 13 [1933]

Dear Mary—

I meant to write this in Mexico before leaving. But a last minute decision to bathe in the Pacific at Acapulco made leaving a rushed affair. So I took your letter with me and its been pointing an accusing finger every time I opened my bag—which is often for I've been making one night stops at San Antonio, Houston, Galveston, New Orleans, Mobile, Montgomery, Atlanta and now Savannah. In another 10 days I'll be home, so it doesn't seem necessary to write at length.

Mexico was a rich time. Outwardly nothing happened and inwardly all was calm, yet I'm left with the impression of having had an enriching experience. It comes, no doubt, from the nature of the country and the people. Europe now seems conventional to me by comparison. Mexico offers something fresh and pure and wholesome—a quality which is deeply unconventionalized. The source of it I believe is the Indian blood which is so prevalent. I sensed the influence of the Indian background everywhere—even in the landscape. And I must be something of an Indian myself or how else explain the sympathetic chord it awakens in me. Of course I'm going back some day.

Travelling in our dear U.S.A. is something of an anti-climax after Mexico.

Perhaps a foreigner would feel differently. A city like Savannah seems glaringly different from the others. (Like Washington, it was planned you know.) Though on second thought, the larger cities all present distinctive physiological pictures and one couldn't confuse Galveston with New Orleans or San Anton with Atlanta. Its underneath that they're all alike, as everybody knows. And the non-existance of any cultural life worth mentioning is depressing even to a passer-by like myself. Perhaps its only dormant and we need a new kind of pioneer down here to awaken the spiritual consciences of the people. I can easily see myself in the rôle. Perhaps there is more 'culture' up where I'm off to—Charleston, Raleigh, Richmond. Isn't that the country where the Tate[2] crowd functions?

Whoever told you I had finished a piece was a bit ahead of the facts. Its only almost done. Two movements are orchestrated and in ink. But theres that damn last movement. I have the themes and the form but the notes have to be filled in.[3] I wish I had finished in time to bring it back with me and play to everyone. Now you'll have to wait. I've promised a piece for the League to be done in April. Its to be a Duo for violin and viola called 'Elegies.'[4] Its going to be a battle to finish all this in N.Y.C.

Well it wont be long now.

Best to Ralph.

Always

Aaron

---

1. Mary Hughes Lescaze was a close friend and loyal supporter of Copland's; the two had met around 1927 through her first husband, photographer Ralph Steiner. She married architect William Lescaze in September 1933 (and it is as Mary Lescaze that she is best known).

2. Poet Allen Tate.

3. The *Short Symphony.*

4. Later used as the basis of "Subjective" in *Statements for Orchestra* and withdrawn as a separate piece from Copland's catalog.

To Charles Ives

Ives/Yale. als.

October 7, 1933

Dear Mr. Ives—

I told Miss Lederman of 'Modern Music' of my desire to write an article on the 114 Songs and she enthusiastically encouraged my [sic] to do so. Before starting work on it I should be very glad if you could clear up some of the following points for me.

1. Could you tell me the date of, and reason for, reprinting the volume of 50 Songs?

2. What in the main governed your selection of the 50 Songs you chose. (Why, for example, was 'Where the Eagle' omitted.)

3. Your reason for omitting the postscript.

4. Does your attitude in the postscript hold good today?

5. Why did you include certain songs written in 1921 in the back of the volume with the earlier ones.

I would appreciate your helping me with these few points.[1]

Yours sincerely,

Aaron Copland

---

1. Mrs. Ives, serving as Ives's amanuensis, answered on October 10:

1. The book of 50 was published about two or three years after the larger book, as there were not many of the latter, and to send to some who . . . weren't musically interested that asked for copies principally because the book was not sold.

2. . . . I don't remember exactly. . . . Why was "Where the Eagle" omitted? I don't know.

3. . . . probably to save space, cost of reprinting & trouble to the reader!

4. . . . <u>Yes.</u> Except possibly in some details.

5. . . . a mistake of the binder and partly mine.

To Carlos Chávez

AC/LC. Photocopy of als.

209 W. 57 St.
c/o Cos Cob Press
N.Y.
Dec 16 '33

Dear Carlos—

I was so glad to have your long letter—to hear from you at first hand—to know of your various activities—and to feel again how close we are in ideas, ideals, and understanding. I see your problem so clearly;—to work for Mexico or to work for yourself I can understand is no easy problem to solve—but you can be sure that I wait for the outcome with absolute confidence that when the moment comes you will know how to solve it. When I was in Mexico I was a little envious of the opportunity you had to serve your country in a musical way. Here in the U.S.A. we composers have no possibility of directing the musical affairs of the nation—on the contrary, since my return, I have the impression that more and more we are working in a vacuum. There seems to me less than ever a real rapport between the public and the composers[,] and of course that is a very unhealthy state of affairs. So you can see that for me your work as Jefe de Bellas Artes is a very important way of creating an audience, and being in contact with an audience. When one has done that, one can compose with real joy.

I was very interested to get the prospectus and programs that you sent and I hope you will always keep me posted of artistic happenings in Mexico. Unfortunately I have the sad news to report that Silvestre [Revueltas]'s record that you sent me came <u>broken</u> in <u>pieces</u>! Won't you please send another and this time have it wrapped in such a way that it <u>cannot</u> be broken. It was a keen disappointment to me—also to Victor.

You ask about my plans. I have none in particular. Everyone is now in New York—Varese, Antheil, Roy Harris, Sessions, Cowell etc.—but the feeling of camaraderie is not too strong. The younger group of composers who I brought together have even less of an 'esprit de corps.' Last year they were very busy getting famous—this year they are students again, several of them studying with Sessions. There is one thing I wish to talk to you about if you come here in January—Mrs Wertheim has turned the Cos Cob Press over to me and has asked me to run it on a very reduced budget which allows for the publication of only a few works each year. Outside of that I occupy myself with helping to run the League of Composers concerts though it is hard to put new life into the old girl!

In the back of my mind always is the idea of going to Mexico again. There is so much of the country that I didn't see. And I should like to come knowing Spanish better. Well, it will happen, I am sure—and even sooner, if there wasn't this damn Depression.

I wrote Revueltas a little about my 'Salon Mexico' piece. Did he tell you? At the same time I am working on the 5 movement piece for orchestra that I think I told you about—to be called 'Statements.'[1] Three movements are done. But between these two very different works I do not succeed in finishing either.

The 'Bounding Line' as you call it—its now entitled 'Short Symphony'—is supposed to be played here by Koussie during the second part of the season. I have a second copy of the score which you may have when you come here. If you dont come I will send it to you. I hope you will like the last movement of the work. You know how pleased it will make me to have it played in Mexico.

Thats all the 'news.' Remember me to all the friends. And please <u>try</u> to come here in Jan.

Always affectionately

Aaron

My temporary address is 138 W. 58 St, but will probably not be good after Jan 15.

---

1. Copland's plan for the number of movements in *Statements for Orchestra* varied; in a later letter (October 15, 1934) he suggests that there will be seven movements. The completed *Statements* has six movements.

During the summer of 1934, Copland lived in his cousin's lakeside cottage in Lavinia, Minnesota, with his companion, Victor Kraft.

To Charles Ives

Ives/Yale. als.

June 28, 1934
Lavinia, Minnesota

Dear Mr. Ives—

Thank you for your very kind letter about the article. I'm sorry if I mis-quoted you on the subject of the 'business man.'[1] It served my purpose so well that I must have misread its meaning.

Has anyone told you of the performance of some of the songs at at [*sic*] League of Composers Concert in March with Julius Huehn, baritone. I wish you could have witnessed the enthusiasm of the audience.

I have talked with Mr. Koussevitzky[2] about the possibility of a performance of one of your scores and hope something comes of it. At any rate I intend to keep the issue alive with him.

I hope you wont forget to get in touch with me on one of your visits to New York. I should very much enjoy knowing you personally. I can always be reached c/o Cos Cob Press 209 W. 57 St.

Cordially yours,
Aaron Copland

---

1. Aaron Copland, "One Hundred and Fourteen Songs," *Modern Music* 11 (January–February 1934): 59–64. Copland questioned why Ives "chose to glorify the businessman composer as opposed to the so-called professional composer" and felt that Ives's music suffered from a lack of contact with an audience. Ives wrote Copland in response, explaining that in praising the businessman he "was paying my respects to the average man (there is one) in the ordinary business of life" who seemed to possess "more openmindedness" than many professional musicians. Ives to Copland, May 24, 1934, as quoted in Howard Pollack, *Aaron Copland: The Life and Work of an Uncommon Man* (New York: Henry Holt, 1999), 110–11.

2. Copland has finally learned to spell the name.

To Israel Citkowitz

AC/LC. als.

Lavinia, Minn
[September 1934]

Dear Israel—

I couldn't figure out from your letter whether or not you realized that my question to Minna [Lederman] about you was just a joke. It never oc-curred to me that there was any serious danger of your becoming a fas-cist![1] Anyhow, I was awfully glad to have you write me at such length, and I must say the contents of your letter interested me enormously, particularly the Mass. part and the arguments with Roger [Sessions].[2] When I think of

Roger and communism I immediately think of Elie [Siegmeister], who is I fear the symbol of Communism to Roger—whereupon all is lost there and then! He'll be 'confused,' as you say, just so long as he neglects to read the 'classics.' Then at least he'll have a real basis for a choice, whatever that may be.

I've had an interesting summer from that angle myself. I cant write all about it now, as I should like, because I should be writing a ballet for Ruth Page at this moment.[3] But anyway—it began when Victor spied a little wizened woman selling a Daily Worker on the street corners of Bemidji. From that, we learned to know the farmers who were Reds around these parts, attended an all-day election campaign meeting of the C.[ommunist] P.[arty] unit, partook of their picnic supper[,] and [I] made my first political speech! If they were a strange sight to me, I was no less of a one to them. It was the first time that many of them had seen an 'intellectual.' I was being gradually drawn, you see, into the political struggle with the peasantry! I wish you could have seen them—the true Third Estate, the very material that makes revolution. What struck me particularly was the fact that there is no 'type-communist' among them, such as we see on 14th St. They look like any other of the farmers around here, all of them individuals, clearly etched in my mind. And desperately poor. None can afford more than a 10¢ pamphlet. (With that in mind I appealed to the Group[4] for funds and they sent me a collection of $30. which I presented to the unit here for their literature fund.) When S. K. Davis, Communist candidate for Gov. in Minn.[,] came to town and spoke in the public park, the farmers asked me to talk to the crowd. Its one thing to think revolution, or talk about it to ones friends, but to preach it from the streets—OUT LOUD—Well, I made my speech (Victor says it was a good one) and I'll probably never be the same! Now, when we go to town, there are friendly nods from sympathizers, and farmers come up and talk as one red to another. One feels very much at home and not at all like a mere summer boarder. I'll be sorry to leave here with the thought of probably never seeing them again.

I expect to spend the month of October in Chicago. This ballet of mine that the Chicago Opera plans to produce on Nov 16 will keep me desperately busy until then. In times like these, having a definite objective to ones music is best—is easier anyhow.

I look forward to seeing you too.

Fraternally

A—

My address after Oct 5
540 North Michigan Av
Chicago
Tenth Floor

1. Citkowitz's letter of September 15, 1934, contains a lengthy history of his relations to the various communist orthodoxies, starting with "First of all, I haven't become a fascist."

2. Citkowitz had attributed his conversion to communism to his having stayed with Theodore Chanler's mother and sister in Massachusetts during the summer of 1934.

3. *Hear Ye! Hear Ye!* (1934).

4. The Young Composers' Group or perhaps the Group Theatre.

To Carlos Chávez

AC/LC. Photocopy of als.

Chicago, Ill
Oct 15 1934

Dear Carlos—

I too have been thinking of you! and reading about you and the Theatre— (the Palace, rather)—and your new work (Llamadas)[1]—and everything—and I could easily imagine how terrifically busy you have been and still are. So your letter (which came today) and the programs were very exciting.

I am writing to Kalmus[2] today to tell him to send you a score of the 'Music for the Theatre.'

I am sending you also today the score of the Short Symphony. This is a copy I made especially for you which I want you to keep. Some day, if your copyist has time I should like to have a copy of the score made for me. The performance of the work which Koussevitzky was to have done last season was postponed because of what he told me was the extreme difficulty of the work. He expects to do it here this season, but as yet, it has never been played. (Kouss—has his own copy of the score.) Are you sure you can prepare the performance in so short a time? Otherwise perhaps it would be better to wait— as I am afraid that with this work a shaky performance would give an incoherent impression to the public. Of course, I leave it absolutely in your hands to do as you like.

I almost had two new orchestral works finished (I was working in Minnesota) when I had to interrupt them to do a ballet to be performed at the Chicago Opera in November.[3] I have written it very quickly and included some old jazz of mine, but perhaps it will 'go over' as they say.

The two orchestral pieces are 'Seven Statements' (very simple—for me anyhow—of which five are finished) and a ten minute 'light piece' called 'Salon Mexico' which only needs to be orchestrated. I am terribly afraid of what you will say of the Salon Mexico—perhaps it is not Mexican at all and I would look so foolish. But in America del Norte it may sound Mexican!

I will be in Chicago until about Nov 1 and then N.Y. Please come in Dec. and

Jan.—I am sure it will rest you and I am very anxious to see you. If you don't come I'll have to come to Mexico soon again.

Victor wants to be remembered to you and Revueltas.

Always affectionately

Aaron

---

1. The first performance of Chávez's "sinfonia proletaria," *Llamadas,* for small orchestra and chorus on Mexican revolutionary ballads, had taken place on September 29.

2. Edwin F. Kalmus, manager of the Cos Cob Press.

3. The ballet *Hear Ye! Hear Ye!* was premiered on November 30, 1934.

To Paul Bowles

AC/LC. als.

Hubbard Woods, Ill.

Oct 24 '34

Dear P

The card that came this morning was the coup de grâce. For weeks I'd been telling V.[ictor] how we were neglecting you frightfully. And he agreed. Every day I've been saying that we really <u>must</u> write. And he agreed. Why we didn't will be clear presently. It had nothing to do with Africa. I understand the attractions of Africa and I'm sure you know the disadvantages, so I took it for granted that you went with both eyes open. These are difficult times for young composers, and I'm sure its better to eat in Africa than starve in N.Y. So theres no reason for 'disapproving' as you seem to suggest—only the natural desire to have you back soon where I can look at you.

The reason for the long spell of silence was a ballet. Out of a clear sky, toward the end of August, Ruth Page who is a dancer in Chicago asked me to do a ballet for her to be ready by Nov 1. To talk it over V and I drove to Duluth and took a train from there to Chi[cago]. After a week, I had signed on the dotted line and have been working like a Trojan ever since. We dashed back to Bemidji and stayed there until about Oct 4. In those 5 weeks the music was done almost entirely. You can see I worked fast. Its 40 minutes long—not all new—I've used some of the early ballet in it. Now we are staying out at Miss Page's country place on Lake Michigan and I'm orchestrating and orchestrating. The ballet is to be put on at the Chicago Opera on Nov 23. Page did the scenario and a Russian by the name of [Serge] Remisoff the sets and costumes. The scene is a law court—the first dance that of the Prosecuting Attorney. The whole thing is a satire on justice and how she functions. If it goes over they'll take it on tour to lots of small cities, which would be fun.

Thats why, you see, there was no time to write anyone. And you being so far away . . .

I received the Stein songs.[1] I'm curious to know how they happened to be published. You never wrote a word about all that. Why, I wonder, of all your things, did you print those two little things. I have no doubt Kalmus will 'handle' some for you. That is, he'll put them on his counter probably, and they'll collect dust with all the Cos Cob things. Its surprising how little 'modern' music he does sell. I doubt whether Schirmers would take many copies. Write to Kalmus if you like and say I suggested it. Or should I talk to him for you?

The Cos Cob Song Volume has been delayed by my not being in N.Y.[2] When I get back—which should be around Nov. 1—I'll try to get it out finally. But you have never written a <u>word</u> about whether or not you got permission to use that poem of yours. Dare <u>I</u> go ahead just the same?

I've just reread all your letters and p.[ost]cards. But they only tell what you <u>have</u> been doing—and I'd like to know what you're doing now. Write me a nice, long, <u>explicit</u>, letter and say what you're up to in Fez. Describe your 'duties,' as your mother called them. Have you a piano there? Are you writing anything new? As soon as this damn ballet is finished I promise you a really long letter in return.

Chicago is all agog about the opening of [Virgil Thomson's opera] 'Four Saints [in Three Acts]' which takes place on the 7th. I hear Virgil is coming, and perhaps G.[ertrude] S.[tein].

Love and kisses

A

P.S. Address me at 55 St.

---

1. Paul Bowles, *Scenes from the Door* (1933), settings of poems by Gertrude Stein.
2. The volume contained Paul Bowles's "Letter to Freddy," with text by Gertrude Stein.

To Paul Bowles

AC/LC. als.

Jan 8 [1935]
63 W 55

Dear P.B.

Heres the Mamoulian[1] letter you ask for. I hope it's a help. I liked the picture of yourself you sent me and the letter. Apparently Hollywood <u>can</u> be lived in. When you do come back, and stop in Chicago, I think you should play some of your music for Ruth Page as she is looking for a composer for next year. She's awfully dumb (entre nous) but she does need music for ballets. She's in Jamaica (W.I.) now, but I think will be in Chicago the first three weeks in Feb. They still talk of bringing her in my ballet to N.Y. in April.[2]

The only news is about me and Harvard. I'm taking over [Walter] Piston's composition class for the second term of this year—Feb to May. Its only 3 hours of teaching a week—on Teusdays and Thursdays—and as I am practically broke—and the job is well paid—I couldn't very well refuse. I think it was very brave of them to have me, dont you? I'll probably commute for Feb and March and live in Cambridge in the Spring. You know my weakness for college 'atmosphere'!

Last night the League started its season with a reception for Stravinsky. Virgil [Thomson] and everybody was there and I missed you badly. Theres no doubt about it—you do something 'indicible' to the N.Y. air which makes it more potentially exciting when you're here than when you're not.

In general N.Y. gets more and more Berlinish every year. V.[irgil?] can tell you about the Barrel House and Flamencos, etc. Only the bull-necked Nazis are missing.

Its hopeless to expect performances if you don't stay around here a while. All the young composers are in Roger [Sessions]'s 'crib' (with the exception of Jerry Moross) and you'd have the field to yourself. You can spend 9 months of the year anywhere you like but I think you ought to plan to be here for at least 3 during each season if you want to feel like a composer. Oh well, I feel so foolish giving you advice, & you seem like such a big boy now.

The Kafka joke is an old one between Mamoulian and myself.

Write soon

Aff—nately

A—

---

1. Rouben Mamoulian, director of stage (*Porgy and Bess*) and screen (*Love Me Tonight*).
2. In fact, *Hear Ye, Hear Ye!* was not performed in New York until 1936.

To Carlos Chávez

AC/LC. Photocopy of als.

MacDowell Colony
Peterboro, New Hampshire
Aug 28, 1935

Dear Carlos—

I was so pleased to be given your envelope this morning—and so surprised and upset when I opened it and read 'my dear Copland.'[1] But naturally I didn't receive the first letter you sent me c/o the League[2] or you would have heard from me before this. Is it possible that only because you got no letter from me in reply to the first one you sent you should be so offended—or have I unknowingly offended you in some other way?

I'm sure you must know how dear you are to me in every way—how close I feel to you mentally and spiritually and musically—and the idea that anything whatever should mar our friendship even temporarily is very painful to me. Even tho I may not write for long periods you are always in my thoughts,— people are always asking me how you are—and I never feel really separated from you. This is particularly true now when I realize that you must have been going through a very difficult period of your life. Paul Strand came back last June with news of your struggles and since then I have often wondered how the new political situation in Mexico has been affecting you and your plans. I have always remembered our conversation on top of the pyramids of Tloti- huacan when you told me that the future—whatever it was to be—did not frighten you. I believed you then—and it has given me confidence that you will know how to manage even in these difficult times.

We have been going through a difficult period here also—though of course not in the same way as you have. It becomes increasingly difficult for instance to have that sense that there is any public for our music—in any case, the public that can afford to pay for concerts is quite simply not interested. Its impossible to have ones music played (on the rare occasions when it is played) before a 'dead' public without getting a feeling of isolation—which is so bad for an artist to have. In a period of such economic and general social tension music itself seems unimportant—at least to those middle class people who up to now have been our audiences. Is it the same in Mexico?

All this has personal repercussions too. It is no longer easy to be published (The Cos Cob Press has discontinued publishing for a year already and I don't know when they will resume)—I must make some money in order to live which uses up much valuable time and energy. I mention all these things not to give you the idea that I am 'discouraged' in any essential way, but merely to show you that I have good reasons to feel sympathetic with your own struggles. It is just in such times as these that friends like we are should encourage and sustain each other. I can tell from your letter that you have felt I was too distant. Please know better now.

This winter I will lecture again at the New School using records as illustra- tions. As you see from the enclosed list I am using the 'H.P.' set you sent me.[3] But in order to make a musical analysis and perhaps play themes for the audience I really need the piano arrangement. Could you possibly send it to me? I will take good care of it and return it. Also can you tell me who in N.Y. would have the Revueltas record 'El Renacuajo Paseador'? The copy you sent me has been cracked. If no one has it in N.Y. could you possibly send me another copy? And if anyone in the audience should want to buy the records are they on sale? By the way, the Columbia Phonograph Co. is about to issue a recording of my 'Variations.' Later they will bring out the Vitebsk Trio and the Violin Pieces.[4] I should like to send you these when they come out.

In June I finished my 'Statements'—six short movements for orchestra. It is to be done by Ormandy and the Minneapolis Symphony this winter.[5] As soon as I have an available copy of the score I will send it to you as I am anxious for you to see it. Just now I am finishing up the orchestration of 'El Salon Mexico' which I wrote you about last summer. What it would sound like in Mexico I cant imagine, but everyone here for whom I have played it seems to think it is very gay and amusing!

I wonder what you have been composing recently? I saw 'The Spiral' piece[6] in New Music and liked it very much. I will arrange to have it performed in N.Y. this winter. If there is any new music by Mexicans which we should hear in N.Y. I wish you would send it to me and I will do my best to arrange performances either at the League or elsewhere.

The only permanent address I have just now is c/o E. F. Kalmus, 209 West 57th St. N.Y.C. I will be in N.Y. around Sept. 1.

Does Ansermet remember my 'First Symphony' from the performance he gave in Berlin? I will have the scores you ask for sent to him as soon as I can.[7] But I wish I could send some of my more recent things. (By the way, Stokowski has the 'Short Symphony' now and I hope he will perform it this season. I want to hear it enfin!) Also you shall have your 'First Symphony' score.

I am certain that I have no copy of the cello Sonatina because we corresponded about that once before and I examined all my music carefully but without success. I hope its not lost.

I am hoping for a long letter from you. With much love
Aaron

---

1. Chávez's letter of August 23, 1935, opens with this unusually formal salutation.

2. Chávez's earlier letter, dated August 9, is now in AC/LC.

3. Chávez's ballet H.P.—the title stands for "Horsepower"—was given its premiere in Philadelphia under Stokowski on March 31, 1932.

4. The Piano Variations appeared as Columbia 68321–D, *Vitebsk* as Columbia 68741–D, and the violin pieces as Columbia 68742–D.

5. Eugene Ormandy conducted only the two final movements, "Jingo" and "Prophetic." The complete work was first performed in 1942 by Dimitri Mitropoulos and the New York Philharmonic.

6. Chávez's "Spiral for Violin and Piano," later part of *Three Spirals for Violin and Piano*.

7. In his letter of August 23, Chávez asked for copies of Copland's First Symphony for himself and conductor Ernest Ansermet. He also requested the return of his own Cello Sonatina if Copland had a copy.

Copland at the MacDowell Colony, 1935. Provided courtesy of the
Aaron Copland Collection at the Library of Congress.

To Carlos Chávez

AC/LC. Photocopy of als.

[Mayo probablemente, 1936][1]

Dear Carlos—

I was extremely pleased to have your wire—and many, many thanks for the generous fee.[2]

I am planning to sail on the 'Yucatan' on June 11, to arrive in Mexico City June 17. If you must have the parts of the Concerto before then, please wire me immediately and I will mail them to you. If I dont hear from you, I'll just bring them with me.

Please keep your ears open if you hear of any little house which can be rented in the country, even two hours from the city. I am tired of the city and want to get some country air.

We have had much excitement since you left—I will tell you all about it when I see you. Big Business suddenly discovered the American Composer and almost ate us alive!

You can't imagine how pleased I am to be coming back to Mexico and how pleased I am with you for making it possible.

Always yours

Aaron

Best to Colin and Jane.[3]

---

1. Date in later hand.

2. Copland's remuneration for performing his Piano Concerto.

3. Composer Colin McPhee and his wife, Jane Belo. McPhee was in Mexico City finishing his orchestral work *Tabuh-Tabuhan*, which received its premiere on September 4, 1936, by the Orquesta Sinfónica de México, conducted by Chávez.

To Serge and Natalie Koussevitzky

SK/LC. als.

Apartado 5
Tlaxcala, Tlax.
Mexico
July 9, 1936

Mes chers amis—

I was so sorry not to have seen you the day you sailed from New York, but I was in Princeton at the small American Music Festival at Harris' school on that day.[1]

I have settled for the summer outside of a provincial town in Mexico. Chavez invited me to play my Piano Concerto with his orchestra (July 24th)[2] and I made that a pretext for working here during the summer. I have a house on top of a high hill, on the site of an ancient Aztec palace, with magnificent mountains all around. The town of Tlaxcala is very old itself, full of ruins of former days, and very picturesque. The conditions for composing are ideal, and I hope to finish my high school opera here.[3]

I hope you are both taking a good rest in the short time before coming back to the Berkshire Festival. And afterwards? Is there really any chance of your coming to Mexico? That would be wonderful!

Always affectionately and devotedly

Aaron

---

1. Roy Harris was teaching at the Westminster Choir School.
2. The concert was later postponed one week.
3. *The Second Hurricane* (1936).

To Carlos Chávez

AC/LC. Photocopy of als.

Tlaxcala, Tlax.
July 15, 1936

Dear Carlos—

I was glad for the postponement—it gave me just the extra week I needed for practicing the Concerto. I think now I can do a good job.

Could you ask Ortega or Armando to arrange the following things for me:

1. That I may have a place to go for practicing in Mexico City on a baby grand. I ask this because I dont want to lose any time when once I get there, on the 24th.

2. Could a notice be sent to the N.Y. papers saying that I am to be soloist with the orchestra. It might help to give someone the idea for future performances. —One never can tell.

3. Could you tell me what sort of clothes I should wear—full dress (with white tie and tails), or tuxedo? I have both with me.

4. Last, but most important of all: I need a big favor of you, if you can possibly arrange it. The money that I brought with me from the U.S. is all used up, and I find myself on the verge of being without funds. Could you arrange to let me have 100 pesos as an advance on my fee for playing with the orchestra. I know this is irregular, and I hope it won't cause you too much trouble to arrange it. If it is impossible to arrange please be quite frank and say so, and I will cable to the U.S. But if it is possible, please send the money by postal money order immediately. (If it isnt possible, you had better wire me.) I would be very embarrassed to make such a request if I didn't know how well you will

understand it, just as you know that I fully accept in advance any decision you may make.

Sorry to bother you with all this just when you must be extra-busy.

Always

Aaron

P.S. I saw the enclosed clipping in the Sunday Times and thought you might want it.

To Carlos Chávez

AC/LC. Photocopy of als.

[Hotel Empire stationery]

Dec 11 '36

Dear Carlos—

Victor just wrote me from Vera Cruz of his visit to you. I do hope he didn't cause you any trouble. He seemed in such a state of exaltation about his trip to Europe that I believe he may have made a nuisance of himself. I sent you to-day a money order for $4.20 according to Victor's instructions.

Anyway, this brings on a letter from me which I have been meaning to write you in any case. I am living at this hotel, but I work in a studio I have in a business building near by. It has been fun to fix up the studio and I hope you'll like it. One thing is sure: I dont have to worry about disturbing the neighbors!

Since coming back, I've been doing little more than lecturing,—which has been well attended, I'm glad to say.[1] My last lecture is next week, and then I plan to start on the work which was commissioned by the Columbia Broadcasting System.[2] You may have read about it.

Well, I suppose you want some 'news' of N.Y.

We are all looking forward eagerly to your visit. The season has been quite unexciting so far. The League has put me in charge of the hour's program for your reception—and if you have any wishes concerning that I wish you'd let me know.

[John] Barbirolli I heard [conduct] once. Once was enough! Later I met him—and had the same impression as from his conducting—very unimpressive. No depth or real distinction in his conducting—only a certain spectacular, 'show-off' side, which would be more at home in Radio City Music Hall. Imagine my complete astonishment when I opened this morning's paper and read that he was made permanent conductor [of the New York Philharmonic] for 3 years! It really is scandalous. The entire explanation is 'box-office.' The Philharmonic has been selling more tickets, and Barbirolli gets the credit, in spite of continuous poor reviews by [New York Times critic Olin] Downes and others.

One more word about the Philharmonic. I sent the 'Salon Mexico' to the competition (under a different name) but Messrs. Smallens and Lange did not find anything worthy of the prize money.[3] Thats that.

Colin [4] is leaving for Bali on Monday.

I am planning to go to Russia myself about April 15th.[5]

We read about your Pan-American Festival and it sounds simply swell.

Are you coming here soon? I'm getting lonesome for you.

With best regards to all the friends—Agea, Ortegas, Armando.

Always yours

Aaron

---

1. Copland was again teaching at the New School for Social Research.

2. This became *Music for Radio* (1937).

3. Conductors Alexander Smallens and Hans Lange, judges of the New York Philharmonic composition contest.

4. McPhee spent the majority of the decade researching the musical traditions of Bali.

5. Copland had previously expressed an interest in going to Russia in a letter to Nicolas Slonimsky of June 8, 1935. He did not go to Russia until 1960, however, when he and Lukas Foss were chosen by the U.S. State Department as cultural ambassadors.

To Carlos Chávez

AC/LC. Photocopy of als.

[Hotel Empire stationery]

May 18 '37

Dear Carlos—

Two days ago I mailed you the score of the 'Salón México' by parcel post. I hope you get it safely. To-day came Agea's letter asking for program notes—so I see we are thinking of the same thing! As for the orchestral parts, they will be ready by about June 15th. I hope that is not too late. I will leave instructions here to have them sent directly to you.

I am still in N.Y., as you see. First, I decided to put off my sailing so as to be present when they broadcasted the opera [*The Second Hurricane*] on May 9th. Then Harold [Clurman] sent an offer from Hollywood for me—$3,000 for a picture. I said I would come for $5000, not less. So I am waiting to hear what will happen. If nothing happens—I will sail for Europe around May 25. But just think—if they should accept my terms I will be seeing you at the Hollywood Bowl! So its either Moscow or Hollywood for me.

I was so sorry you missed the opera. It seemed to go off very well—even better than I had hoped—considering how quickly it was all put together. [Herbert] Weinstock heard it twice—perhaps he's written you about it. When I first heard the chorus and orchestra together I said 'My God, it sounds like the Ninth Symphony'! By that I meant it had a surprisingly big sound, and a highly dramatic one. Also, the end has something of the same 'Freude, Freude' feeling, tho in completely different terms. Of course the kids had everyone completely interested. Kids are like Negroes, you cant go wrong if they are on the stage.[1] Well, someday I hope you'll hear it. C. C. Birchard is publishing it.

I suppose you must have wondered how I happened to write that piece for the N.Y. Times on Silvestre [Revueltas].[2] As a matter of fact I had no idea the Times would use it. The publicity secretary of the Filmarte Theatre where Redes[3] was playing, called me up and asked if I would not give some publicity material on Redes in order to bring customers to the show. I did it rather hastily—and was very surprised when she called to tell me she had sold it to the 'Times.' Apparently anything about Mexico is of interest now.

Nothing very much has happened since you left. I went up to Boston to hear Koussie read thru the 'Statements' as a rehearsal. He said that the orchestration was 'masterly,' but the music as a whole was rather 'cerebral.' Perhaps he is right, but I liked it anyway. He says he will 'surely' do it next season, and this time I believe him, because he's actually heard it.[4]

Mrs Reis is still muy tonta [literally, "foolish"] on the subject of electrical instruments of the future[.] Dukelsky is being very active with an idea for putting on 3 concerts of 'entertaining' modern music for the fashionable people next season.[5] I am thinking about the Composers Union we must definitely get started next season.

I hope the Festival will be a big success. Also, that you'll enjoy working on the 'Salon Mexico.' Be sure to have Armando send me all the reviews—even those of Senor Pollares!

Remember me to all the amigos. I hope that Ortega is all recovered by this time.

Love

Aaron

P.S. I'll let you know my summer address.

---

1. Copland may have had in mind *Four Saints in Three Acts*, which sustained Gertrude Stein's modernist libretto and Virgil Thomson's music by means of its black cast, and perhaps Gershwin's *Porgy and Bess*.

2. Aaron Copland, "Mexican Composer," *New York Times*, May 9, 1937.

3. A film to which Revueltas had written the score.

4. Koussevitzky never performed *Statements for Orchestra*. Another performance was announced (and canceled) by Dimitri Mitropoulos, and the work was not heard in its entirety until 1942.

5. Copland wrote an opening fanfare for the "High-Low Concerts," organized by Vladimir Dukelsky (later Vernon Duke). The musical material of this fanfare was later used in *An Outdoor Overture* (1938).

It was for Hollywood, rather than for Moscow, that Copland left in June 1937. He then traveled to Mexico in the beginning of July—without a movie contract.

To Carlos Chávez

AC/LC. Photocopy of als.
[California Limited (Santa Fe Railroad) stationery]

June 2 [1937]
Near Kansas City

Dear Carlos—

All my plans are changed! I am coming to Mexico via Los Angeles.

Harold [Clurman] convinced me that if I come to Hollywood now it would surely end up by getting me a job sometime before October. The money arrangements are O.K. It is just a question of finding a feature film which needs my kind of music. So I said I would come to 'look over the ground' until July 1st. Then to Mexico. Mrs Coolidge invited me to be her guest during the week of the Festival[1] and I am hoping I can hear the Salon Mexico also. I will stay in Mexico all summer, unless I get a call back to Hollywood suddenly. Perhaps nothing will happen really but I thought it was worth taking a chance. Anyway, it gives me an excuse for coming back to Mexico!

My address is:

c/o Clurman

249 SOUTH MAPLE DRIVE

BEVERLY HILLS, Cal.

I hope you have the score of the Salon by now. Knowing how long packages can remain in the Customs office I am a little worried. The parts I hope to send you by the 15th at the latest.

I'm looking forward to seeing you again. And hope that the Festival will be a big success.

Love

Aaron

Excuse my poor handwriting. Its the train.

---

1. The First Festival of Pan American Chamber Music, held in Mexico City and sponsored by chamber-music patron Elizabeth Sprague Coolidge.

CHAPTER FOUR

Musical Triumphs, 1937–42

The years between 1937 and 1942 were some of the busiest and most productive of Copland's career. In 1937, he returned to Mexico to attend the First Festival of Pan American Chamber Music at the invitation of its sponsor, Elizabeth Sprague Coolidge, and on August 27, he attended the world premiere of *El Salón México,* performed by Carlos Chávez and the Orquesta Sinfónica de México. Also in 1937, Copland attended the premiere of *The Second Hurricane,* composed a piece for CBS radio (*Music for Radio*), lectured at the New School for Social Research, and was instrumental in the founding of the American Composers Alliance, an organization formed to collect performance fees for concert composers. These activities stemmed in part from his commitment to bridging the gap between the composer and his audience. Copland embraced the cause of music education in his New School lectures, titled "What to Listen for in Music" and later collected into a book of the same name. Inspired by the resounding success of *El Salón México,* he continued to write in an accessible, folkloric style and experimented with writing music for children as well as for the new media of radio and film. His first trip to Hollywood in the summer of 1937 had yielded no offers, but in 1939 Copland had the opportunity to compose a score for a documentary film, *The City,* for the New York World's Fair. This project caught the attention of producer Hal Roach and director Lewis Milestone, who hired Copland to write the score for *Of Mice and Men.* Copland left for Hollywood in October 1939. His first commercial film score was nominated for an Academy Award, and he later wrote music for several other major motion pictures.

Copland described 1939 as "the year my name became better known to the American public" (C & P I, 291). In that year he wrote incidental music for two stage productions: Orson Welles's Shakespearean adaptation *Five Kings,* and Irwin Shaw's *Quiet City,* directed by Elia Kazan. He also composed the score for a puppet show, *From Sorcery to Science,* heard along with *The City* at the World's Fair. In May 1939, Copland's ballet *Billy the Kid,* choreographed by Eugene Loring, had its New York premiere. The ballet inaugurated a trio of certifiable hits; along with *Billy, Rodeo* (1942) and *Appalachian Spring* (1944) have forever associated the Brooklyn-born Copland with the American West.

This was a fruitful period in Copland's personal life as well. On November 14, 1937—Copland's birthday—the composer met a young man, then a junior at Harvard, who was already an ardent fan of the *Piano Variations.* Leonard Bernstein and Aaron Copland were seated near each other at dancer Anna Sokolow's New York debut, and after the recital Bernstein attended Copland's informal birthday party. This chance meeting initiated a spirited correspondence and enduring friendship. Bernstein's effusive letters from Harvard reveal a passionate crush on the older composer, while Copland often adopted the role of mentor, even offering advice about Bernstein's undergraduate thesis on Americanism in concert music. When Bernstein graduated in 1939, he moved to New York City for a brief period; there, he and Copland met regularly, and Copland hired his young, destitute friend to make a two-piano arrangement of *El Salón México.* Their relationship seems to have cooled around 1942, likely marking the end of a love affair, but the two men stayed close throughout their lives, discussing all matters personal and professional.

Underlying these triumphs, however, was the tension and crisis of World War II. Copland was acutely aware of and interested in world events. He had hoped for a commission in the Army Specialist Corps, and so was in touch with Harold Spivacke, who was not only head of the Music Division at the Library of Congress but also chairman of the Subcommittee on Music of the Joint Army and Navy Committee on Warfare and Recreation. Copland was not entirely averse to army service—so long as he could continue to compose. He never did enter the military, however, and instead offered such works as the *Fanfare for the Common Man, Lincoln Portrait, The North Star,* and *Letter from Home* as his contributions to the war effort.

To Elizabeth Sprague Coolidge

ESC/LC. als.

[Hotel Reforma, Mexico, stationery]

Tlaxcala, Tlax
Mexico
July 26, 1937

My dear Mrs Coolidge—

May I thank you most warmly for an unusually interesting 12 days in Mexico City. Without having heard all six programs in that particular setting, it will be difficult for you to appreciate how original in conception and in execution the whole Festival seemed to us.[1] I think you are to be hugely congratulated on the outcome of the entire affair.

Having lived in Mexico before, I think I can understand what a profound influence such a series of concerts is most likely to have on the musical life of the country. Merely hearing the Coolidge Quartet in the series of classics, would have been sufficient to stimulate their interest in the art of chamber music. But what the concerts as a whole did for Mexico, as I see it, was to give the musical life of the country a less provincial aspect. It was as if they might have justly said "you see, the outside world takes us seriously as a musical center, therefore we must be more serious about ourselves"!

Chavez worked hard and well, under trying circumstances. I do not refer only to the desperate illness of his mother, but also to the quality of the musicians with whom he has to work here. It would be foolish to think for a moment that the orchestral men here are of Philharmonic calibre. Chavez asked me to conduct my own work,[2] so that I was able to attest the fact from personal experience. Some of the men are excellent (certainly the Ruvalcaba Quartet fits into that category) but others, though willing, are simply not able to give finished performances, by American standards. There is no doubt that some of the works for chamber orchestra suffered from this unevenness among the men. But I dont see how this could be avoided in a country like Mexico. And certainly it was far better to have given the Festival here, even with an occasional lapse in performance standard, than not to have given it at all.

The general concensus of opinion seemed to be that the North American and Mexican composers showed to better advantage than the South Americans. I'm not sure that I can be completely impartial in any such judgement. Certainly the prize quartets left much to be desired. But I was glad to become familiar with numerous South American names, to know that they were composing in far off Chile and Brazil and Argentina, and to have some idea of their present stage of development.

On the whole, from my own standpoint, (which is that of a musician who has closely followed the American and Mexican musical movement for the past 15 years) the most important aspect of the Festival, was the opportunity it gave me for a cross section view of the present status of our own music. I came away feeling strongly encouraged for its future. The music of Harris and Revueltas already show signs of a distinctive American idiom, the works of Sessions and Piston prove that Europe has little to teach us in the matter of expert craftsmanship.[3] I could not help thinking that if our younger men take up the task where these men will have left off, all will be well with us.

I could, of course, continue to write at much greater length, but I have no wish to tire you. Needless to say, one of the most delightful aspects of the Festival was our stay at the Reforma. I was happy to make the acquaintance of your son and daughter-in-law, and though they did all that was humanly possible to make up for your absence, we all felt it most keenly, nonetheless.

I am staying on in this small town in Mexico for the rest of the summer, so it will be easy for me to keep fresh the memory of the impressions of the last 12 days.

Allow me once more to thank you most sincerely for a fascinating and stimulating Festival.

Yours faithfully
Aaron Copland

---

1. Health concerns prevented Coolidge from attending the festival herself.

2. *Music for the Theatre.*

3. Works performed at the festival included Roy Harris, Trio for violin, cello, and piano; Silvestre Revueltas, *Homenaje al Federico García Lorca;* Roger Sessions, Quartet in E minor; and Walter Piston, Trio for violin, cello, and piano in E.

To Carlos Chávez

AC/LC. Photocopy of als.
[Hotel Isabel stationery]

[Fines Sept o principios Oct][1]
Esperanza
Wed [1937]

Dear Carlos—

I was sorry to have missed you when I telephoned last night. I arrived in town late—had a lot to do arranging my trip home—became quite exhausted—and called you too late. It would have been nice to see you before leaving.

Anyway, this is just a good-bye note—and to thank you again for the pleasure of hearing the Salon Mexico in a really authentic performance—to say the least.

It was a good summer for me—I finished the arrangement of the Short Symphony for string quartet clarinet and piano before leaving Tlaxcala.[2]

Here's wishing you lots of luck for Cleveland.

Always yours

Aaron

My address in N.Y.[:] Hotel Empire—63rd & B'way.

---

1. Date in later hand. Dated September 10 on the Library of Congress *American Memory* Web site, although September 10 was a Friday in 1937.
2. Published as the Sextet for string quartet, clarinet, and piano in 1948.

To Leonard Bernstein

LB/LC. tls.

[Hotel Empire stationery]

March 23, 1938

Dear Leonard,

What a letter! What an 'outburst'! Hwat a boy! It completely spoiled my breakfast. But it couldn't spoil the weather, so thank Marx for that. The sun has been shining in a way to defy all wars and all dictators, and theres nothing to be done about it.

That "female" you tell of.[1] I've never seen her, but I had reports of her at a time when she played the Variations here, which I studiously avoided attending. I see that did no good, since she continues to 'play' them. But what can a poor composer do? I know of no way of stopping her once the piece is published, do you? Think what people do to the three B's etc. and nothing can be done about <u>that</u>. As for your general 'disappointment' in Art, Man and Life I can only advise perspective, perspective and yet more perspective. This is only 1938. Man has a long time to go. Art is quite young. Life has its own dialectic. Aren't you always curious to see what tomorrow will bring?

Of course, I understand exactly how you feel. At 21, in Paris, with Dada thumbing its nose at art, I had a spell of extreme disgust with all things human. Whats the use—it can't last, and it didn't last. The next day comes, there are jobs to do, problems to solve, and one gets gradually inured to things. At my advanced age (37) I can't even take a letter like yours completely seriously. But I'm glad you wrote it, if only to let off steam. Write some more!

Now its definite that I'm not due to be up in Boston. I've been bought off with promises of a performance at the coming Berkshire Festival.[2] (Don't mention this around, will you[.]) I'm vaguely thinking of a trip to England in

May. Sir Adrian Boult is to conduct my Salon Mexico at the I.S.C.M. Festival in June, and previously on the BBC on April 20th; also here when he conducts the NBC orchestra in May. I hope you're coming to New York soon. I always enjoy seeing you.

Always,

[signed] Aaron

---

1. Cara Verson, who had performed the *Piano Variations* in Boston's Jordan Hall.

2. The Berkshire Music Festival was inaugurated in 1934 in Interlaken, Massachusetts, by Henry Hadley and members of the New York Philharmonic Orchestra. In 1936, the Boston Symphony Orchestra replaced the Philharmonic and performed three concerts. The following year the festival was moved to the Tanglewood estate in Lenox, Massachusetts, and by 1938 the festival had increased to six concerts. Copland's *Music for the Theatre* was performed on August 7, 1938. The Berkshire Music Center (now known as the Tanglewood Music Center) was inaugurated in 1940 as a summer music academy for young instrumentalists, singers, conductors, and composers. Copland was a member of the composition faculty nearly every summer between 1940 and 1965.

To Leonard Bernstein

LB/LC. tls.

[Aug, 1938][1]
115 West 63rd St.
New York

Dear Lenny,

I hope this reaches you all right. I really should have written you from Europe, and sent the enclosed letter of Mrs. MacDowell's,[2] which shows anyway that I did write her about you.

What have you done with your summer? I read your name in a paper, saying you were to play with [an] orchestra at Lynn. But what else have you done? I hope it hasn't been too awful.

I'm ashamed to say I had an awfully nice time in London and Paris. Its all so relaxing after the drive of a winter in New York. I had forgotten how charming it could be. And I met at least one new and talented young composer in London, Benjamin Britten. (Of course, you probably know all his works by heart.)

Now I'm back until Sept. 1st, correcting proofs on the opera and the book, both of which are to come out in October; and working at top speed on a new cowboy ballet for the Ballet Caravan outfit.[3]

I'm going to spend September at the [MacDowell] Colony in Peterboro. Couldn't some angel lend you $16 a week so that you could come too? They always have room after Labor Day. At any rate, its so near Boston that you must come up for a week-end if nothing more. They don't take week-end guests at the Colony, but you could stay some place in the village, as <u>my</u> guest. And perhaps, if I go up by way of Boston, I could see you then. Anyhow we must make Peterboro a pretext for seeing something of each other, don't you think?

Let me hear from you soon.

[in ink] Always,

[signed] Aaron

---

1. Date in later hand.

2. Marian MacDowell, widow of the composer Edward MacDowell and driving force behind the MacDowell Colony; her official title in 1938 was Corresponding Secretary and Manager of the Edward MacDowell Association.

3. The opera is *The Second Hurricane*, the book is *What to Listen for in Music* (New York: McGraw-Hill, 1939), and the ballet is *Billy the Kid*.

To Leonard Bernstein

LB/LC. als.

[Hotel Empire stationery]

Dec 7 [9?, 1938]

Dear Lenny—

I know I'm late in answering but I've been swamped with things to do and your letter asked so many questions!

Aren't you coming down to N.Y. during Christmas holydays? And since it would be so much better to do this viva voce than by letter, could it wait till then for my grandfatherly advice?

You sound as if you were very much on the right track anyhow both as to ideas and composers' names.[1] Dont make the mistake of thinking that just because a Gilbert used Negro material, there was therefore nothing American about it.[2] Theres always the chance it might have an 'American' quality despite its material. Also, don't try to prove too much. Composing in this country is still pretty young no matter how you look at it.

Good luck and lets hear if you're coming down.

Consider yourself missed.

A.

---

1. Bernstein had written Copland for advice on his senior thesis at Harvard, which concerned nationalism in American composition.

2. American composer Henry F. Gilbert (1868–1928) wrote such pieces as *Comedy Overture on Negro Themes* and *The Dance in Place Congo*. The section about Gilbert from Bernstein's completed thesis may be found in Bernstein, *Findings* (New York: Simon and Schuster, 1982), 45–47.

To Virgil Thomson

Thomson/Yale. tls.
[Hotel Empire stationery]

May 1 [1939]

Dear Virgil—

It was lots of fun to get that long letter from you. We talk about you all the time of course—and little trickles of news leak through—but that's not the same as hearing from the source itself.

I enjoyed reading your strictures on the book more than much of the praise it has had.[1] All the wrong people like it very much—which makes me suspect you must be right. I won't argue the merits of your sonata-form analysis—this is hardly the moment.[2] My tendency always is to stress the similarities of things rather than their differences. The whole book is a kind of outline of musical facts. It never occurred to me that anyone would look for an original contribution to musical theory in it. I quite agree that "any music teacher" could have written it. The damn thing was never meant for you to read in the first place— so it doesn't surprise me to know that you found it a bore. Still I'm glad you read it and sent me the low-down on it. I was about to think that so much praise must be deserved when your letter arrived. Thought I: we can always depend on Virgil.

Its been a very busy winter for me or you would have heard directly about the Arrow Music Press[3] and the A[merican] C[omposers] A[lliance] long before this. Its been busy partly through your fault, because I've been doing all the things you would have done if you had been here. Like music for the Five Kings (that calamitous thing!) and a Steiner documentary film.[4] I also orchestrated my 'Billy the Kid' ballet, wrote an Outdoor Overture for a high school orchestra, and incidental music for Irwin Shaw's 'The Quiet City' (which is not opening). My career in the theater has been a flop—through no fault of my own I hasten to add. The Five Kings story is long and involved and rather dreary. Orson [Welles]'s stock is very low at the moment. No one knows where it will all end—but he's going to have to do a lot of pulling himself together. Last year's hero arouses very little sympathy.

The ACA has been moving slowly—mostly because its directors have all been so damn busy writing music—including the chairman.[5] We've taken some decisions recently: (1) to lay off ASCAP—in other words, not to press for an open fight[6] (2) to set ourselves up as a permanent organization with constitution, officers, etc. (3) to accept performing rights assignments according to our plan. By next September, if we can raise the money for an office and secretary (about $1500) we should be ready to start fee collection. I have spoken unofficially with the lead royalty man at CBS and they speak of taking out a license. We are collecting our catalogue in the meantime. (Have you filled out your list, by the way?) We've been agitating for American music at the [1939 New York World's] Fair, and have had 2 composers accepted as functioning composers on WPA. Its slow going I admit, but I think that we are getting to be a force gradually, and there are no signs of defections in the ranks. (I wish to hell you were here to help on all this!!) We badly need a plan at the moment for distributing monies collected. I lean toward the English point system, tho it means lots of book keeping. What think you?

Affectionate glances from Victor and my own embracements

[signed] Aaron

---

1. Copland is responding to Thomson's letter of March 20, 1939, concerning Copland's new book, *What to Listen for in Music,* which Thomson described as "a bore." Thomson's letter is published in Virgil Thomson, *Selected Letters,* ed. Tim Page and Vanessa Weeks Page (New York: Summit, 1988), 127–29.

2. In his letter to Copland, Thomson explained: "I do not believe, for instance, that the loose and varied sonata-form practiced by the great Viennese has very much relation to the modern French reconstructed form that d'Indy made up for pedagogical purposes. The first kind, even in its final Mahlerian decay, retained a spontaneity, a Viennese *désinvolture* [casualness], that enabled it to be written consecutively. . . . The modern French version, on the other hand, is really written as you describe, that is to say, pieced together like a picture-puzzle."

3. The Arrow Music Press was founded in 1937 by Copland, Thomson, Lehman Engel, and Marc Blitzstein. Copland served as treasurer, Engel as president. In 1938 Arrow took over the publications of the Cos Cob Press; in 1956 its publications were in turn taken over by Boosey & Hawkes.

4. In 1939 Copland composed the incidental music for Orson Welles's *Five Kings,* a short-lived adaptation of Shakespeare. He also composed the score to the documentary film *The City,* by Ralph Steiner and Willard Van Dyke.

5. Copland helped to found the American Composers Alliance (ACA) in 1939 and served as its chairman until 1945. The organization was charged with the mission of collecting royalties for the performance of concert music and of promoting American music.

6. The ACA was involved with the American Society of Composers, Authors, and Publishers (ASCAP) in a bitter dispute about the rights to collect royalties for composers of "serious" music.

To Leonard Bernstein

LB/LC. tls.
[Hotel Empire stationery]

Tuesday [July? 1939]

Dear Lenny:

Your letter made me feel a louse. But it isn't as if I hadn't thought of writing each day. But a) my plans have only just been definitely set, and b) I wasn't sure where to address you. So there!

You write—just incidentally—awful cute letters when you want to.

Well, its Woodstock, New York. It almost was West Redding, Conn. It was never possibly Long Island. But now its Woodstock, just above Kingston, where all the artists go, unfortunately. Its just a small bungalow house, but I hasten to add that I saw another small bungalow house 10 minutes walk away which looked just right for you. That is, if you can find $125. someplace, which is what they are asking for the rent till Oct. 15.

I am going up to-morrow with Victor. We have just bought a car together and we'll drive up in state. My address is simply Woodstock, N.Y. If the very worst comes to the very worst you will still have to come for a visit to my house. And don't forget that I am at the Loft in N.Y. every Wednesday. Will you listen in to the broadcasts and tell me whats wrong with them?

Benjamin Britten arrives to-night!

Always affectionately,

[signed] A—

[in pencil] P.S. Write soon again.

Copland had first met English composer Benjamin Britten in 1938. During the summer of 1939, Britten and tenor Peter Pears rented a house near Copland and Kraft in the small town of Woodstock, New York.

To Benjamin Britten

AC/LC. Photocopy of als.

Woodstock—Sept 6 [1939]

Dear Benjie—

I've been wondering where you are in this miserable world! I keep marvelling how it has all turned out just exactly as you feared it would. The question is: do you have to go back? I mean—does the Conscription go into immediate effect. Because if not—I think you absolutely owe it to England to stay here. Whatever anyone may think now, I'm sure the future will justify your looking upon your own case as a special one. After all anyone can shoot a gun—but how many can write music like you? Of course, for all I know, you may be gone already. But if not—and I hope not—then remember what I say as to how you can best serve la patrie!

Nothing very different about Woodstock, despite the War. Ned Chase asks after you when we go down for tennis. You must write and say where you are, if only to allay his anxiety! Of course, it is colder—much—and we have stored in wood for the fireplace.

I find it hard as Hell to go on putting down notes on paper as though nothing were happening.

Victor sends his best. We both want to know what happened to Peter [Pears]?

Love

Aaron

To Leonard Bernstein

LB/LC. als.

Saturday [September or October 1939]

Dear Lenny—

Am back from Saratoga and conferences with the 'Boss' [Koussevitzky] about the Berkshires, etc. What are people saying in Boston about the ASCAP mess, I wonder?

Something new has come up. I've been approached from Hollywood. Actually! To do the music for 'Of Mice and Men.' I've asked a _fat_ price, which they are unlikely to accept. (I thought if I was to sell myself to the movies, I ought to sell myself good . . .) This may necessitate a sudden departure for the West. But as I say, its unlikely. In which case, I shall want you to come for a week to Woodstock. Hold yourself in readiness for a telegram in case it has to be sudden.

A—

To Leonard Bernstein

LB/LC. als.
[Chateau Elysée, Hollywood, stationery]

Nov 12 [1939]

Hello Pal—

How ye gittin on? Are they treating you as well as they did? And is Reiner behaving himself? And are you learning anything?[1]

Saw your old friend Al here a couple of times. I suppose he's written you how we met on the MGM lot—and how he toured us around the studio. Nice boy. Not a very enviable situation for him though—such a very small fish in such a very big pond. He talks passionately about N.Y.

In usual Hollywood manner they brought me out here about a month too soon. I'm just about to begin work. The picture I've seen numberless times in rough cut. Its honest anyway—no happy endings and no boy-girl romances. But its pretty grim as entertainment. Anyhow, I needn't be ashamed to be connected with it—which is plenty to be thankful for. There isn't much music needed, but where its used I think it will count.

Who do you see in Philie? What do you do for a social life. Do you want any letters to people—or had you better not get too involved outside school things.

I hear your friend Dmitri [Mitropoulos] has scheduled the Salon [México] for April next. Is that your work? First all-high-school performance of The Second Hurricane is happening in Akron Ohio of all places.

Best to you and write me

A—

---

1. Bernstein was at the Curtis Institute of Music in Philadelphia studying with conductor Fritz Reiner.

Copland at typewriter, Palm Springs or San Diego, 1939. Provided courtesy of
the Aaron Copland Collection at the Library of Congress.

To Virgil Thomson

Thomson/Yale. tls.

115 West 63 St
New York
Feb. 15, 1940

Dear Virgil:

I was just thinking that I should have written you a personal note about the book instead of just letting you read my reactions in M[odern] M[usic], when your letter came.[1] So all is well. I meant every word of what I said. At the moment everybody is discussing the Oscar Levant book,[2] which had very nice things about Four Saints in it. It has sold 33,000 to date, which leaves us far behind.

I wrote the review on the train out to Hollywood! Ones experiences out there are no good to generalize from, since everything depends on who you work for. I worked for Lewis Milestone who let me do exactly as I pleased. There was no Musical Director at the Hal Roach studio where Mice and Men was filmed so there was none of the usual 'advice.' In other words I had ideal conditions so if the music is lousy it is all my own fault—no alibis. Its opening on Friday at Roxy's so I guess you'll be getting r[e]actions from others. For a first job I don't think I did a bad job. (Important note: we did three previews with stock music track; when all cuts were made I then timed my own music. Therefore no cutting up of the score after it was written.) I was offered a second picture at the same studio for more money but I turned it down because the picture stank. My agent was shocked.

I've took a little house in the country an hour out of New York. Trying to write a piano sonata and a second book—mostly collected from articles.[3] Also trying to keep track of ACA and Arrow [Press].

To write you very much detail about either or both would take too long, and a lot of it might be stale. I sometimes wish passionately that you would come home and help, instead of sending all that good advice from Paris. Arrow is doing O.K., except that we haven't allowed enough for running expenses and so we are running dangerously close to being in the red all the time. However, we are staging a little benefit for the press at Constances on the 27th. Five bucks a ticket to hear Marc do excerpts from his new opus (which by the by, is his best so far from the sheerly musical standpoint).[4] From all reports they will be packed in like sardines. I am publishing my Two Pieces for String Orchestra at some considerable figure, and we are all hoping that you will be able to do the Christmas choruses.[5]

The ACA is moving to its new office at 17 West 42 St, which is part of the new American Music Center, which is a store where they specialize in American music, books, records, etc. You know about the fight between ASCAP and the Broadcasters, I assume. Well, Ernst[6] says that we may be able to sell our catalogue to the new rival to ASCAP set up by the Broadcasters themselves.[7] He has quoted them $25,000 as a likely price. Whether or not this works out the ACA badly needs money for a publicity man, a business manager, etc. 103 members have paid their second year's dues out of a possible 180. I think that a fair showing.

There is a rumor that you are thinking of coming home this Spring. Would to God t'were true. Love from V and me.

[signed] Aaron

---

1. Thomson to Copland, January 5, 1940. "Thanks for [the] glowing review of my book and I'm delighted you liked it." The book in question is Thomson, *The State of Music* (New York: W. Morrow, 1939); and the review is Copland, "Thomson's Musical State," *Modern Music* 17 (1939): 63–65.

2. Oscar Levant, *A Smattering of Ignorance* (Garden City, New York: Doubleday, 1939).

3. Aaron Copland, *Our New Music* (New York: Whittlesey House/McGraw-Hill, 1941).

4. Marc Blitzstein performed *No for an Answer* at a benefit for Arrow Press hosted by Constance and Kirk Askew on February 27.

5. Thomson's *Scenes from the Holy Infancy According to St. Matthew* (1937).

6. Morris L. Ernst, attorney for the ACA.

7. Broadcast Music Inc. (BMI) was founded in 1939 by leaders in the broadcast industry to collect fees for the performance of music on commercial radio.

In 1940 Copland became involved with government organizations devoted to cultural exchange between North and South America. He was appointed to two Advisory Committees on Music, one under the State Department Division of Cultural Relations, and a second within the Office of Inter-American Affairs (its usual, though not invariable, name) under the Council of National Defense and the direction of Nelson Rockefeller.

To Carlos Chávez

AC/LC. Photocopy of tls.
[Hotel Empire stationery]

Nov. 19, 1940

Dear Carlos:

It has been a long time since I have heard from you and I've been wondering how you are. I received the Boletins of the O[rquesta] S[infónica de] M[éxico] and thought the programs looked fine. I'm particularly curious to hear how the Stravinsky visit came off.[1]

The reason I am writing you now is connected with Nelson Rockefeller's work as Coordinator of Cultural Relations with Latin America. (I am a member of his Advisory Committee on Music.) The suggestion has been made to the Committee by Mr. Henry Coke, President of the Dallas Symphony Orchestra, that we should consider the possibility of sending the Dallas Symphony to Mexico for some concerts. What do you think of this idea?

It was thought by Mr. Coke that the proximity of Texas to Mexico would give such a visit a significance that one from another state would not have. Also, he says in a letter: "The cost of sending an orchestra from Texas, rather than a more remote point[,] has its advantages. Likewise, the people of Texas would be interested by the sending of a local orchestra, whereas that interest would not exist, or would be of little value, should the orchestra come from a region without contact with Mexico."

All this is open to further suggestion from you, of course. I believe that if you think the idea is worth developing, the best way to pursue it might be for the Dallas Symphony to invite you as guest-conductor, at which time you could really discuss the project with the Dallas people. The interest of our committee is to further cultural relations, and to help with the financing of the Dallas Orchestra's trip. If the trip should materialize, it might be a good idea for you to share the podium with Jacques Singer (the regular conductor of the Dallas Symphony) in their concerts in Mexico. While writing you the further idea occurs to me that perhaps an exchange of orchestras could be effected,—the OSM to visit Dallas, while Dallas visits Mexico.

Anyway, think about the whole problem, and let me know if you can, by Wednesday next, so that I can report back to the Music Committee.

Any chances of our seeing you this winter in New York? I certainly hope so. My best greetings to you always!

[signed] Aaron

---

1. Chávez replied November 26: "The Strawinsky visit was a great success. He undoubtedly enjoyed his visit and his concerts. He recorded for us Le Baiser de la Fée for R.C.A. Victor."

To Carlos Chávez

AC/LC. Photocopy of tls.
[Hotel Empire stationery]

Nov. 28, 1940

Dear Carlos:

I've been waiting to get your answer to my letter before answering your first one sent to me care of Minna [Lederman]. There are many things so perhaps I had better list them.

1. Absolutely delighted that you want to repeat the Short Symphony next year, and naturally I hope that the recording can be arranged, also. I believe I could come to Mexico to hear it in late August or September. The Berkshire

Music Center, where I will probably be teaching each year, is finished around August 15th, so I am free after that.

2. About the American Music Rental Library: it is still only in the organizing stage, and exists only on paper so far. Miss Hull is new in the field and no one can tell how effective she will be in producing performances. If you have no other possibilities for Energia or Soli,[1] I would like to think they are in a place where we can get at them, if necessary.

In general, I wish you would think seriously about publishing your works. Boosey, Hawkes[2] is now looking around for new composers to further, and they are under the impression that the Sinfonia India, Antigona, H.P. etc. are all tied up at Schirmers. Is there any way of freeing those works for actual publication, or do you still wish to restrict performances as in the past. Boosey-Hawkes is particularly interested in orchestral works right now, but later that could lead to publication of chamber works too. Anyhow, think about it and let me know.

3. As for the Dallas Symphony: I will show your letter to Carleton Sprague Smith, who is the head of the Music Committee. Personally, I think you are probably right—either a first class orchestra or none. At any rate, you answered just as I predicted you would! But I was asked to suggest the idea to you, so I did so. The Committee also has discussed briefly the possibility of asking you to head a small group of people to collect Mexican folk song material among the Indians in remote places—this to be financed by the Committee. What do you think, or who would you suggest if you are not interested yourself. Any other bright ideas you may have, along the lines of furthering cultural relations between Latin American countries and the USA, via music, would be very welcome. It is very possible that the Committee may send me down to visit South America in the Spring for a few months. I am curious to see what their musical life is like.

I have kept myself free for composing this winter, living on my Hollywood gold![3] I've nearly finished two movements of a three movement Piano Sonata, and I wrote an 8 minute slow movement for trumpet solo, English horn and string orchestra called "Quiet City." I've been going to lots of committee meetings (unfortunately), of one kind or another, and I'm right in the middle of the ASCAP-BMI fight which becomes more 'passionant' each day. Outside of that you know New York,—its always different, but always the same.

Everyone tells me how much they like the new records of the Museum concerts of last Spring.[4] Its very good to know that the piano concerto is progressing. Work hard on it!

Always yours,

[signed] Aaron

[in ink] P.S. The news of Silvestre was shocking.[5] It is a great pity that his work should remain unfinished.

1. Chávez's nonet *Energía* (1925) and his quartet *Soli* (1933; later *Soli I*).

2. In 1938 Copland began his relationship with British publisher Boosey & Hawkes, which would become his sole publisher. Chávez's *Sinfonía de Antígona* was eventually published by G. Schirmer in 1948, as was his *Sinfonía India* in 1950.

3. The money paid Copland for composing the music to the film *Our Town*.

4. Chávez had organized a series of concerts in May 1940, in conjunction with the exhibit "Twenty Centuries of Mexican Art."

5. Silvestre Revueltas died on October 5, 1940.

To Serge Koussevitzky

SK/LC. tls.

[Hotel Empire stationery]

Dec. 16, 1940

Dear Sergei Alexandrovitch:

I was in Boston last week to give a lecture at the University Club, and was so disappointed to find that you were gone on the trip. I had several things to talk to you about—but I will try to make it short in this letter.

1. I hope Mrs. Grant[1] spoke to you about the plan I had to have the U.S. government bring a number of the best students from South American countries to the [Berkshire] School this summer. I am a member of the Music Committee established by the State Department under Nelson Rockefeller for cultural relations with South America. This idea would be similar to that of Mrs. Bok[2] and the Curtis Institute, except that the government would take the place of Mrs. Bok, and we would have all South America to choose from. I have spoken with the Music Committee, and they are very enthusiastic about the plan. If you have any further ideas along this line I wish you would let me know, so that I can present it to the Committee.

2. The I.S.C.M. is planning a Festival for the Spring in New York. They have enough money for three chamber music concerts, but nothing for orchestral concerts. In order to get orchestral works performed, they are asking each of the major orchestras to perform one work on their regular programs, preferably in New York and in the Spring. The work would of course be chosen by the International Jury, and would be announced as being part of the festival idea. Assuming always that you approved of the work suggested for performance [added in ink: by your orchestra,] do you think it possible that the Boston Symphony would take part in this plan? Please write your reactions to Miss Dorothy Lawton, 121 East 58th St., in New York. I know that everyone would be delighted if you gave your support to this idea.

3. I wonder whether you have any definite date for the STATEMENTS. Naturally I want to reserve that week so that I can be at rehearsals, and it would help me a great deal if I knew the date well in advance.[3]

I hope Madame is feeling well. Remember me to her and Olga.

[in ink] Always devotedly

[signed] Aaron

Aaron Copland, Serge Koussevitzky, and Nadia Boulanger, ca. 1939.
Photographer: Victor Kraft. Used by permission of Mrs. Victor Kraft.

Aaron Copland and Leonard Bernstein, ca. 1940. Photographer: Victor Kraft.
Used by permission of Mrs. Victor Kraft.

1. Margaret Grant, executive secretary to Serge Koussevitzky.

2. Mary Louise Curtis Bok (later Zimbalist), patron of the arts and founder and president of the Curtis Institute of Music.

3. Koussevitzky never did perform *Statements*.

To Leonard Bernstein

LB/LC. tls.

[April 9?, 1941]
Larchmont
Wed.

Wed dead lead dead led wed lead dead wed dead led wed[1]

HELLO!

Fooled you—I'm going to Havana. First to Key West, and then across the waters to Havana. I'm leaving Saturday—and I'll be in KW on Sunday. Book's half done.[2] I'll finish it, do a little swimming, hear a little music, and investigate the painting situation in the tropics . . . . .

Flabbergasted by the double-header in Philie on Friday.[3] I feel as if I ought to send a telegram to the Mayor or something. Can't come down—much as I'd like to[—]because I'll be busy cleaning up my affairs in NY. I'll be gone a month and stop off in Atlantic City on the way back to be at a M[usic] E[ducators] N[ational] C[onference] conference to hear kid's bands, on May 3rd. When do you graduate?—maybe we could connect on the boardwalk.

Has it ever occured to you that nobody ever plays Liszt paraphrases any more?[4] There must be a reason! Still you have all my blessings so why not try. Whether Boosee likee or not I ain't got no idea.

You <u>would</u> like the Britten[5]—you old romanticist you. But I agree. Its definitely got something—and the second movement orchestration is phenomenal. Very Mahlerian finale . . .

Its wonderful about the painting lessons. As soon as I send you a southern address you must write me all.

I'm clearing out of Larchmont to-morrow. Awful to think I won't be seeing you for a whole month more. What are your plans for May and June if any? I tried to get you a job playing the piano part of the Sextet for CBS in the ISCM Festival in May, but I think they have to give it to their staff pianist (Vera Brodsky) if she'll take it. Was tempted to have you do the piano concerto in an all-Copland program I am to conduct of the NYA Orchestra over WNYC, also in May, but not enough rehearsal time allowed.

Well, anyhow, good-bye—and wish me good Spanish lessons.

[signed] Me

1. From the procession ending Act III of *Four Saints in Three Acts* by Virgil Thomson and Gertrude Stein.

2. *Our New Music.*

3. Two performances of *Vitebsk* were to take place that Friday in Philadelphia, one with Bernstein as pianist.

4. Bernstein had proposed doing a "piano version of *Billy* . . . a kind of paraphrase in the style of the Liszt ones (formally only, I mean)."

5. Probably the *Sinfonia da Requiem*, premiered by the New York Philharmonic (conducted by John Barbirolli) on March 28, 1941.

To Leonard Bernstein

LB/LC. als.

[Hotel Royal Palm, Havana, stationery]

el martes [Tuesday]—15 [April 1941]

Querido amigo:

This is the address until May 1st, so please write.

Havana is fun—you'd like it here. Key West is like a country village compared to this. I had forgotten how big it was—and how much like Paris in many ways. Its a crazily mixed-up city with skins of all colors, clothes of all varieties, and everybody jabbering away at top speed.

It just doesn't make any sense to be writing about the works of one R. Sessions in this atmosphere.

What the hell are you up to across all that blue sea I can so clearly see from my window.

Is there any chance of our connecting in Atlantic City on the 3rd & 4th? It'd be nice if you'd let me invite you.

Alles gutes

A—

To Leonard Bernstein

LB/LC. als.

[Hotel Royal Palm, Havana, stationery]

Sunday [April, 1941]

Dear L

Naturally, I missed your broadcast because I was out at the Beach getting sun tan. Isn't that a good excuse? One works in the morning, beaches in the afternoon, and listens to Cuban music at night. Perfect program, No? Oh, yes, and I mustn't forget my Spanish lessons—excellent teacher, still not out of high-school!

I wish you were here to share the music with me. I have a slightly frustrated feeling in not being able to discuss it with anyone, and a sinking feeling that noone but you and I would think it so much fun. Anyway, I'm bringing back a few records, but they are only analogous to Guy Lombardo versions of the real thing. I've sat for hours on end in 5¢ a dance joints, listening. Finally the band in one place got the idea, and invited me up to the band platform. "Usted musico?" <u>Yes</u>, says I. What a music factory it is! Thirteen black men and me— quite a piquant scene. The thing I like most is the quality of voice when the Negroes sing down here. It does things to me—its so sweet and moving. And just think, no serious Cuban composer is using any of this. Its awful tempting, but I'll try to control myself.

Margaret Grant writes that Kouss really did Quiet City in Boston,[1] and we'll hear it at the Festival.[2] Ain't that good?

I'm leaving here Thursday by boat for Miami, and will be in N. Phillie around 9:23 A.M. on Sat. I assume thats where I change trains for Atlantic City. (I wish you had a phone.) I'll try to get more dope before sending this. In Atlantic City, I'll be at the Hotel Traymore, which is the headquarters for the Penn M[usic] E[ducators] N[ational] C[onference] meeting. The invitation is still open if you want to come. (P.S. I just found out that the trip is only 1 1/4 hours from North Phil. I can make direct connection with only a 5 minute wait between trains. So I'll be taking a 9:29 that morning. Come then or come later if you can.)

Hope you're making a lot of money out of the Joe Wagner affair—because the idea appalls me.[3]

Listen in to Bob Palmer's[4] piece and Quiet City over CBS on Sat. at 3—if you're still in Philly. What peculiar graduation exercises there will be at Curtis!

Love—

A—

---

1. Friday, April 18, and Saturday, April 19, 1941.

2. *Quiet City* was not a part of the official programs of the eighteenth festival of the ISCM, held in New York in May 1941 (Copland's *Music for Radio* was broadcast as part of the festival), nor did the Boston Symphony perform it in New York that month.

3. Bernstein had been hired to perform American composer Joseph Wagner's *Triptych for Piano, Percussion, and Strings* (as well as Beethoven's First Piano Concerto) with the Women's Symphony Orchestra of Boston in May 1941.

4. Robert Palmer (1915–) is an American composer best known for his chamber music.

From August 19 to December 13, Copland traveled throughout South America on a grant from the Office of Inter-American Affairs.

To Leonard Bernstein

LB/LC. acs.

Santiago—Oct 25 '41

Leonard Bernstein!—why don't you ever write to me. Here I am far away from home—and nary a word from you. Shame!

Spent most of Oct. in Buenos Aires and Montevideo. Flew back across the Andes yesterday to spend 10 days here. I'm conducting; and playing the Piano Concerto with the orchestra. I'll be in Rio on Nov. 6. (Write care American Consulate, Rio de Janeiro, Brazil.) Home by the 15th of Dec.

Finished the [Piano] Sonata! Played the world premiere in B[uenos] A[ires]. Slonimsky was there. Musicians said nice things.

What are you up to? The silence is ominous. Write me what everybody is saying, thinking and doing. Including you.

Did you receive my book?[1]

Sweet remembrances to all the friends. For you—un embrazo.

A—

---

1. *Our New Music.*

To Nadia Boulanger

AC/LC. als.

[Palace Hotel, Rio de Janeiro, stationery]

Nov. 24, 1941

Dear Nadia:

It was so nice to receive your birthday note,—so far from home. I was delighted also, that you liked the book.[1]

My trip through South America has been fascinating. It has been like discovering a new continent. If one is interested in growing things, one must be interested in these countries where all musical effort is just beginning.

You are well known here. I saw a great deal of Camargo Guarnieri, who is certainly one of the finest talents down here.

I also had time to complete my Piano Sonata, which I am anxious for you to hear.

I'll be back before Christmas if all goes well.

All my affection to you

Aaron

---

1. *Our New Music.*

Copland returned from South America in December 1941, spent the spring in New York City, and returned to Tanglewood in the summer of 1942.

To Leonard Bernstein

LB/LC. acs.

[postmark: Stockbridge, June 10, 1942]

Stock—

Wed.

Lensky love:

I'm leaving for 2 hectic days in N.Y. to-morrow—no time to write now. Its heaven here and I have a cook—de coleur—and perfect.

I'll be down on Wed. the 17th when I conduct the Goldman Band and will be returning here the 19th. I'll write soon again so we can arrange something. I'm writing a ballet—very frothy one—for the Monte Carlo people.[1] How to have you and finish that at same time is my problem. But je meurs aussi [I'm dying too]—so

Love—

A—

---

1. *Rodeo* (1942).

To Elizabeth Sprague Coolidge

ESC/LC. tls.

Box 104

Stockbridge, Mass.

July 31, 1942

Dear Mrs. Coolidge:

Thank you for your letter and for the offer of a commission for a Martha Graham dance score. I am, in principle, happy to accept. I have been an admirer of Miss Graham's work for many years and I have more than once hoped that we might collaborate. It particularly pleases me that you should make this possible, and also that I should be invited to take part as composer in celebration of the twenty-fifth anniversary of the historic Pittsfield Festivals.[1]

However, this being a stage work, I think it would be wiser for me to contact Miss Graham before definitely committing myself. For example, I ought to know the subject matter of the dance piece, how long it should be, set for how many instruments, how soon it must be ready, etc. Also, since this is a stage work, I would have to assume that the commission of $500. covered only the composing of the work especially for the Festival occasion. Miss Graham and I would have to work out performance fees for her use of the work subsequent to the premiere. As soon as these details are arranged, I shall write to Dr. Spivacke in order to formally accept the commission from the Foundation.[2]

In the meantime, please accept my appreciation of your extraordinary efforts for contemporary music in our country, and my sincere thanks for being invited to take part in the celebration of your unique contribution.

Yours most cordially,

[signed] Aaron Copland

---

1. It was first intended that the Graham ballets be presented in Pittsfield, Massachusetts, celebrating the twenty-fifth anniversary of Mrs. Coolidge's Pittsfield Festivals.

2. Harold Spivacke was chief of the Music Division of the Library of Congress and thus director of the Elizabeth Sprague Coolidge Foundation in the Library of Congress. In consultation with Coolidge herself, Spivacke arranged the commission of *Appalachian Spring* from Martha Graham and Aaron Copland.

To William Schuman

Schuman/NYPL. tls.

Box 104
Stockbridge, Mass
Aug 6, 1942

Dear Bill—

Sorry you couldn't come here, but I quite understand. Its swell, that you've finished the Piano Concerto already.[1] Of course I'd like to have a copy of the two-piano arrangement. I'm going to be here until Sept 8, and then I don't know where.

I finished the ballet for the Monte Carlo people,[2] but still have the orchestrations to do. It's a pure theatre piece, not likely to interest fellow-musicians very much! If you have nothing better to do, listen in on the afternoon of the 16th at 4:30, when Kostelanetz is broadcasting my Lincoln piece,[3] for the greater glory of Coca-Cola. They have mesmerized Carl Sandburg into delivering the Speaker's part. I am terrified by your reports of signs outside Town Hall, since not a note of that there piece is written.[4] However,—

Tell me more about the house in New Rochelle (which I suppose is really in Larchmont). But what would I do with a "big house," even though for very little money. And how to heat it if fuel is hard to get? And suppose I get drafted? (Tell Frankie[5] not to snort.) Of course its furnished. And of course I need it from Oct 1.

Kouss has done miracles with the kids and is in fine fettle. A famous storm blocked out the Toscanini broadcast of Shostie's 7th [Shostakovitch's Seventh Symphony], so all that is still to be revealed up here. I stop playing at being teacher end of next week and go back to composing again. Its always a relief.

Best to you both.

[signed] Aaron

---

1. Copland had urged Schuman to write a piano concerto to cure his dislike of composing for piano.

2. *Rodeo.*

3. *Lincoln Portrait* (1942).

4. Copland had promised to write a piece for Schuman's chorus at Sarah Lawrence College.

5. Schuman's wife.

To Harold Spivacke

Army/LC. tls.

Stockbridge, Mass.
Sept. 3, 1942

Dear Harold:

Your letter cheered me up considerably—I mean the part about composers in the Army being given "time for composing."[1] You can't imagine how right I hope you are. But I should warn you that "composing" to me means a private room with a piano and some consecutive time for writing. (Unlike Beethoven and Hindemith I don't work in the fields.) If the Army can provide that, its set-up is even more intricate than I thought. Well anyway, I'm only too happy to take your word for it that army life and composing are not incompatible.

I am returning to New York next week (after Tuesday my address is the Hotel Empire). I'll be seeing Martha Graham in N.Y., and as soon as I get a clearer picture of what she plans to do for you I'll write you an "official" letter to settle up the matter of the Coolidge Commission. I'm quite willing to go through the making of arrangements for the commission, always assuming that it can be carried out—army life permitting.

In the meantime I hope you will do whatever you can to press for action in the matter of my personnel questionaire for a commission of another sort.

Yours cordially
[signed] Aaron
Aaron Copland

---

1. On August 21, 1942, Copland wrote Harold Spivacke, "I contemplate the giving up of my composing activities with the greatest reluctance, but if I must be used in the war effort, I wish to

be as useful as possible." In a letter of August 28, Spivacke jokingly replied, "As Chairman of the Sub-Committee on Music of the Joint Army and Navy Committee on Welfare and Recreation, I wish to take this opportunity to advise you to change your attitude toward service in the Army. I admit that you will not have as much time for composing as you had in civilian life but I see no reason why you will have to give it up entirely. No matter what branch of the service you end up in, whether as a commissioned officer in the Army Specialist Corps or even as a buck private in the Infantry, there will be time for composing. It may be difficult, but it will be important that you carry on. For this reason, I urge you in my dual capacity now as Chairman of said committee and as Chief of the Music Division and therefore Director of the Coolidge Foundation to accept the commission and plan to carry it out irrespective of what happens. For once I feel myself in a better position to advise on a composing matter than you are."

To William Schuman

Schuman/NYPL. tls.

Stockbridge, Mass
Sept 3, 1942

Dear Bill:

I've taken the same house that I had two years ago in Oakland, NJ, for Oct to Jan. That is I've taken it if the army doesn't take me first. Being single and without dependents, I begin to feel as if I were sitting on a red hot spot. As far as I can see, its only a matter of time before they get me. Since you've been to Wash. perhaps you could relay some pointers as to what I ought to do to make myself as effectively used as possible. It wont be via potato peeling! The only person I've contacted thus far who had any suggestions is Harold Spivacke. He thinks there is some chance with the Army Specialist Corps. Anything else you may know aside from that would be helpful. I hate like hell the idea of giving up composing—at least until NY is under attack. Any bright ideas? (I'm not classified as yet.)

Marc Blitzstein has went. He is now Pvt. B of the Air Force—landed some sort of a musical job and seems quite happy at the end of his first week.

Nice to hear what "everybody says" about the Lincoln piece. Your friend Lawrence covered himself with glory by writing the first criticism I ever got without any "buts" or "ifs" in it.[1] Any theories? I'm deep in a sea of notes— there are 180 orchestral pages in this damn [added in ink: 25 min.] ballet[2]— thats what I get for writing 10 minutes worth of fast music. I pass sleepless nights about the S[arah] L[awrence] choral piece. Can't find a "vigorous" poem for lady singers. Any leads?

I'll be in NY from Tuesday on—at the Empire. If you come into town ever, lets have lunch. And let me at some more of that ig-noble music of yours. Lenny is settled in NY at 158 West 58—looking desperately for work. What are we going to do about that guy?

[signed] Aaron

1. Robert Lawrence, reviewer for the *New York Herald Tribune*. His review appeared on August 17, 1942.

2. *Rodeo.*

To Harold Spivacke

Army/LC. tls.

[Hotel Empire stationery]

Sept. 17, 1942

Dear Harold:

I wanted you to know that I have had my army physical examination and came through with flying colors. Of course my eyes would limit me to what the doctor calls "limited service," but I assume that that only improves my case with the Army Specialist Corps.

I had a letter from Charlie Thomson in which he said the two of you had been "exploring possibilities" in relation to me. If there is anything more you can tell me without breaking confidences, of course I'd like to know it.

Thanks a lot for expediting matters in regard to the commission. You would help me enormously if you could tell me what your guess is as to the earliest possible date for my relinquishment of civilian life. In other words, in making plans for the immediate future I badly need to know up to what date I can safely promise to be around. Naturally I know your answer can only be approximate and only a guess, but even that would be a help.

I am seeing Martha Graham to-morrow and will communicate with you again.

Best regards to you.

Yours cordially,

[signed] Aaron

Aaron Copland

CHAPTER FIVE

During and After the War,
1942–48

A fter the success of his film scores for *Of Mice and Men* and *Our Town,* Aaron Copland returned to Hollywood in 1943 to compose music for *The North Star.* William Wyler had originally been slated to direct *The North Star* but was called to military service, so Lewis Milestone, with whom Copland had worked on *Of Mice and Men,* was brought in as a replacement. With a story by Lillian Hellman, *The North Star* was a work of wartime propaganda, intended to foster pro-Soviet and anti-Nazi sentiment. Unlike Copland's previous film scores, the music for *The North Star* included several vocal numbers, for which Ira Gershwin wrote the lyrics. Neither the film nor its music proved a success. The film was in effect disowned by its studio after the war, when cold-war politics rendered films about heroic Russian resistance an embarrassment to Hollywood, and Copland never transformed the score into a concert suite, as he had once planned. Copland and Milestone later worked together for a third time on *The Red Pony,* based on John Steinbeck's novel, and that same year Copland collaborated with Wyler on *The Heiress,* for which Copland was awarded an Academy Award in 1950 for best film score.

Copland was enjoying a similar string of successes on the stage. Following on the heels of *Billy the Kid* (1938) and *Rodeo* (1942), Copland accepted a commission in May 1943 from Elizabeth Sprague Coolidge for a new ballet to be choreographed by Martha Graham. The genesis of *Appa-*

lachian Spring is long and complex, dating back to 1941 when Graham first contacted Copland about writing a ballet based on the character of Medea. Once discussions about a commission from Coolidge were under way, Graham sent Copland a potential script inspired by the ancient tale of betrayal and murder. Copland rejected these ideas, and it was a year later before he and Graham finally agreed on an acceptable scenario: a portrait of a young pioneer couple in rural Pennsylvania.

Though busy writing for stage and screen, Copland never abandoned concert music. He worked on the Piano Sonata while composing scores for *Of Mice and Men* and *Our Town* and while traveling throughout South America in 1941. The Violin Sonata was also written while Copland was in Hollywood working on *The North Star.* Around 1943, he expressed a desire to write a large-scale concert work and briefly considered composing a piano concerto for the New York Philharmonic. That project was never realized, but in 1944 Copland accepted a commission from the Koussevitzky Music Foundation for a new symphony. The Third Symphony was, despite its appellation, Copland's only traditional, four-movement symphony. Koussevitzky wanted an expansive work in "the grand manner," and Copland delivered just that—reusing his *Fanfare for the Common Man* in the finale of the Third Symphony. The work was generally well received, as was Copland's subsequent major concert piece, the Clarinet Concerto, written in 1948 on a commission from Benny Goodman but not premiered until 1950.

To William Schuman

Schuman/NYPL. tls.

Dellbrook Farm
Oakland, NJ
Oct 28, 1942

Dear Bill:

Is it possible that those dumb clucks at the [Hotel] EMPIRE gave you the impression I was still there?!! I've been here since a month—thought you knew, imagined I told you—and of course I havent had any messages from you via telephone. I was in NY until yesterday, so only received your card today. Is all explained?

I've been on the verge of writing you for the past two weeks. First because my conscience has been troubling me about the choral piece,[1] which I knew was due on Sept. 21st. It's the first time I've ever fallen down on a commission—and its awful that it should be you who is involved. I never was able to find a poem that at the same time attracted me for ladies voices and was 'fast and virile' by nature. So I got stuck. You'll have to tell me when I see you whether I ought to keep on trying, or whether its too late to bother. But we may have to compromise on something 'slow and feminine.' Anyway, my humble apologies. I hope that Piston came through all right.[2]

The other thing that I wanted to talk to you about was our Town Hall Forum evenings.[3] I begin to feel that more is at stake in their being a success than our own private careers. That is, if we can manage to fill the hall for the series, even sell out, and generally surround the evenings with a successful air, much good will be done for the "cause" in general. We've got to put our heads together and see what can be done.

I'm going to be in town next Tuesday and Wednesday. Can we have lunch on either of those days? Or see you any other time that is convenient for you, except from 4 PM on, on Tuesday.

Best to you—

[signed] Aaron C

PS I'm not a captain yet—only a cowboy-composer from Brooklyn.

---

1. For Schuman's chorus at Sarah Lawrence College.

2. Walter Piston, who generally disliked writing vocal music, did not come through.

3. New York's Town Hall was planning to start a series of single-composer concerts of new music called the Town Hall Music Forum. Schuman and Copland were to be the first two composers honored. Copland's concert, which took place on February 17, 1943, included the premiere of his *Music for Movies*.

To Carlos Chávez

AC/LC. Photocopy of als.
[Samuel Goldwyn stationery]

March 3 '43

Dear Carlos:

[Charles] Seeger wrote me that you were coming to Washington and planned to conduct "Billy the Kid." I hope it all works out as you wish, and am so sorry I can't be there for the concert.

As you see, I have landed another job in Hollywood—after 3 years! I am doing the music for a Russian film called "The North Star," produced by Goldwyn. It's a big production, and I hope will have a good result. Write me when you get a chance—and all best luck on the concert day. (Send reviews, if any!)

Always affectionately

Aaron

P.S. I've asked Heinsheimer[1] to send you a copy of the 'Lincoln Portrait'—which has just come out.

P.P.S. I have just heard that the Berkshire Music Center won't be opened this summer—so if the job is finished here, maybe I can come to Mexico for the summer! I would like that very much.

---

1. Hans Heinsheimer, then artist representative of the American office of Boosey & Hawkes.

To Marcelle de Manziarly

AC/LC. als.
[Samuel Goldwyn stationery]

March 18 1943

Dear Marcelle:

You were awfully nice to send me that letter gratuite. Particularly since my conscience has been killing me because I left N.Y. without our having the famous luncheon date! But if you only knew how sudden it all was—coming out here, I mean. I am still not entirely acclimated—after 7 weeks—(already!)[.]

You wrote some very pretty things about my music—which touched me very much. I know how critical you are—so that your praise is that much more valued.

Isn't it wonderful about the success of Guarnieri's concert.[1] It went far beyond my most optimistic hopes. If only he could stay for the night of the opera. It seems idiotic to have to leave a day before. Is there nothing to be done?

And I was pleased as Punch to read that your quatuor is being done at the Serenade.[2] I hope the performance succeeds in thawing you out, so that you will compose more. I wish I could be there to help with the thawing out process, but there seems little chance. The picture is only just begun and there are weeks ahead yet.

I feel very proud because Stravinsky invited me to dinner. Unfortunately it was cancelled for some reason, but I am proud nevertheless. I assume it will take place later.

My life here is oh so different from N.Y. Quiet, country-like—almost anonymous. Though the town is full of famous personalities—musical and otherwise—they seem never to see each other. Each is an island—complete in himself. If I were to live here I would break it down—but as a visitor, its outside my province.

All my best to you—and keep me in touch with goings-on in the center of all things.

Yours
Aaron

1. Brazilian composer Camargo Guarnieri, whom Manziarly probably met when he was studying in Paris (1938–40).

2. La Société de la Sérénade, an important Paris society devoted to new music.

To Andre Kostelanetz

AC/LC. carbon.

April 8, 1943
Mr. Andre Kostelanetz
322 East 57th Street
New York, New York

Dear Andre:

I have been meaning to write in order to thank you for releasing the Lincoln Portrait to Koussevitsky ahead of time. My friends have been writing me about the performances in Boston and New York and from what I can gather Will Geer[1] must have been rather on the hammy side. I wonder what you thought about the performances?

I have been thinking about you in connection with the picture that I am working on now, "The North Star." The subject matter has to do with Russia on the first day of the attack by Germany in June, 1941. It has a serious script by Lillian Hellman and is being directed by Lewis Milestone. All indications point to an outstanding film.

Aside from the musical background score which I am to do, there are to be interpolated four or five vocal numbers—songs and choruses—for which Ira Gershwin has supplied me with the lyrics. It would please me personally a great deal if something could be worked out between Samuel Goldwyn, Inc. and you so that the first radio broadcast of these vocal numbers would take place on the Coca-Cola program. Aside from a chorus, which could be used in several numbers, we would need the services of some outstanding singer like Nelson Eddy or Jan Pierce.[2]

I mention this now, not because there is any immediate rush, but because I would like you to have plenty of time to think about the matter.

Heinsheimer writes me that you are planning to do a performance of Lincoln at the Stadium on July 12th.[3] I hope I can be there.

Always cordially,

AARON COPLAND

1. The actor Will Geer narrated *Lincoln Portrait* when it was performed by the Boston Symphony Orchestra on March 26–27 and April 9–10 in Boston and during the intervening week in Brooklyn and in New Brunswick, New Jersey.

2. Tenor Jan Peerce.

3. Kostelanetz performed *Lincoln Portrait* at Lewisohn Stadium on July 26, 1943, with Carl Sandburg as narrator.

To Arthur Berger

AB/NYPL. als.

Hollywood, April 10, 1943

Dear Arthur:

The other night, while walking down Hollywood Blvd., I happened on a copy of the Partisan Review. Imagine my surprise when I came upon your piece on the Piano Sonata.[1] I wonder what made you not tell me about it—just neglect? Or was it "fright" at my reaction? Anyhow it was lots of fun to be surprised like that. Subsequently Victor [Kraft] wrote me that you had mentioned it to him.

I don't know what others will think, but I liked it. My one objection is that it came to a rather sudden end, just as things were getting along. Were you cramped for space? It gives that impression.

There are a few things I'd like to comment upon. One of the meaning of my articles and "pronunciamentos." When I call for a "style that satisfies both us and them," I am mostly trying to goad composers on toward what I think is a healthy direction. I am emphatically not laying out an a priori plan for my own future compositions. I reserve the right always to practice not what I preach, but what the music dictates.

I think also that for the sake of drawing sharp distinctions you rather overdo the dichotomy between my "severe" and "simple" styles. The inference is that only the severe style is really serious. I don't believe that. What I was trying for in the simpler works was only partly a larger audience; they also gave me a chance to try for a home-spun musical idiom, similar to what I was trying for in a more hectic fashion in the earlier jazz works. In other words, it was not only musical functionalism that was in question, but also musical language. I like to think that in Billy and Our Town, and somewhat in Lincoln, I have touched off for myself and others a kind of musical naturalness that we have badly needed—along with "great" works.

The reference to David [Diamond]'s and Harold [Shapero]'s building up the "thinned out musical substance" needs to be expanded to be clear. I didn't understand it myself. But I'm sure they were pleased with the plug!

Did Victor tell you Stravinsky had me and [George] Antheil to dinner? (After reading Kazin's book[2] I've come to the conclusion that Stravinsky is the Henry James of composers. Same "exile" psychology, same exquisite perfection, same hold on certain temperaments, same lack of immediacy of contact with the world around him.) He was extremely cordial with us. We played S's

Symphony[3] from off-the-air records. I don't think he's in a very good period. He copies himself unashamedly, and therefore one rarely comes upon a really fresh page—for him, I mean. I know this is blasphemy in the Berger household, but there it is—so make the most of it.

Love to Esther,

Aaron

---

1. Copland's letter was prompted by Berger's article, "Copland's Piano Sonata," *Partisan Review* 10, no. 2 (1943): 187–90; see also Berger, *Reflections of an American Composer* (Berkeley: University of California Press, 2002), 13–15.

2. Alfred Kazin, *On Native Grounds: An Interpretation of American Prose Literature* (1942).

3. Stravinsky's Symphony in C (1940).

To Harold Spivacke

ESC/LC. tls.

[Samuel Goldwyn stationery]

April 13, 1943

Dear Harold:

Your letter, sent to Stockbridge, just reached me out here. Since I hadn't heard from Martha Graham in several months, I was going on the assumption that the idea of a ballet was in abeyance. Your letter now brings the whole thing to life again.

When I last saw her in New York, she promised to send me a scenario which we could discuss. That was around Christmas time and I haven't heard from her since. We also agreed that when the rights to the ballet are released after the first year, she would be willing to pay me a royalty performance fee on a per performance basis. Therefor, as far as Miss Graham goes, everything is set, except that I have nothing to work with, until she prepares a scenario suitable to us both.

Because of the job I have out here, doing the score for a picture called The North Star, my time will be pretty much taken up until the middle of June. However, I can probably sneak in some work on the ballet nevertheless. I assume that the performance date is still planned for late September.[1]

As far as the terms of the commission go, I think the Foundation should take into account the fact that this is a stage work, and therefore ought to be handled somewhat differently from the commissions given for chamber music. I think that the $500. fee should cover three points: 1) the writing of the work especially for the Foundation, 2) the premiere performance, and 3) exclusivity for a year from the premiere performance. I believe however, that in fairness to the composer, a small royalty fee of $15. per performance should be paid the composer each time the work is given after the premiere. That is the customary procedure with the ballet companies, though of course the rates are about double that for regular commercial outfits. Such an arrangement also provides more incentive for a publisher who might be interested in bringing the work out immediately.

My suggestion is that you write to Miss Graham, finding out the present status of her scenario, and then let me know how the whole matter stands.

Best greetings to you!

[signed] Aaron Copland

---

1. *Appalachian Spring* was eventually premiered in October 1944.

To Leonard Bernstein

LB/LC. als.

May 6 '43

Dear Lensky—

We must stop this business of crossing letters. Did you get my last, sent to 15 W 52?

Somehow it doesn't seem so odd to have you in the Chelsea. Particularly when I think of who is on the 2nd floor![1]

You never wrote me a word about "Lark."[2] How did it sound? And what impression did you have of Stravinsky in the long talk V[ictor Kraft] says you had with him after that concert.

Also I don't understand what brought the break with Edys[3] just now. Explain.

The 2–piano Salon is out. Ask Heinsheimer for a copy if he hasn't already sent you one. It looks very pretty with Antonio's cover.[4] But V is upset because you (we) forgot to add the dedication.[5]

Of course—you were right in the argument with the Askews.[6] "Hollywood glamour" couldn't get me in a million years. Its just that the picture goes on an[d] on, and as long as it lasts, I have to be here. I have visions of being done by August 1st, but thats just a guess. Think of the mess I'd be in if Kouss hadn't decided to close down Tanglewood . . .

I keep being properly impressed by all the offers, interests, contracts, personalities that flit through your life. But don't forget <u>our</u> party line—you're heading for conductoring in a big way—and anybody and everything that doesn't lead there is an excrescence on the body politic.

Whats been happening with the Frau?[7] Sum up for me what she has contributed in the last 3 months.

Isn't [it] wonderful how Bill Sch[uman] is walking off with all the prizes?[8] He must be in 7th heaven. You can't say they dont encourage the young men nowadays—or anyway, one young man.

I can't remember what I wrote you a few days ago—and since I have a horror of repeating myself, I'd better quit here.

X and + and S[9]

A—

---

1. Virgil Thomson, who had in fact moved to the ninth floor early in 1943.

2. Copland's chorus on words of Genevieve Taggard.

3. Edys Merrill, dedicatee of Bernstein's song-cycle *I Hate Music*.

4. Bernstein's two-piano arrangement of *El Salón México* had appeared in print, with a line drawing by Antonio Álvarez of two Mexican dancers on its cover.

5. The *Salón* is dedicated to Victor Kraft.

6. On March 6, 1943, Bernstein had written to Copland: "I had a long fight with Kirk and Constance Askew about whether you could hold out to the Hollywood glamour. They were skeptical. I was, of course, loyally adamant."

7. Bernstein's psychoanalyst.

8. Schuman's *A Free Song* had just won the 1943 Pulitzer Prize in Music, the first such prize to be given for a musical work. In 1942 he had won the first Music Critics' Circle award for his Third Symphony; in April 1943 he had been awarded a grant of $1,000 by the National Academy of Arts and Letters.

9. The letter S formed by three straight lines.

To Harold Spivacke

ESC/LC. tls.

[Samuel Goldwyn stationery]

July 21, 1943

Dear Harold:

Two days ago I sent a long letter to Martha Graham, and was just about to write to you when your wire arrived. I can easily understand your anxiety about the score, but the situation was too complex to be taken care of in a wire.[1]

I wrote to Martha because I had just received the final version of the scenario. As I think I pointed out to you, I had suggested certain changes in the first version she sent me, and she promised to make them. Then there elapsed about a six week interval. She realized, of course, that the delay was serious because of the pressure of time, but apparently couldn't make the revisions any sooner. The new scenario is an improvement, and I wrote her my acceptance.

In the meantime I was at work on the score, and have perhaps a third done. If I had nothing to do between now and Sept. 1st but write the ballet, I wouldn't hesitate to promise it for that date. But through a series of unforeseen incidents the picture score I am contracted to do is just now getting under way. In another week I shall be in the midst of it—and there are a lot of notes to write!

Martha wrote that the Chavez score is still not in her hands.[2] Knowing him well, and the heavy season he has in Mexico at this time, I can hardly hope that his score will arrive soon[,] giving Martha something to work on until I am ready. As you probably know, he is famous for getting things done at the last possible moment.

In view of all this, I told Martha I thought she ought to write to you with the idea of finding out whether there was any chance of postponing the performances until Spring. I was very reluctant to make the suggestion, and only did so because I thought we could all do ourselves greater justice if we took a few more months time.

As I see it, if the postponement is out of the question, I can let Martha have about half the ballet to work on during the first weeks of September, and will finish up by Oct. 1st. This is on the assumption that the movie score will be out of the way by Aug. 31st. By "score" I mean piano reduction, from which I later make the instrumentation. In my case the instrumentation comes last, and all I can say is that it will be ready in time for orchestra rehearsals.

There is one other detail that hasn't worked out as I had hoped. Because of the nature of the scenario I have decided that the best possible instrumentation for my ballet would be piano and strings. In the case of the premiere that could mean piano and double string quartet. Since you have a flute and clarinet for the Chavez anyway, I may decide to add those two instruments. This means an addition of five players to the Chavez group, and I hope won't cause too much upset in the finances.[3]

I hope this gives you a clear picture of the set-up. Let me know what is decided as soon as you conveniently can.

Greetings,

[signed] Aaron

---

1. Copland had wired Spivacke "AM SENDING YOU AIR MAIL SPECIAL DELIVERY LETTER TODAY EXPLAINING SITUATION IN FULL."

2. Chávez had also been commissioned by Coolidge and Graham to write a new ballet. He did not finish the work on time, however, and it was not premiered with Copland's as had been planned.

3. The final scoring for the original version of *Appalachian Spring* was flute, clarinet, bassoon, piano, four violins, two violas, two cellos, and double-bass.

To Carlos Chávez

AC/LC. Photocopy of tls.
[Hotel Empire stationery]

Oct. 23, 1943

Dear Carlos:

I've been thinking of you, and wishing that I could have been in Mexico during the Festival. But the job in Hollywood took so long, and I had been away from New York for so long a time, that I felt I had to come back here before doing anything else. Well, in any case I finished the score for the movie—The North Star—and I hope you will keep an eye out for it. (There is more than an hour's music in it!)

I saw Martha Graham yesterday and played her the part of my score which is finished. Naturally we talked about you, and we are both very anxious to hear what progress you have been making with your own score. She tells me she hasn't heard from you since July. Maybe you had better write directly to me as to how soon you figure you can have the music in her hands, and I will pass on the information. Of course if you wish to write her directly that is all right also. In any case, she wants some kind of word, which is understandable enough. As for me, I will be very disappointed if we do not premiere our ballets together. Now that the concert season is done, I am hoping you will quickly finish what you have started.

I had a letter from Stokie [Stokowski] today—he has programed the US premiere of the Short Symphony for Jan 9th with the NBC Symphony. After ten years! Well, one must have patience if one is a composer.

[in ink] Any chance of seeing you this Winter in N.Y.?

All my best to you

[signed] Aaron

To Carlos Chávez

AC/LC. tls.
[Hotel Empire stationery]

March 28, 1944

Dear Carlos:

I had your nice wire, your letter—and today the Boletin.

I was delighted that you liked the score for North Star. I was in Hollywood for seven months, and sometimes I used to wonder whether any movie score is worth that much of one's time. It was a difficult job because of the Russian atmosphere that had to be in the score. Sometime I hope we can see it together so that I can get your detailed reaction. Later on, I hope to make a Suite from the music.

Its been an active winter for me. I finished a Violin Sonata, and am still working on the Martha Graham ballet, which is almost done. Naturally I am terribly disappointed that you haven't sent your completed score to her. The idea of our being presented on the same program with two new ballets was awfully nice. I just assume that your activities in Mexico are such that there just was no time to work on the piece. Too bad!

I am about to go to live in Cambridge until the end of June. I am teaching at Harvard for the Spring term, and giving some lectures there. I am trying my best to keep myself free for the summer so that I can come to Mexico, and settle in some quiet place to work on a large new orchestral work.[1] If you happen to hear of anyone wanting to rent a suitable house, let me know.

[in ink] All my best to you.

[signed] Aaron

---

1. The Third Symphony (1946).

To Harold Spivacke

ESC/LC. tls.
[Hotel Empire stationery]

July 8, 1944

Dear Harold:

At last I am able to write you that the complete score of the ballet has been mailed to you. Since I put the score on thin master sheets I hope you will send a copy to Martha Graham soon, so that she may have some idea of the sonorities. I am also planning to make some piano records for her, so that she will know my tempi. Unfortunately, she had left for Bennington before I had arrived back here, so I had no opportunity to play the completed score for her. Also I hope you are planning to send me a photostat of the score for my "collection."

I hope also that you will be able to send her a copy of the piano version of the ballet made from master sheets that I am about to send you. (I have had to hold on to them for a few more days so as to make the recording.) Martha has the ballet complete already,—but since sending it to her there have been some minor changes made, so that she ought to have this final version for comparison. Please return the originals of the piano version to me with the orchestral score copy, as I never know when I may need further copies.

I am about to leave for Mexico for the summer, so hold everything until you get an address from me. That goes for the check also!

I hope the ballet all turns out well, and that you and Mrs. Coolidge will feel properly rewarded for all your pains!

Yours,

[signed] Aaron C—

P.S. I wrote Martha that if the orchestration for 13 players is too much for her on the road, the score could be played (with slight rearrangements) with only a single string quartet for the string section, instead of the double string quartet and bass now called for. That would reduce the number of players to 8.

To Leonard Bernstein

LB/LC. als.

Mexico DF
Wed.—July 26 '44

Dear Lenotch:

Wonder where this will reach you—probably California. We got here after 10 days but the trip turned out to be a sad one. Five days after I left, my mother died suddenly, and I didn't get the news in time to attend the funeral. I was relieved to know that the end came so painlessly—but I've been left with a depressed feeling, nonetheless.

We are going out to Tenancingo tomorrow to visit houses with Peggy Riley[1] and her sister Heather. Hope its a good one we get. Everyone agrees that the town itself is una joya, but the road that goes there is lamentable.

Heinsheimer sent the Whiteman contract.[2] Looks as if it would happen after all. How's about you?

I wish I knew what version of Our Town you did at the Stadium—and what the final advice is.[3] Saw nice notices someplace on the trip about you & the piece. How did it all go?

Mexico City is different, but the same. I feel as if I know it all so well that theres no point being here. Of course, what I need is a house and a piano . . .

This is a short letter—but the first I've written. Write me back—

Love

Aaron

care Orquesta Sinfonica, I. la Catolica 30, Mexico D F. Mexico

---

1. Copland's close friend Rosamund ("Peggy") Bernier, at that time married to Louis Riley.

2. For the piece that would become *Letter from Home* (1944), commissioned for radio broadcast by bandleader Paul Whiteman.

3. The precise content of the suite from *Our Town* was still not decided. Bernstein's reply (August 16) does not indicate which version he had used but said, "*Our Town* was nice at the Stadium, but it's not a piece, I guess. There's nothing to be done, except strike out on a new tack. Perhaps a real suite. I still adore that music."

To Leonard Bernstein

LB/LC. tls.

ADDRESS: Calle J.G. Rojas #1,
Tepoztlan,
Morelos,
Mexico
Aug. 11, 1944

Lentschk:

It turned out not to be Tenancingo, after all. We went there and saw houses, but though it was charming, it reminded me too much of Tlaxcala. Also, the road was filthy horrible, and Posh[1] never would have lived through the summer. Besides it was terrifying to ride on, with hairpin turns over bottomless arroyos, and I never would have pulled through the summer.

Peggy's sister Heather brought us to Tepoztlan, and we fell for it. I was saying to Victor the other day what an amazing experience it would be for you to take a plane and come directly here, with no stopover in Mexico City. It would be like stepping off into the middle ages. The town is just a village, and though its only 60 miles away from Mexico City, it might as well be 600 as far as any relationship goes. Only a few years ago it took 4 hours on horseback to reach here from the nearest rail station. Now they've built a beautiful carretera [access road], and nobody seems to have discovered it but us.

The village itself is pure Aztec—a kind of museum piece. There are no paved streets—therefore no traffic, except the pitter-patter of bare feet. Theres no electricity—therefore no radios. There is one telephone—but it doesn't work—its decompuesto [busted]. The only sign of civilization as we know it is the afternoon rugby game that takes place in the courtyard of the church. The church itself is hoary with age. Its snuggled, like the town, between two imposing mountains that have a curious formation. They seem to bulge with the turrets of mediaeval castles. From the top of the main street one looks down on a wide open valley below. The gesamt [whole] impression is unforgettable.

Our house is of course the only liveable one in the town. If that sounds too snooty, I'll amend it by saying that we boast the only bathroom in the town. Its built in Mexican patio style—so that everybody's room is independent, and gives off on the patio. The 'family' consists of an elderly lady cook from Yucatan, an Indian girl helper, and Vicente the gardener. I have a separate studio away from the main house. The whole set-up almost collapsed because it appeared for awhile that there was no renting a piano in all Mexico. Because of the war-scarcity of pianos, commercial houses will only sell, not rent. An angel man, by the name of Cameron O'Day MacPherson, came to the rescue. I've never met him, but he lives in Cuernavaca, which is our nearest neighbor town, and it was rumored that he owned three Steinway grands, a Hammond organ, and a novachord. A visit proved the rumor true, (I counted them), but C. O'D. MacP. was in New York. Frantic wires with explanations did the trick—I get one. It isn't here yet, but its coming.

All this settling in has taken endless time and energy. It makes no sense unless I settle here for life. I would at that, except that its impossible to get a New York Times ever.

And what about you? Have you written me all? You'd better.

[in ink] Love and everything

[signed] A—

---

1. Apparently a nickname for Copland's car.

To Leonard Bernstein

LB/LC. als.

Tepoztlan,
Morelos
Mexico
Aug 25, '44

Dearest L—:

Its your birthday—(or I think it is)—so the least I can do is scribble you a note. Twenty-six—hmm. . . .

I got the letter you sent from Hollywood—. Why is it that when I'm in Hollywood you are in N.Y. and when you're in Hollywood I'm in Mexico and—no doubt, when you're in Mexico I'll be in Russia. It doesn't seem right.

Its amazing how often I think of you in this Aztec No Man's Land. Just think, not a single soul in all this town has ever heard of you or me. And I moan when I think how good it would be for you to spend a month in this utter tranquility of anonymity.

When tranquility gets too boring I go to Mexico City. Last week I heard [Vladimir] Golschmann conduct Carlos' orchestra as guest. He got a terrific hand—as do all visiting conductors. The orchestra has changed—it plays more correctly and better in tune—but with a certain student-like carefulness that spoils half the fun. (Don't quote me.) In the old days (1932) they made a mess—but it was a pretty mess.

While in town I saw an old Harvard architect friend, name of John Mc-Andrew. Somehow your name came up—it generally does—and I asked him if he had ever heard of you—(he's lived here for the past 5 years). Reply: "Oh isn't he the boy who can never say no? I hear he's gone into musical comedy . . ." That floored me. . . .[1]

I'm working on the Whiteman piece. Its slow and sentimental and I'm calling it "Letter from Home." (You'll just <u>have</u> to get used to the title!) I'm afraid it will fall between two stones [*sic*, "stools"]: too distingué for P[aul] W[hiteman] and not distingué enough for the Arthur Bergers of this world.[2] Well, that's a composer's life for you . . .

Your little paragraph about Our Town was very unilluminating. Didn't tell me what to do! As a result I think I'll publish it as is. And for a little birthday present I'll dedicate the thing to you. After all, its your baby . . .

What are the tentative dates on the opening of your show? What else is coming up that I don't know about?

Write much & often

Love

A—

P.S. Twenty-six—hmm

---

1. Bernstein was in fact working on his first musical, *On the Town* (1944).

2. Composer and critic Arthur Berger preferred Copland's acerbic earlier works to his more accessible music of the later 1930s and 1940s.

To Harold Spivacke

ESC/LC. tls.

> Tepoztlan,
> Morelos,
> Mexico
> Sept. 7, 1944

Dear Harold:

I am planning to fly up to Washington for the sole purpose of attending the Festival.[1] Therefore, if anything should happen to change plans for the event at the end of October, <u>please</u> make me the first person to be told about it.

However, on the assumption that all is to go ahead on schedule, would you let me know as soon as possible, what date Martha Graham will be having her first rehearsals in the Library Hall? Thats the day I should like to arrive. Also, it would be nice if your secretary could make me a reservation in the likeliest hotel for the period of the Festival.

One more request: would you have an invitation sent to Dr. Hans Heinsheimer of Boosey & Hawkes, 43 West 23 St., NYC. Since he is the eventual publisher of the ballet, he naturally wants to be there for the premiere.

The other day I visited the library of the National Conservatory in Mexico. The librarian assured me that no books had ever been received from the USA from the (Cowell) Distribution Project, or any other source.[2] Could you tell me where in Mexico such grants, if any, were made? The day I was at the Conservatory the library was filled with students. They have an excellent collection of the classics (or so it seemed to me), but no funds available for contemporary music. Since the Conservatory is one of the prime centers of musical activity in Mexico, and an ideal depository for American music, I very much hope that you will use your influence to see to it that they get an allotment of material whenever it starts going out.

Thats all for now!

Best regards,

[signed] Aaron

---

1. The Tenth Festival of Chamber Music at the Library of Congress, at which *Appalachian Spring* was premiered on October 30, 1944.

2. Henry Cowell was running "the Music Distribution Project at the New School for Social Research, which disseminated the music of U.S. composers to Latin America under a grant from Nelson Rockefeller's office" (Michael Hicks, *Henry Cowell, Bohemian* [Urbana: University of Illinois Press, 2002], 142).

To Arthur Berger

AC/LC. Photocopy of tls.

Tepoztlan,
Morelos,
Mexico
Sept. 8, 1944

Dear Arthur:

Theres no particular point to this letter—only a sort of blind instinct that if I can elicit a letter from you I can thereby keep in touch with the musical center of the world. Tepoztlan is definitely off the main road. In fact its about 400 years behind the procession. I doubt whether they ever even heard of Schostie, as Harold [Clurman?] would say.[1] And even if they heard of him, I doubt whether they'd care.

I found out most about the place by reading a book about it, written by an American, of course.[2] He spent 8 months here 15 years ago, before the road was opened. You can't find out much from the Indians themselves, they're so tight-lipped. The Mexico City Mexicans say they are unfriendly, but I suspect they are just shy. In any case my presence here is remarkable only because no American has lived here since Redfield wrote his book.

I imagine life here is closest to Italian hill town life, or what I suppose Italian hill towns are like. No newspapers and no radios, no telephones and no tele-grams. That simplifies life considerably. Theres no traffic because the streets are unpaved. A kind of pitter-patter of bare feet on rock can be heard all day through. Its the women on their daily round. The men wear guaraches, but then they only work in the fields, and are mostly not to be seen until around 5 in the afternoon, when they emerge to make conversation with their friends on the corner of their street. Nights are dark—there's no electricity. In spite of that, twice weekly there is a kind of public dance that takes place in the open air market. Its the only modern touch in town—and I can't say it's very gay. Instead of doing jarabes and huapangos I was amazed to see them attempting a kind of Tepoztlan version of a fox trot. The nearest movie house is 15 miles away, but obviously its had its effect. The "jazz" is better than the dancing— perhaps because Redfield mentions phonographs with horns when he was here. But the whole thing is hardly conducive to inspiring a Salon Tepozteco.

I don't suppose you're interested in any of this, but at least it tells you where I am. Esther[3] will be relieved to know that our house is quite perfect— complete with cook and gardener, and a bathroom. I have a separate studio with a baby grand. Unfortunately the old days are gone when one used to pay $8. a month for the whole thing—but then, you can't have everything.

We are only two hours from Mexico City so I have heard the Sinfonica several times. Chavez played a piece of Revueltas' called Ventanas (Windows). Its very amusing to listen to—chuck full [sic] of orchestral color—but the form isn't very good, I'm afraid. He was like a modern painter who throws marvellous daubs of color on canvas that practically takes your eye out, but it doesn't add up. Too bad—because he was a gifted guy. Also heard a Symphony No. 1 by young Pablo Moncayo. He adds a gentle note to what is generally the grim or boisterous Mexican palette, but the whole thing is still rather unformed, despite charming moments. I am disturb[ed to][4] note that there doesn't seem to be any youngest generation of [Mex]ican composers—fellows in their twenties, I mean. Galindo and Moncayo are the thirty generation. I spoke to Chavez about it, but he doesn't seem to have any explanation. It may be the lack of [an] outstanding composition teacher—nobody who teaches really seems to know his stuff. Chavez and Revueltas went abroad and the young men stay home. Something ought to be done about it.

What goes on where you are—thats really the point of this letter. I feel as if I had been gone for ages, and everything has changed. Of course it hasn't, but I need reassuring. [Music critic Irving] Kolodin isn't back from the wars, is he? Have you been composing anything? Has anybody been composing anything? I wrote a seven minute piece for Whiteman's commission called "Letter from Home." Its very sentimental, with five saxophones that are sometimes five clarinets and sometimes four flutes—but it modulates!

Now all I have to do is to take care of the Koussie commission.[5]

Love to Esther from me and Victor.

[signed] Aaron

P.S. Wild coincidence. Just came back from the P.O. and foun[d] a letter including the two I sent you in 1934 and 1943.[6] Very amused to reread them. Now I see why I wrote you—trying to [get?] printed, thats all!

1. Dmitry Shostakovich, whose *Leningrad Symphony* was the sensation of wartime American concert halls: he appeared on the cover of *Time* magazine in July 1942.

2. Robert Redfield, *Tepoztlán, a Mexican Village* (Chicago: University of Chicago Press, 1930). Copland may also have known a second book on the same village, Stuart Chase, *Mexico: A Study of Two Americas* (New York: Macmillan, 1931).

3. Berger's wife.

4. Page 2 of the letter is torn in the upper-right corner.

5. The Third Symphony.

6. *Letters of Composers: An Anthology,* edited by Gertrude Norman and Miriam Lubell Shrifte (New York: A. A. Knopf, 1946), included Copland's letters to Berger of August 6, 1934, and April 10, 1943, as well as a letter from Copland to Slonimsky. The letter that prompted this postscript was doubtless from one of the editors of the anthology asking Copland's permission to publish and enclosing transcripts of the letters to be published.

To Harold Spivacke

ESC/LC. tls.

Tepoztlan,
Morelos,
Mexico
Sept. 25, 1944

Dear Harold:

Thanks for the prompt reply to my last letter. Also for the check that came through safely.

I had no idea Martha would be coming for rehearsals as early as five days before the event. Naturally I don't intend to make a nuisance of myself during all that time!

My present plan is to fly up from here on the 25th, reaching Washington the following day. So please reserve a room for me from Thursday the 26th. (Even if I'm put off the plane for a day through lack of priorities I can still make the dress rehearsal.) My budget will stand $4. or $5. a day for a room—but the main thing is to put me where "everybody" will be. Half the fun of going to festivals is bumping into people in your hotel lobby.

If anything happens to make me change my plans I'll wire you. I hope you'll do the same. Please ask your secretary to write me the name of the hotel I'm to go to, in the event that I reach Washington at some ungodly hour, not knowing where to go. I'd like it if she could include some sort of announcement of the Festival, so that I can mull over the events to come in quiet contemplation.

Best greetings to you!

[signed] Aaron

Minna Lederman, editor of the magazine *Modern Music*, often turned to Copland for advice. The following is by far the longest of the letters from Copland still extant in the *Modern Music* Archives.

To Minna Lederman

MMA/LC. tls.

Tepoztlan,
Morelos,
Mexico.
Oct. 6, 1944.

Dear Mink:

If this reply seems late, try to remember that your letter, mailed on the 26th, only reached here two days ago. I hope this one goes a bit faster so that my measly suggestions may be of some help for issue no. 1.

I do feel kind of swamped by the variety of questions you fling at me.[1] Don't forget that I am rather rusty—not having been in the center of activities for a good many months. So—take all this for what its worth:

1. About Latin America: I don't get the impression that very much has been happening in Mexico. Still if you want a round-up of events I'd suggest you ask Salvador Moreno. He's a young composer in the Chavez camp, a Mexican of Spanish antecedents. He's bright and amusing, and has recently been writing criticism for one of the Mexican dailies. The catch is that he is ill at the moment with some sort of eye disease, and I have no way of knowing whether he will be up to turning out an article right away. He can be addressed care of the Orquesta Sinfonica.

I recently had news of a new "Grupo Renovacion Musical" that has been formed in Cuba. They gave two concerts of works by the new generation of composers. I doubt whether the works are very significant, but I think its worth reporting on. José Ardévol could write an article about it. You could address him care of the Grupo at Compostela 156, altos, La Habana, Cuba.

Argentina's season is just over and I think we ought to have a report on the new works introduced. It could be written by Roberto Garcia Morillo, who is assistant critic on La Nacion of Buenos Aires. You can write him care of that paper.

From Chile I think you might have a study of Domingo Santa Cruz' new Piano Concerto. I spoke with [pianist Claudio] Arrau here and he seemed very impressed by it. Santa Cruz writes the sort of music that analyses well. The article should have some musical illustrations. I think you could take a chance again on young Juan Orrego [Salas], who once flopped on a round-up of the season. This is more in his line, I think. Write him care of Santa Cruz, if you don't have his own address in your files.

From Brazil I should think Carleton S[prague] Smith ought to have a thousand words inside him about life in Sao Paulo, where I understand he is cultural attache to our consulate. Also I have just heard that Everett Helm, a young composer pupil of Piston, is being sent down to Brazil on a travel grant from the State Dep't to "write a book about Brazilian music." You might contact him for a piece for a later issue. His US address is: 702 East 17 St., Santa Ana, Cal. I don't know whether he is still there or has already left for Brazil.

I also wish that we could have a note from Montevideo but I don't know who could write it. Even Curt Lange has left, and is now living in Brazil. My only idea would be to write to the Uruguayan pianist Hugo Balzo, care of the S.O.D.R.E. Orchestra in Montevideo, and he undoubtedly could suggest someone intelligent for the job.

If you want something from Lima why not go back to the man who wrote so amusingly last time. Wasn't it Raygada??[2]

2. About Europe: The only composer I've heard about is in Rome. He is Nino Rota, who once studied at Curtis and is a good friend of Sam Barber. (Barber would supply his address.) I'm not sure of the kind of article he'd write—he's the delicate rather than the forceful type; but I know he's gone through a lot, and recently communicated with Barber.

I should think that one good source for material would now be Switzerland, since they'd know more than before, and would probably be more ready to tell what they know. But I don't have names to suggest.

As for Paris I'm stumped. Why don't you ask Milhaud if he doesn't know of someone who could write for you. You might even persuade Poulenc to say what it was like, since according to TIME, he wasn't a collaborator.[3]

Too bad about London being such a pain in the neck. But I think its time that Marc [Blitzstein] came across with a piece. Or you might even attack Benjamin Britten again. After all, he once wrote for you. I don't have other ideas because most of the younger men are in the Army now—fellows like Humphrey Searle or Henry Boys. If you are desperate you might ask Erwin Stein, who works in an editorial capacity for Boosey & Hawkes' London office. He's an experienced writer but I don't know how unbiased. (Heinsheimer would probably be willing to discuss his capabilities frankly with you.) Theres another fellow in the B & H office by the name of Campbell—forgotten his first name. He also has written—but he's a rabid Bloch fan, and I don't know whether anything else pleases him. Heinsheimer would know about him too.

For a stab in the dark about Brussels, you might ask Desire Defauw whether he knows of any musician in Belgium capable of writing for you.

I wish we had someone in Spain who could send some dope. I'll ask [Adolfo] Salazar whether he has any suggestions about that.

3. About the Harris article by [Robert] Evett, I'm all for it. Everybody knows that Roy has a harmonic system, and nobody knows what it is. It should be an article with illustrations that completely satisfies the curiosity.

4. About the Portrait series:[4] if you are to have Quincy Porter don't have Hans Nathan do it. He's a dyed in the wool European and I don't think Quincy would like being written up by him. Douglas [Moore] would know whom to suggest for Quincy. For a new name in the series I'd be for an article on Burrill Philips'[5] work. I think its significant, and has character. Robert Palmer knows the work well, but whether he can organize an article about it I don't know.

5. I have heard the new Sonata for 2 pianos of Stravinsky. Its a charming but slight work. Whether it rates a whole separate article for itself I doubt, but if you're hard up for material it would pass. I don't happen to know Prof. Tangeman.

6. About correspondants from American cities: Boston should be written up by Irving Fine of the Harvard Music faculty. They've had a new Hindemith Uraufführung [premiere] during the summer.[6] Also private hearings of new piano works by Harold Shapero. Fine is fine for those things. His address: 15 Everett St., Cambridge 38, Mass. (There were other things too, of course.) I think Persichetti is OK from Philie, but have nobody better to suggest from Pittsburgh and Cleveland than the people you already know. When I am in Washington I'll keep my eye open for somebody to recommend from there.

I assume you'll be writing up the Musicians' Congress concerts on the campus of UCLA, in Sept.

7. About general articles my mind is blank, mostly because I have had little contact with musicians these last months, and therefore no stimulation. Why not try to get Sam Barber to write an article. His last symphony showed him to be getting less stuffy.[7] He is very articulate with the pen and might have something he wants to write about. Anyway, I'm sure he would like being asked.

Later on I might want to do one myself—something about the men who have come "back from the wars." A kind of welcome home article that would give them a send-off into civilian life. But its too soon yet—so forget about it. [added in ink: (Just an idea, anyhow!)]

I'm planning to fly up to Washington for the Coolidge Festival and then on home to N.Y. No one has seen a public announcement of the event, but Spivacke keeps saying it will come off at the end of Oct. In any case I am coming back then. Thats just around the corner so theres no sense in prolonging this already long letter.

I sent a letter to Claire [Reis] urging her to close up shop at the end of this season. I haven't heard her reaction, but am curious.

Glad you've been writing and selling things. But what things??

I leave Tepoztlan and the primitive life on the 23rd, and I ought to be back in New York by Nov. 1st.

Love and all that,

[signed] A—

---

1. Lederman had apparently requested Copland's advice about articles for upcoming issues of *Modern Music*.

2. It was indeed Carlos Raygada in "The Curse of Virtuoso Routine," *Modern Music* 20 (1943).

3. "La Musique et la Politique" (*Time*, Sept. 18, 1944, p. 60): "Poulenc . . . maintained an unimpeachable record of resistance."

4. *Modern Music's* series of articles, "American Composers." The article on Quincy Porter was finally written by Herbert Elwell.

5. Composer Burrill Phillips.

6. Hindemith's *The Four Temperaments*, for piano and string orchestra.

7. Barber's Second Symphony (1943; rev. 1947), originally titled *Symphony Dedicated to the Army Air Forces*, premiered by Koussevitzky and the Boston Symphony Orchestra on March 3, 1944, and later withdrawn by the composer from his catalog.

Copland flew to Washington from Mexico City on October 26 and attended the premiere of *Appalachian Spring* on October 30 as part of a festival honoring Elizabeth Sprague Coolidge on her eightieth birthday.

To Jerome Moross

JM/Columbia. tls.
[Hotel Empire stationery]

Nov. 7, 1944

Dear Jerry:

It was awful nice to get that letter from you in Tepoztlan, just when I needed it most. I left there at the end of October, and stopped off on the way home in Washington for the Coolidge Festival. Martha Graham put on three new ballets, including the one I wrote for her. People seemed to like it so I guess it was all right. I plan to get a suite out of it to be called Ballet for Martha. (She called it Appalachian Spring.)

I didn't do so very much work in Tepoztlan. Finished a piece for the Paul Whiteman radio series. Called it Letter from Home. I recently heard an off the air record of his performance—sheer murder it was too. I dread to think the impression it must have made on the unsuspecting listener. Also, like you, I began a Symphony—so we can weep on each others shoulders together. Its tough going even without having to sandwich in movie music. All I need is another two years.

I've been back only a week and am catching up on NY's musical doings. Things don't seem to have changed much. Virgil [Thomson] is still at it, David Diamond had quite a success with his second Symphony, Lenny Bernstein has written his first musical show,[1] Bill Schuman is to be head of Shirmer's [*sic*] editorial board, Paul Bowles has a new ballet,[2] etc., etc. But you probably know all this better than I do.

My best to H & S.

[signed] Aaron

[in ink] P.S. If you hear of any outstanding picture assignment thats available for the Spring—let me know.

1. *On the Town.*
2. *Colloque Sentimental* (1944).

To Nadia Boulanger

AC/LC. als.

[Hotel Empire stationery]

March 1, 1945

Dear Nadia:

It was wonderful to get your letter and to find you so enthusiastic about the new ballet.[1] I was a little unprepared for so much enthusiasm because some friends who know my music well have been rather severe about my 'copying myself.' It is a difficult point—to say exactly what line divides the justifiable and unjustifiable repetition of manner, procedures, ideas, in an artist's work. So I am delighted that you found 'fraicheur' [freshness] there.

Forgive me if I jump from the above to the enclosed clipping in to-days paper.[2] Imagine how excited I am! It is a unique opportunity to bring back to Paris at such a moment some of the fruits which were nourished there.

You must give me all your ideas as to what would be most effective from a French point of view. We are planning to present Stravinsky's Symphony[3] as part of the Festival—and to send his own recordings to Paris as a guide for the conductor. (I so much enjoyed seeing him here, amidst an admiring group of jeunesse americain [young Americans]. That is how it should be!)

Have you any messages to send, any greetings, any errands for me to do? It will be a pleasure to carry out your wishes. Have you any news of Gargenville or of 36 rue Ballu? I shall be leaving about April, and plan to stay 3 months.

In haste, and with all my affection

Aaron

P.S. Some time you must tell me your negative feeling about my Violin Sonata. I am just as interested in your disapprovals as in your praises.

The copy of the ballet you have was formerly mine. The Library of Congress then presented me with a second copy, so I am <u>delighted</u> to present the first to you—

It will seem very strange to be in Paris without you there!

1. *Appalachian Spring.*
2. The clipping is no longer with the letter, but was probably Mark A. Schubart, "U.S. Music Festival Planned in Paris," *New York Times,* March 1, 1945. Copland had been asked to direct a festival of American music in Paris, to be jointly sponsored by the French government and United States Office of War Information. The event was eventually canceled.
3. Stravinsky's Symphony in C (1940).

To Nadia Boulanger

AC/LC. als.

Box 294
Bernardsville
New Jersey
April 14, 1945

Dear Nadia:

Its very sad—but I'm afraid the Festival in Paris is not to happen after all—at any rate, not this Spring, as planned. Perhaps in the Fall, altho I am not too optimistic. You can imagine how disappointed I am!

Just between ourselves I fear the O[ffice of] W[ar] I[nformation] made something of a mess of its own plans. They were venturing into what was a new field for them—concert giving—and unforseen and serious financial complications arose. Since I am not a member of the OWI I have been able to do nothing but watch our plans go wrong. There is still some chance for the Fall— so I shall wait and see.

In the meantime I am in the country. It is beautiful here—and I am working hard on my Symphony. Quel travail! [What a job!] Also—I am making a Suite for orchestra of the "Appalachian Spring" ballet.

So—unlike Mr. Hurok[1]—I have my composing to console myself for the disappointments of an impressario's life. Still—it would have been nice to go to Paris now. Dommage! [A pity!]

Always devotedly
Aaron

---

1. Sol Hurok, New York impresario, noted particularly as the arranger of American tours for major ballet companies.

To Harold Clurman

Adler/HRC. als.

Box 294
Bernardsville, New Jersey
May 8, '45

Dear H—

I should have written sooner—but I had nothing better to say than that I wasn't going to Paris after all. You showered such envy on my head that I was a little ashamed to have to admit it was all to no purpose.

The annoying part of the affair was not so much my abrupt change in plans— but the reason given by OWI for abandoning the project: namely, the U.S. government will not directly sponsor and pay for a Music Festival. (I assume the reason for that is: its never been done before, or that Congress couldn't be made to see it.) For a while we were making desperate attempts to collect a mere [$]25,000 backing from private sources; in which case the OWI promised complete support in Paris from itself + the State Dep't.

Well, finally, it all fell thru—and I went to New Jersey instead of Paris. I have a cottage—beautifully situated on a big estate and I console myself with writing a Symphony (same one!).

In my off moments I made a Suite from Appalachian Spring arranged for full sized orch. which the Philharmonic is to premiere next season. Martha [Graham] is doing the N.Y. premiere of the ballet on Monday. Yesterday—out of a clear sky—I read in the Times that the ballet score had won me the Pulitzer Prize for music! Obviously theres a conspiracy to turn me into an academician before my time.

Now about You. I had a letter from Clinton Simpson at Knopfs saying that your book would be off the press in another 2 weeks and that I would get an advance copy immediately.[1] So I'll be writing about it to you soon I hope.

The Sartre play that Paul Bowles adapted is to be produced by Oliver Smith, who is also to do "my" musical.[2] I spoke with him about the possibility of your directing it (Sartre) and he seemed definitely interested. I asked him to send you a script. (His address is 28 W. 10.) I like his kind of theatre sense. He is a very gifted set designer—but beyond that has a general feeling for the theatrical without any of Orson's[3] "profundities." Oliver has no pretensions but in his own way I think he's "theatre-wise."

It was disappointing to hear that you haven't started directing your picture as yet.[4] The notes I had read in the papers made it sound as if it were already beginning. About a month ago I had Waldo [Frank][5] for lunch. He seemed in good spirits + [illegible due to water damage] was about to leave for Truro.[6] I also went to see the Paul Strand show and came away wishing I had your article to read again. The pictures looked shiney new on the walls—even the 20 yr old ones.

Its the quiet life I'm leading—do lots of book reading and sun-relaxing. In spite of you I continued the Santayana autobiography, jumped on the H.[enry] James revival bandwagon, was fascinated by a Christopher Isherwood tale of public school life called "Lions + Shadows," amused by a new 20 yr old novelist Denton Welch whose Maiden Voyage was well-named, and now engaged on a biography of Byron by [André] Maurois.

I hope you come back to civilization soon.

Love

A—

---

1. Harold Clurman, *The Fervent Years: The Story of the Group Theatre and the Thirties* (New York: A. A. Knopf, 1945).

2. Bowles was the first to translate Jean-Paul Sartre's *Huis clos,* giving it the title *No Exit.* Oliver Smith produced its premiere in November 1946. Copland's musical is *Tragic Ground;* see headnote to letter of July 9, 1945.

3. Orson Welles, with whom Copland had worked on *The Second Hurricane* (1936) and the Shakespearean adaptation *Five Kings* (1939).

4. Clurman was the director of *Deadline at Dawn* (1946).

5. Waldo Frank, American radical writer. Copland saw his *Our America* (1919) as instrumental in bringing modernism to America. The two had known each other since 1924 and had both taught at the New School for Social Research in 1927.

6. Truro, Massachusetts, a small town near Provincetown on Cape Cod.

To Irving Fine

IF/LC. als.

> Box 294
> Bernardsville
> N.J.
> June 15 '45

Dear Irving:

It would be nice to see you in N.Y. Let me know when you'll be there and maybe we can connect—I come in occasionally. If not—why not plan to spend a day out here. My phone is Bernardsville 981—and you could call me from town if necessary.

I liked your article in M.[odern] M.[usic] very much.[1] (I wonder what was cut?) I know from experience that articles on the young are not easy to do. Yours was definitely on the kind side—but why not? How about one on H. Shapero for next year?

By the way—M.M. is in financial difficulties for next year and has appealed to the Weymouth Fund via Walter [Piston]. If you think it will do any good—or is at all necessary—drop a note to Woody[2] backing the appeal (I'm assuming you think it a worthy project!)[.]

Did the Guerrilla Song[3] ever happen at the Pops?

I suppose Lenny [Bernstein] gave you as dramatic an account as possible of my back ache. It was bad for about 5 days. Seems I have to have some teeth yanked out—so you may find a toothless Aaron when we meet.

Try to read Harold Clurman's book—The Fervent Years. Its part of my youth and I think it'll amuse you.

You don't say what you are composing. Be modest—but don't exaggerate![4]

Best to Verna

Aaron

---

1. Irving Fine, "Young America: Bernstein and Foss," *Modern Music* 22 (1945): 238–43.
2. G. Wallace Woodworth, conductor of the Harvard Glee Club.
3. From *The North Star.*
4. A Koussevitzkyism.

To Mary Lescaze

AC/LC. tls.

Box 294
Bernardsville, N.J.
June 19, 1945

Dear Mary:

Big surprise—and very pleasant—to hear from you. Thanks for all the kind words about the Graham piece. You'll have a chance to hear the music without the benefit of dance next season. Rodzinski has a Suite I arranged from the ballet and says he will play it in October with the Philharmonic.[1]

I was thinking of you because of that nice pose of yours in the frontispiece of Harold [Clurman]'s book.[2] Have you read it yet? I wonder what you will (or do) think of it. Naturally I'm prejudiced, particularly since I love reading the events of my youth as if they were history. But considering what a hard job he set himself I think its a moving book. With all those people still around, and each one of them certain to have their own version of how it all happened, and having to be reasonably detached about his own role, I thought he gave a remarkably urbane and psychologically interesting performance.

I'm afraid I don't have much to contribute to the problem you pose about kids and contemporary music.[3] As for new music for recorder I'm sure there is some, but offhand I can't say what. If interested enough call the American Music Center, talk to Miss Dower, tell her you're calling on my advice, and ask if she can send you a list of new music for recorder. Also, big stores like Schirmer or Fischer generally have special folders containing new publications in different categories and I assume that would include the recorder too.

None of the organizations that I know of have any program specifically designed for modern music listening in schools. I've heard it discussed several times, but no general solutions were ever arrived at. The only sensible thing I suppose is to make certain that when the kids get to the record listening stage that they have the opportunity to hear music styles of every period including our own. Not much help, am I?

I'm living in New Jersey for the summer, about 30 miles below Oakland. Have a cottage on a big estate and its all very beautiful. Not a thing to do all summer but write a Symphony and dream about the house I want to build in the not too far-off future.

You were very nice to relay the sayings of Patsy O'Neill. Please relay back to her and Blackie affectionate greetings from me.

Yours,

[signed] Aaron

---

1. Conductor Artur Rodzinski gave the premiere of the Suite from *Appalachian Spring* on October 4, 1945, the opening concert of the New York Philharmonic's 104th season.

2. *The Fervent Years.* The frontispiece is an informal photo of "the Group Theatre Company, at one of Harold Clurman's afternoon talks, Brookfield Center, Summer, 1931." Clurman ("wielding stick"), Clifford Odets, Stella Adler, and Franchot Tone are identified in the caption; Mary Lescaze is not.

3. Lescaze had written "Next year, in the second grade, [the Lescazes' son] Lee, like most progressively educated children, will begin to blow into a recorder. But unless a little pressure is exerted . . . he'll be singing and blowing early English, folk song, simple classics, period. . . . Surely there must be some blowable, singable pieces from living composers. Is there an available list?"

In 1945 Copland was at work on the score for a planned musical theater piece, *Tragic Ground,* based on Erskine Caldwell's novel of the same name. Agnes de Mille was to be the choreographer, Lynn Riggs the playwright. Due to a lack of financial support, the project was abandoned in late 1946.

To Lynn Riggs

Riggs/Yale. tls.

Box 294
Bernardsville, New Jersey
July 9, 1945

Dear Lynn:

Thanks for sending Act I complete. The Bus and White Turkey scenes read well, though of course a hell of a lot depends on production. Whether or not I can write a low-down blues number remains to be seen.

I have to admit to being skeptical about the final scene between Jim and Libby as you now have it. It seems glaringly conventional by comparison with the rest of the act. Not in the writing, but in the general idea of finishing act I with the usual musical comedy misunderstanding between He and She. Also it looks to me as if it would be very anti-climactic coming after all that Turkey noise—particularly since it must serve to ring down the curtain on Act I. You've undoubtedly thought of all this yourself. And have beautiful reasons why you did it the way you did. Anyway I thought I'd give you my reactions just in case they stimulate you to further inspirations on the subject.

In doing Act II try to avoid deciding on actual lyrics for Florabelle's song and Floyd's number. It occurred to me we might try the other method of putting words to music, since I think I have musical ideas for the general style of both songs. I won't try to develop them further however until we get a chance to talk over what you think ought to go into them. At the moment I'm in trouble because I have some ideas for Alone at Night that don't always fit the lines to a T. But I'm sure we can make adjustments later. I don't expect any trouble with the Figgerin' number which seems to sing itself. However, I haven't sat down to listen to it sing as yet!

I should think with Act I behind you the worst is over. Keep a-goin' . . .

[signed] Aaron

To Irving Fine

IF/LC. als.

Box 294

Bernardsville, N.J.

Sept 5 '45

Dear Irving:

Thought I'd try to get you this before Fall term starts. Your letter sounded frustrated. Maybe you've written some music in these last weeks—after all.

I'm the proud father—or mother—or both—of a second movement.[1] Lots of notes—and only 8 minutes of music—such are scherzi—pfui! Its not very original—mais ça marche du commencement jusqu'au fin [but it works from beginning to end]—which is a help.

Also I've started work on the show: arranged a song for kids to sing that Lynn Riggs picked up in his home state—Okla.[2] But Agnes de Mille is in London so all is suspended until her return nobody seems to know when.

Occasionally, I get lazy and have visitors—Lenny's been out—full of plans for his new City Center orchestra. Ain't that sumpin? David Diamond arrived also—with a finished 3rd Symphony—and already at work on a short 4th. They get more and more classical—and I told him that if he's not careful he'll turn into the Glazunow of Amer. music. He was horrified. . . .

Weyman Fund came thru with [$]1000 for M[odern] M[usic] with the proviso that the full budget can be raised. MM's future seems precarious at the moment—very![3] Did you see an article on P. Bowles in Music & Letters by Mrs. Stanley Bate (P. Glanville Hicks)?[4]

If you come to N.Y. give me warning.

Best to Verna

Aaron

---

1. Of the Third Symphony.

2. This would become "I Bought Me a Cat" from the first set of *Old American Songs* (1950).

3. *Modern Music* ceased publication in 1946.

4. Peggy Glanville Hicks, "Paul Bowles: American Composer," *Music and Letters* 26 (April 1945): 88–96.

In late 1945, William Schuman, then president of the Juilliard School, offered Copland a teaching post. Copland first tried to negotiate a more flexible position, but Schuman refused the terms. Copland turned down the offer of employment altogether and never held a permanent full-time position at a university.

To William Schuman

Schuman/NYPL. tls.

Limestone Rd.
Ridgefield, Conn.
Jan 2, 1946

Dear Bill:

The reason I haven't written sooner is very simple: I've been having the great inner struggle of all time and you might as well know about it. At the eleventh hour, faced with the job of tieing myself down to a 30 week job, I got the jitters. I'm torn between two desires: to be connected with you and the School and not to lose my present freedom of action. The fact that the inner dichotomy didn't come out more strongly in our previous discussions is proof of how much I want to be there with you, and to what a degree I wanted to be talked into it. But now, faced with the white sheet of paper and fixing my name to it I can't quite bring myself to it.

I've been trying, ever since I got the official invitation, to work out a compromise solution—and this is what I figured out:

1) Since I am not to start actual teaching this coming Sept. in any case, I would rather be put into the announcement as a special guest lecturer for the student body as a whole. In that way I could be available for a few lectures sometime during the course of the academic year.

2) If you care to, you could also announce me as a guest-teacher for composition students starting in 1947–48 term. The advantage of that arrangement is that it is more honest from the student standpoint—not promising things we can't perform—and the term "guest-teacher" leaves me with a sense of freedom that I don't seem to have when I think of myself as a regular faculty member. The point is, that I have no objection whatever to being around for a few terms, (and it may turn out I'll want to be around forever) but my deepest inner concern seems to be a need to think of myself as free to move about when and where I please and to let my mind dwell solely on my own music if I happen to feel that way.

I hope this won't come as too great a shock. You'll probably think it uncharacteristic of me not to know my own mind for so long but put it down to my real wish to work with you and your own potent charm! If you don't like any of this just throw me out on my ear.

Affectionately
[signed] Aaron

To William Schuman

Schuman/NYPL. als.

> Limestone Rd
> Ridgefield, Conn
> Jan 10 '46

Dear Bill:

I'm returning the invitation of Dec 17th as requested.[1]

I note that you decided to "put me out on my ear"—which is undoubtedly what I deserved. I guess my compromise solution was no good. But still, I'll be reading that announcement with a certain nostalgia for what might have been. . . .

I'll call you for a lunch date and you can talk about nothing but school.

Don't be too mad at me.

Best

Aaron

---

1. The invitation to join the Juilliard faculty.

In the spring of 1944, the Koussevitzky Music Foundation had offered Copland $1,000 to compose what would become the Third Symphony. As commissioner of the work, the foundation had certain proprietary rights to the score, but Hans Heinsheimer, Copland's representative at Boosey & Hawkes, was eager to offer the symphony to other conductors as well and began promoting the work before its completion.

To Serge Koussevitzky

SK/LC. tls.

> Limestone Ridge
> Ridgefield, Conn.
> April 5, 1946

Dear Sergei Alexandrovitch:

Here is a letter on a personal matter.

It seems—according to Boosey & Hawkes—that there is great interest among the conductors about my new Symphony. I know you are anxious to spread the Foundation's commissioned works as widely as possible. Obviously they all want to do the work as far as possible while it is still fresh and new, and being talked about. So it is natural that they want to know when you will have given the first performances in Boston and New York. It would be wonderful from my angle— and also of course for Boosey—if you could say now that by December first the

Symphony can be generally available. I know that that means the Symphony would have to be scheduled for the first trip to New York, but perhaps you would be willing to do that.

In any case—if convenient—write me or Boosey & Hawkes direct what your decision is.

Affectionately,

[signed] Aaron

P.S. We went up to visit the Barrington School in Great Barrington yesterday. The buildings and accommodations are first-class. The only drawback is the half-hour journey to Tanglewood, but considering the beauty and comfort of the living conditions I think the students would agree, especially if we put there the composition students and the auditors. In any case, I gave my opinion to Mr. Judd[1] that I am in favor of renting the School for our purposes. I think you would also agree if you saw the place.

[in ink] P.P.S.—Looking forward to Wednesday night![2]

---

1. George E. Judd, manager of the Boston Symphony Orchestra.

2. Koussevitzky was to conduct *Appalachian Spring* in Hartford, Connecticut, on Tuesday, April 9. Copland has either mistaken the day of the week or is referring to a social get-together the night after the concert.

To Carlos Chávez

AC/LC. Photocopy of tls.

Care Boosey and Hawkes
668 Fifth Ave.,
New York, N.Y.
[September 1946]

Dear Carlos:

I received the issue of Nuestra Musica with your translation of the Berger article.[1] I must tell you how touched I was—first at all the space devoted to the article, and second, that you bothered to do the translation yourself. The magazine itself looks so well, and I am delighted at the thought that there is now in Mexico an organ of expression for the writings of Mexican composers.

I received programs and reviews of the performance of the Short Symphony that you gave this summer. I am touched once again at your devotion to that piece. (Did you see your letter of 1934 printed in the volume that Knopf published "Letters of Composers"? If you don't have that book I'd be glad to send it to you.)[2] Its now almost twenty years that we know each other and I must say that I know of no other fellow-composer who has given me firmer support or more continuous encouragement in my work. Un abrazo, querido amigo! [A hug, dear friend!]

The work at Tanglewood was finished only recently. I still regret that no one came from Mexico as student at the school but perhaps it can be arranged next summer. Now I am settled near Tanglewood for a few more weeks, finishing up my Symphony. It should be done about October first. It has four movements and lasts about 40 minutes—my longest piece of absolute music so far. I hope you'll like it. It has taken two years of my time, and I am anxious to get busy on other projects.

The temporada [concert season] will soon be over, and I hope you will find some time for your own composing. What is the next piece to be?

You heard, I suppose, about the sudden death of Paul Rosenfeld in July. It doesn't seem natural not to have him there on 11th St., worrying quietly about the state of music. I'm sure he didn't approve of my music of the last years, but it is sad to think of him no longer there to disapprove.

All my best to you,

[signed] Aaron

---

1. Chávez had translated Arthur Berger's article "The Music of Aaron Copland," originally published in *Musical Quarterly* 31 (October 1945), for *Nuestra Musica* 1, no. 2 (May 1946).

2. *Letters of Composers: An Anthology* (1946).

Copland's Third Symphony was premiered by Serge Koussevitzky and the Boston Symphony Orchestra in October 1946. The first conductor after Koussevitzky to present the symphony was Leonard Bernstein, who gave the first performance outside the United States in May 1947 with the Czech Philharmonic in Prague. Soon after, Copland himself led a performance in Mexico by the Orquesta Sinfónica de México on June 20 and 22, 1947, at the invitation of Carlos Chávez.

To Leonard Bernstein

LB/LC. als.

Mexico D.F.
June 4, '47

Young charmer!

Just received your forwarded Paris letter and I'm dashing a hasty reply on the chance that it will reach you in Holland. It was fun to read the various reactions to the [Third] Symp[hony]—including your own.[1] I've decided that it is a tough job to write an almost 40 min. piece which is perfect throughout. That's about all I'll concede for the moment! You were an angel to struggle with rehearsals at the tail-end of a Festival. The part of your letter I liked best, of course, was your saying you'd like to do it zum States.

Didn't I tell you I was coming to Mexico to conduct the Symph myself? I've had 3 rehearsals already and the concert is still 2 weeks away. My main trouble is: giving cues for entrances. Well anyhow its very good experience and I'm getting a kick out of it. (Kouss said to me before I left "If you ruin MY Symphony I vill keel you.")

All my N.Y. news is probably stale for you by now. Virgil's opera[2] was original-looking on the stage—no one has ever seen anything quite like it. But I thought there was more music in Four Saints. It's as if a new musical idea hadn't occured to him in 10 years. The prosody, as per usual, is superb—but then its easy to have good prosody if you have nothing else on your mind. (I'm quoting myself.)

D[avid] D[iamond] looked much improved when last I saw him. I suppose Helen Kates told you of our financial crisis which was solved until August.

Bob Shaw did a bee-utiful job with my new chorus.[3] Most people seemed to like it, but the press was only mildly interested. I can't imagine how you'll react to it. Any ho you won't have to conduct it—since theres nothing but voices. (I decided that Bob's conducting technique derives from the football cheer leader. Or did you say that already?)

I was in Cuba the night you played the Symph. in Prague. Mexico seems so naively serious by comparison. I see Jeremiah on display here in the record shops.[4] Chavez spoke of asking you to come to conduct a week in August. Did he wire you? And just before getting your letter I was talking about you—(I seem to be always talking about you!)—with de Spirito and Carrington at lunch. You'll be glad to hear that San Juan de Letran[?] still thrives and that I live one block away.

I'll be at the Stadium concerts. And thank Gawd for Tanglewood so's we can talk—finally. I've lectures all prepared for you about your City Center programs—completely disinterested, since I leave for Brazil on Aug. 14. Your ex-mentor sends you

un abrazo muy fuerte [a great big hug] —

A.

---

1. Writing to Copland from Paris in May 1947, Bernstein had announced, "It's done. Fait. The Symphony's been heard. Two days ago in Prague. First, I must say it's a wonderful work. Coming to know it so much better I find in it new lights & shades—and new faults. Sweetie, the end is a sin. You've got to change. Stop the presses! We must talk—about the whole last movement in fact" (Bernstein to Copland, May 27, 1947, C & P II, 70). Indeed, Copland did make a cut in the coda of the last movement.

2. Virgil Thomson's *The Mother of Us All.*

3. *In the Beginning* for mezzo-soprano and choir was composed for Harvard University's Symposium on Music Criticism in May 1947. Robert Shaw directed the premiere.

4. Bernstein's *Jeremiah Symphony,* recorded by Bernstein leading the St. Louis Symphony Orchestra on RCA Red Seal album DM 1026.

In 1947 Copland undertook another tour of South America at the behest of the State Department. He spent four months in Argentina, Brazil, and

Uruguay, giving lectures about and concerts of American music as well as becoming acquainted with contemporary composers and their music in these countries.

To Irving and Verna Fine

IF/LC. als.

> c/o American Embassy
> Rio de Janeiro
> Brazil
> Sept 6 '47

Dear Angels:

Hope this reaches you before you leave the wilds of N.H.[1] Verna—you were awful nice to write—hope you're still dreaming about me.

The flight down was uneventful. Puerto Rico was pleasant for a day—and there was an unforgettable Blake-like sky at sundown over Dutch Guiana. . . .

Now I'm settled in an incredible apartment on top of a mountain overlooking the Rio harbor. Its all very curious because the mountain is plunked down right in the middle of Rio's Times Sq. Up here you think you are living in the country—but you can walk down to city life in 10 minutes. The view is superb but the piano stinks! Well you can't have everything . . .

I've just been launched on a series of 12 lectures on Amer. music. That, plus extra radio jobs playing recordings and me commenting (in Portugese!) keeps me busy. [Conductor Eleazar de] Carvalho does his all-American program with the orch. next week. So Rio is getting a proper dose of musica norteamericana.

The city itself is beautiful as ever. Streets are always full of people—no one ever seems to want to go home. Coffee every two hours till you are black in the face. A friendly, democratic feeling in the air that comes across because of the lack of color lines. Skins of all shades and faces of all shapes. Its endlessly amusing to sit at a sidewalk café and watch what passes. With all that, the art life in general is provincial, so I guess I'll be back in December!

Did I tell you that before leaving N.Y. I rented a marvellous house on the Hudson for 3 years?[2] Wait until you see it. At last—a home. And by the end of 3 years I hope to have built a permanent one.

The dark side of life: haven't written a note. I have a cook but no secretary—AND—I miss you both.

Write often and long.

Aaron

---

1. The Fines had spent August at the MacDowell Colony in Peterborough, New Hampshire.
2. Copland had rented a house at Sneden's Landing near Palisades, New York.

To Leonard Bernstein

LB/LC. als.

c/o American Embassy
Rio de Janeiro
Sept 24 '47

Dear You—

I thought of you hard two nights ago because it was the start of the new season—and I wasn't there. If I had been near a cable office I would have sent you a wire—but anyhow I thought of it.

V[ictor] says he's seen you—so I assume you have all my news. He <u>raved</u> to me about the Sonata recording.[1] Hope you re-did whatever needed re-doing . . .

Rio is fun—but every once in a while I wake up in the morning and wonder what I'm doing here. I mean theres no terrific necessity for my being here . . . But God knows the town itself is 'sumpin.' I'll be here until Oct 15th. Then on to Sao Paulo, Porto Alegre, B[uenos] A[ires]. I'll be lecturing about you in all those places—till I'm blue in the face.

Eleazar [de Carvalho] did the 3rd [Symphony] on an all-American program.[2] Somehow the orchestra got through it, but nobody was happy about it, including me. They haven't played nearly enough new music, and in general, sound like the Orquesta Sinfonica de Mexico back in 1932. Theres a good chance I may be conducting it [the Third Symphony] myself in B[uenos] A[ires] with the Colon Orch—which is the best in S[outh] A[merica].

I've just about begun work on the B. Goodman piece.[3] Had a hard time getting settled—but now I'm installed in my own ap't on top of one of those fantastic hills right plunk in the center of Rio, with a picture postcard view of Rio from the bedroom window. Its fun to lean out the window with a friend and admire the view.

And how go your own complicated affairs—musical and t'otherwise?? How did G.M. sound in the City Center?[4] (I just imagined you making the whole thing a memorial for LaGuardia.[5]) Couldn't find a single Amer. work mentioned in any of your preliminary announcements. It's a mistake.

Write me where you'll be in Dec—when I get back. (I take in the North coast of Brazil on the way back—Bahia, Recife, Fortaleza.)

Its springtime in Rio and I miss you.

Me

---

1. Bernstein recorded Copland's Piano Sonata for RCA Victor in 1947.
2. For a list of works on this program, see Copland's letter to Koussevitzky of September 27.
3. The Clarinet Concerto, commissioned by Benny Goodman.
4. Bernstein opened his last season with the New York City Symphony Orchestra with a performance of Gustav Mahler's Second Symphony.

5. Fiorello La Guardia, former mayor of New York City and noted supporter of such progressive policies as Roosevelt's New Deal, had died on September 20, 1947.

To Serge Koussevitzky

SK/LC. tls.
[Instituto Brasil—Estados Unidos (Rio de Janeiro) stationery]

Sept. 27, 1947

Dear Sergei Alexandrovitch:

I have been waiting until I was sure you would be back in Boston before writing you. Of course the news of the marriage went all around the world, so Brazil heard it too.[1] Please tell Olga how pleased I am, both for her and for you—and may you both have many years of happiness together.

Since leaving Tanglewood I have been in Rio de Janeiro, where I will stay until Oct. 15th. I've been giving lectures on American music to the Brazilians, playing recordings on the air with my comments in Portuguese (!), and generally getting to know better the Brazilian musical scene.

So far, of course, the big event was the all-American program conducted by Carvalho. He played Schuman's Symphony for Strings, Menin's[2] Folk Overture, and my Third Symphony. An ambitious program,—particularly when you consider that the orchestra here is not used to playing modern music, and is not of a good quality in general. Carvalho did his best, but it was pioneer work both with the orchestra itself and with the public. On all sides I heard people talk of Carvalho's extraordinary improvement as conductor. He talks of you everywhere, naturally, but even without that I think you could get a job as teacher of conducting in Brazil on the basis of this one pupil alone! But seriously, the example of one such case as Carvalho does a great deal for building up the reputation of the United States as a place for young musicians to finish their training.

Until Oct 15th my address will be: care American Embassy in Rio de Janeiro. After that, care of the American embassy in Buenos Aires, Argentina until Nov. 15th. I hope to be back in New York by December first.

This letter will be reaching you at the start of the new season. I hope the European trip was refreshing and restful, and that you will have a brilliant 47–48 season. My warm greetings to Olga and to Mrs. Hirschmann, if she is in Boston.

Always devotedly,
[signed] Aaron

---

1. Koussevitzky had just married Olga Naumova, the niece of his second wife, Natalie, who had died in 1942.
2. Composer Peter Mennin.

Having just returned from South America, Copland left for California in February 1948 to begin work on his newest film score, for *The Red Pony*.

To Serge Koussevitzky

SK/LC. tls.
[Republic Productions Inc. stationery]

March 4, 1948

Dear Sergei Alexandrovitch:

I suppose that you heard that I was in California. While you were in Arizona, I got an offer from the same man who had produced two of my other films [added in ink: Lewis Milestone] to do the score for a story by the well-known American writer, John Steinbeck. I am glad the offer came when it did because it gives me a chance to make some money and to be back before your last concert in New York.

The job keeps me very busy because I have to produce fifty-two minutes worth of music in a comparatively short time. Still it's amusing to write for the films occasionally—and certainly the California weather is wonderful! (You really must try it sometime.)

I've been keeping in touch with Tod Perry,[1] and my impression is that it will be several weeks between the time I come home (April 10th) and the time when decisions about student acceptances [to Tanglewood] must[2] be made. Because of scholarships offered by outside sources we are going to have composing scholarship students from Argentina, Uruguay, Brazil and Palestine.

I recently had a letter from my Norwegian student, who is back in Norway, telling me that the composition that he wrote at Tanglewood last summer has just won him a big prize in his own country.[3]

Fond greetings to Olga and Genia. I'll be seeing you all next month.

Devotedly,

[signed] Aaron

ac/ej

---

1. Thomas D. Perry, Jr., manager of the Boston Symphony Orchestra at the time.
2. "Should" is crossed out here, and "must" is added in pen.
3. Composer Knut Nysteat (b. 1915).

To Irving and Verna Fine

IF/LC. tls.

[Republic Productions Inc. stationery]

March 4, 1948

Dear Kids:

This is just to say hello from that wild place, Hollywood. This letter can't be very wild because it's being dictated to my local secretary[1] who is almost as good as Verna. I would have written sooner, but when you write your first score, you'll know what it's like.[2] Notes, notes, notes, all day long. Fifty-two minutes of music in six and a half weeks is my stint, and when it's over, I'm going to conduct the whole thing myself. It will really be the first time I have ever premiered my own music. Taking a wild chance I know, but it's now or never. The picture is a nice one but no epic or path-breaker.

The trouble from my angle is that it was shot on the same ranch that "Of Mice and Men" was shot on. Now I ask you: if you had to look at the same landscape every day could you think up different music? (Note, I'm getting my alibis all set up in advance.)

How are things back in the rugged climate? What was Harold's symphony like in performance?[3] What is Lukas [Foss] up to? How'd you like the Malipiero?[4]

I'll see you all around the middle of April. Until then my love to the baby and to both of you.

[signed] Aaron

ac/ej

---

1. Erik Johns, who would write the libretto to Copland's *The Tender Land*.

2. Fine was in fact in the process of writing his first major orchestral score, the *Toccata Concertante*.

3. Harold Shapero's *Symphony for Classical Orchestra* had received its premiere in January by the Boston Symphony Orchestra, conducted by Bernstein.

4. Gian Francesco Malipiero's Symphony no. 4 ("In Memoriam"), given its premiere by the Boston Symphony Orchestra in February. Fine reported that it was "a good Grade B symphony."

On March 2, Claire Reis sent Copland her "one and only written letter in twenty-five years of threats and resignations" that declared her intent to step down as chair of the Executive Board of the League of Composers. She asked Copland to return her letter with any suggested changes marked in red pencil.

To Claire Reis

Reis/NYPL. als.
[Republic Productions Inc. stationery]

March 7, 1948

Dear Claire

Your letter came as a bombshell! My first instinctive reaction was to think of trying to dissuade you. But there was something in the tone of your letter that gave me the impression that you were not to be dissuaded—and that you were doing the right thing, for <u>you</u> that is.

Of course, your resignation as chairman puts the League's future in jeopardy. I don't think we ought to attempt to go on along the old lines. But what the future is to be is a big question mark in my mind.

My only suggestion in regard to your letter of resignation is to question the wisdom of including para[graph] 3. Its too negative a note to conclude on—and in any event it is not clear, even to me, as to what 'destructive undercurrents' and 'discouraging rumors' you are referring to. Anyway, think it over—and do as you think best.[1]

This is hardly the moment to get sentimental and expansive—but let me say it right out—we all owe you an unpayable debt of gratitude.

My best to you

Aaron

---

1. Reis replied (her handwritten letter is undated), thanking Copland for his suggestions and his words of praise. She omitted the third paragraph.

To William Wyler

AC/LC. pencil draft.

[final letter sent May 29, 1948][1]

Dear Mr. Wyler:

I saw The Heiress and have read the script you were kind enough to send me.[2] I subsequently gave some thought to the type of musical score a film like the Heiress deserves. I agree with you that the picture will not call for a great deal of music—but what music it does have ought to really count.

I can see that the music would be a valuable ally in underlining psychological subtleties. But it seems important to me that it ought also to contribute its share of tone and style to the picture. My fear is that a conventionally written score would bathe the score in the usual romantic atmosphere. What I would try for would be the recreation in musical terms of the special atmosphere inherent in the James original. That atmosphere—as I see it—would induce a music of a certain discretion and refinement in the expression of sentiments. I had a somewhat similar problem in the writing of the film score for Our Town, where it was necessary to recreate in musical terms the quiet life of a typical New Hamp[shire] town around 1900. My method was not merely to confine myself to the harmonies or melodies of the period, but rather to make use of every musical resource in order to [evoke?] the music of that particular time and place. I would hope to do the same thing for The Heiress.

I understand the starting date in shooting the script was delayed. Could you say now when approximately you calculate the picture would be ready for scoring? It would help me in making my plans—always assuming of course that you are still interested in having me do the score.

Yours cordially

[no signature]

---

1. This date is found in William Wyler's reply of June 19, 1948.

2. Copland saw the play The Heiress, which had opened on Broadway in the fall of 1947.

To Leonard Bernstein

LB/LC. als.

[River Road, Palisades, stationery]

Oct 18 '48

Dear Lensk:

Loved hearing from you—and particularly noted the Swedish contents of your letter.[1] Ah well, alack-a-day. I'm off to Cal. the end of this month.

Nothing much has been happening. I stayed home a lot and finished my Clarinet Concerto—endlich [finally]! Tried it over for Benny [Goodman] the other day. He had Dave O[2] around for moral support. (O what an angelicums that O is!) Seems I wrote the last page too high 'for all normal purposes.' So it'll have to come down a step.[3]

Listen. Me and Mrs Reis are cooking up a big bang-up Carnegie Hall anniversary affair so that composers in de hul vuruld can honor K on his 25th.[4] It is to take place May 4th or 5th with maybe the RCA Recording Orchestra or some other such band. Mrs Reis wants you, Reiner, & Monteux to conduct. As for me, I can't imagine the affair sans toi [without you]. Are you free those days—or <u>must</u> you be in Paris already. (I plan to head for Europe right after the concert.) Let's know pronto please.

How went my 3rd [Symphony]? (Or is it still to go?) Be nice and this time do try to find somebody who liked it. Enyho send reviews.

Heard Munch and the Orchestre National last night. Gave a new Toccata of Piston, which he played too fast. What a hectic man that is (Munch, not Piston!)[.] It was fun to hear the orchestra. They <u>blend</u> so beautifully. The Tombeau[5] was delish.

Saw a letter of yours in my file from Spring 1943. You were just <u>enchanted</u> at the idea that you <u>might</u> be named ass't cond. of the Goldman Band and <u>maybe</u> the Red School House[6] would take you on as teacher . . . Tempus fugit as the feller says.

Love from an
old old old bastard[7]
[no signature]

---

1. Bernstein's letter of September 29, 1948, to Copland contained a photograph (presumably of a handsome man but no longer with the letter) with the comment "How would you like some of the enclosed for a present? It's just for you, it's terribly blond & Swedish, & it will be in America (Philadelphia!) by December."

2. David Oppenheim, clarinetist. He is the dedicatee and first performer of Bernstein's Sonata for Clarinet and Piano.

3. Copland revised the final measures of the concerto to bring the clarinet part down a few steps, one of four revisions that Copland made at Goodman's request. The changes primarily concern the very high range of Copland's original. See Robert Adelson, "The Original Version of the Copland Clarinet Concerto," *The Clarinet* (November–December 1995): 42–45.

4. Koussevitzky's twenty-fifth year as conductor of the Boston Symphony Orchestra. Copland was poking gentle fun at Koussevitzky's thick Russian accent.

5. Maurice Ravel's *Tombeau de Couperin*.

6. The Little Red School House in Greenwich Village, founded in 1921 to enact John Dewey's principles of progressive education.

7. Bernstein had closed his letter of September 29, "You old bastard, I love you."

CHAPTER SIX

The Post-War Decade, 1948–58

In the years following World War II, Aaron Copland assumed the undisputed role of "dean of American composers." He was recognized as the leading figure among composers of his era and as the public face of American music. The 1950s brought many accolades, including a Fulbright Fellowship to the American Academy in Rome (1951), the Norton Professorship at Harvard University (1951–52), membership in the American Academy and Institute of Arts and Letters (1954), and a Gold Medal from the academy (1956). Copland was also awarded his first honorary doctorate, from Princeton University, in 1956. He was in demand both as a composer—nearly every one of his works from the 1950s was directly commissioned—and as a conductor, making his debut with the New York Philharmonic in 1958.

But the decade between 1948 and 1958 also brought its challenges, among them a changed political and ideological climate that called into question many of the values Copland had espoused in the more progressive era of the 1930s and 1940s. The simplified, folkloric style of such works as *Rodeo* and *Appalachian Spring* was no longer in vogue, and Copland's full-length opera, *The Tender Land* (1954, rev. 1955), struggled to find an audience, perhaps because its rural setting and accessible idiom seemed old-fashioned to post-war sensibilities. Anticommunist rhetoric and ideology permeated American culture in the 1950s, and Copland was vulnerable because of his involvement with various left-wing organizations and causes during the 1930s and 1940s. Pressure from Congress caused his *Lincoln Portrait* to be removed from the official concert celebrating Dwight D. Eisenhower's first presidential inauguration in 1953, and later that year, Copland was called to testify before the Senate Permanent Subcommittee on Investigations, chaired by Joseph McCarthy. Despite some canceled performances, isolated protests, and bureaucratic passport difficulties, however, Copland and his reputation emerged unscathed, for the most part, by McCarthyism. The one area in which he experienced major difficulty was his film career. Copland's politics made him unemployable by Hollywood film studios just as his Academy Award for *The Heiress* made him otherwise more desirable. Although Copland planned to do more film work at least as late as 1950 ("price goes up," he commented to Bernstein after winning an Oscar), his one later score, *Something Wild*, was not a studio production: it was released by United Artists, an association of independent producers.

The 1950s also proved challenging in terms of Copland's compositional work, in part because his activities as a conductor and lecturer left him less time to compose. But the era was devoted to major efforts: *Twelve Poems of Emily Dickinson* (1950), The Piano Quartet (1950), *The Tender Land,* and the *Piano Fantasy* (1957). The setting of Emily Dickinson poems was complemented by another set of songs from around the same time: the two volumes of *Old American Songs* (1950, 1952). These folk-song arrangements proved immediately popular with audiences, just as the Dickinson songs have found lasting fame as an exquisite marriage of music and verse.

The Tender Land, an opera intended for television production, was Copland's first musical theater piece since *The Second Hurricane* (1936). Copland completed *The Tender Land* within a scant two years, and it was premiered on stage, rather than on screen, in April 1954. In the wake of decidedly mixed critical reception, Copland and his librettist Erik Johns reworked the opera, finally settling on a three-act version that received its first performance at Oberlin College in May 1955.

Like *The Tender Land,* the *Piano Fantasy* is a large-scale piece, a thirty-minute virtuosic essay for solo piano with which Copland wrestled for over five years. Unlike *The Tender Land,* however, the *Fantasy* embraces a thorny, often atonal language based in part on the twelve-tone method as in the music of Arnold Schoenberg and Luigi Dallapiccola. The *Fantasy* met with immediate critical approbation, and the work remains a landmark in the twentieth-century piano repertoire.

Perhaps the most engaging letters of this period are those to Irving and Verna Fine, whom Copland had met while teaching at Harvard in 1943–44 as a sabbatical replacement for Walter Piston. Copland and the Fines spent much time together during summers at Tanglewood, where both Copland and Irving were on the faculty. Verna often cooked for Copland and even handled some of his secretarial work. She and Copland remained close after Irving's sudden death in August 1962.

By that time Tanglewood had changed. After Serge Koussevitzky's death in 1951, Charles Munch assumed directorship of the festival and music center; he was neither so charismatic a leader nor so committed to the cause of contemporary music as Koussevitzky had been. Nonetheless, Copland spent nearly every summer in Lenox, Massachusetts, at Tanglewood, teaching composition and giving lectures on the subject of twentieth-century music.

Copland's letters in the second half of the century are generally less revealing, less personal and engaging, than his earlier correspondence. This shift is perhaps explained by the rise of the telephone as a preferred means of personal communication. In addition, more and more business began to cross Copland's desk each day: arrangements for Tanglewood in the summers, exchanges about concert programs and schedules for tours throughout Europe, letters of recommendation for various younger colleagues—such matters began to constitute an ever larger proportion of Copland's correspondence.

To Irving and Verna Fine

IF/LC. als.
[Paramount Pictures Inc. stationery]

Nov 21 '48

Dear V & I:

You were awful nice to remember me [on] my birthday. Well, I'm a year older—no help for it. The wire confirmed it—

Ever since I got Verna's letter I've been meaning to write.[1] I had consulted a copyright lawyer on the Cat & Mouse and he told me word for word what Verna figured out all by herself. The coup de grace was the under 21 clause— for I <u>was</u> under 21 by one month when I signed it. Now what? Lawyer said it would wait till '49.

I've been busy like a cockroach. Aside from the picture,[2] I've been lecturing at UCLA and heard the 3rd Symph cond. by [Alfred] Wallenstein. He did a good job—made it sound very American and zippy. I'm even conducting a bit myself! The studio men are all so bored playing movie scores that they form an orchestra for their playing pleasure. Imagine! And invite different conductors each time. I'm one and thats fun.

The picture is good—well acted and serious. Everyone is convinced it will make no money. Its not as easy a job as I had hoped—but anyhow its different from anything I've had to do before. Lots of psychological underpinning. . . .

Lets hear what gives in Boston. Is winter there? Is the W.W. piece[3] done? Any good concerts?

Write all.

Love

Aaron

---

1. Verna had written in detail about the possibility of Copland's regaining the copyright to his early piano piece *The Cat and the Mouse* (1921).

2. *The Heiress.*

3. Irving Fine's *Partita* for wind quintet.

To Carlos Chávez

AC/LC. Photocopy of tls.

[Paramount Pictures Inc. stationery]

6, December 1948

Dear Carlos:

It was wonderful to get your letter—a real long one with much news. I was delighted to have the score of "Antigone."[1] It was shocking to me to realize that none of your other orchestral scores has been generally available, but let's hope that with this beginning the situation will change.

First about your question concerning Koussevitzky and the Boston Symphony—as you know, the symphonic organizations generally make their concert plans six months in advance of the opening of the season, and Boston is no exception—particularly this year because of the fact that it is Koussevitzky's last one. It is difficult for me to imagine that any dates are still open. The only guest conductors that he has announced are his three former students, Thor Johnson, Bernstein and Carvalho. Next year with Munch at the head of the orchestra it is not at all certain what the situation will be. Now that you have the picture in mind you can see for yourself how it is.

I was glad to hear of the recordings being finally issued and look forward to hearing them.[2] Knowing your patience and persistence I'm confident about your getting around to the "Short Symphony" some day.

Of course I've realized for some time how difficult your situation is in regard to the Instituto, the Orquesta and your composing. What you cannot realize is what it will seem like in the perspective of the years. You alone can know what the cost has been, but all Mexico will someday realize the full extent of the achievement. You know how happy it makes me to know the firmness of your convictions about your need to compose. I recently finished a "Clarinet Concerto" that I was writing for Benny Goodman. It's in two movements and lasts about fifteen minutes. I think you will like it.

Just now I'm in Hollywood again until January in order to compose the score for a film based on Henry James' story "Washington Square." It's my second film this year, and now I will have done enough Hollywood jobs for some time to come. I plan to go to Europe in May and June. I haven't been in eleven years.

Did I ever thank you for sending me the issues of Mexico en el Arte? It adorns my table at home, and I show it to all my friends as a shining example of what an art magazine should be like. Would that we had such a publication in the United States. I hope somehow to be able to see you soon.

Affectionately,
[signed] Aaron
ac:ej

---

1. Chávez's *Sinfonía de Antígona*, which had just been published by G. Schirmer.

2. Chávez and the Orquesta Sinfónica de México had recorded several works (none by Copland) for a Mexican recording company.

To Nadia Boulanger

AC/LC. tls.
[River Road, Palisades, stationery]

20 January 1949

Dear Nadia:

A short time ago I mailed you a copy of my Sextet which was recently published by Boosey & Hawkes. You will remember perhaps that this piece was originally my Short Symphony and still exists in that form. I wanted you to have it and hope you like it.

I read that you were recently named Director of Music at Fontainebleau. My congratulations to you—it will mean a great deal to the school.

For the first time since '38 I am planning a trip to Europe in the spring. I expect to be in Paris from May 25 to the end of June with a brief interlude in Rome. If you can think of any ways in which I might be useful in the spreading of knowledge about American music either by participating in concerts or in talks on the radio, please let me know.

I was considerably disturbed to hear the sad circumstances concerning young Joachim. I'm sorry if you were in any way troubled.

I can't tell you how keenly I look forward to seeing you and the Rue Ballu.

Devotedly,

[signed] Aaron

On September 11, 1949, Virgil Thomson published in his column for the *New York Herald Tribune* a set of remarks Arnold Schoenberg planned to give on his seventy-fifth birthday. (Schoenberg's birthday was September 13; Thomson had an advance copy of the remarks.) In his address, Schoenberg complained that his music was being suppressed in America. He concluded: "It should be discouraging to my suppressors to recognize the failures of their attempts. . . . Even Stalin cannot succeed and Aaron Copland even less." Copland responded by writing Thomson a letter, which was published in the *Herald Tribune*.

To Virgil Thomson

Published in the *New York Herald Tribune*, September 25, 1949.

Palisades, New York

Sept. 11, 1949

Dear Virgil:

Imagine my astonishment on reading your column this morning to find Arnold Schoenberg coupling my name with that of Joseph Stalin as one of the suppressors of his art. You were good to have called this attack 'unjustified'; but it is much too negative merely to say that 'Mr. Copland has never, to my knowledge, acted to prevent the dissemination of Schoenberg's work, little as he may approve of it.' I both approve of it and have helped to disseminate it. I approve of it in the sense that, for better or worse, Schoenberg's music has proved itself one of the major influences in the contemporary music world and therefore deserves adequate hearing. I have disseminated it in lectures and in arranging concerts for more than twenty years and was instrumental in seeing to it that the Columbia Recording Company issued 'Pierrot Lunaire' under the auspices of the League of Composers. True, I can't be listed as an apostle and propagandizer for the twelve-tone system; but since when is that a crime? Unless Mr. Schoenberg considers it such he clearly owes me an apology.

After considerable puzzling over the reason for this gratuitous slam I suddenly arrived at the obvious solution: Mr. Schoenberg must have seen my picture in the papers in company with Shostakovich on the occasion of his brief visit here last spring.[1] In America it is still possible (I hope) to share a forum platform with a man whose musical and political ideals are not one's own without being judged guilty by association. What Dmitri Shostakovitch said during that visit, condemning the music of Stravinsky, Hindemith and Schoenberg, may make some sense as the statement of a citizen of the Soviet Union; but it certainly makes no sense over here. I dissociate myself from such an attitude absolutely. If that is the seat of Mr. Schoenberg's misunderstanding of my position it is easy for me to reassure him. Unlike Stalin I have no desire to suppress his music!

Greetings

Aaron

---

1. Copland and Shostakovich both gave speeches at the Cultural and Scientific Conference for World Peace in March of 1949.

Schoenberg replied to Thomson on December 23, denying that his remarks were based on having seen the photograph of Copland and Shostakovich. He explained that "as a teacher who for about fifty years has worked hard to provide young people with the tools of their art . . . I could not stand it to learn that Mr. Copland had given young students . . . the advice to 'use simple intervals' and to study the masters. Much damage has been done to an entire generation of highly talented American composers, when they . . . were taught to write in a certain style. . . . And only in this respect did I couple Mr. Copland with Stalin: they both do not consider musical composition as the art to present musical ideas in a dignified manner, but they want their followers to write a certain style. . . . This I must condemn." Thomson gave a copy of Schoenberg's letter to Copland, who wrote to Schoenberg directly.

To Arnold Schoenberg

AS/LC. tls.
[River Road, Palisades, stationery]

Feb. 13, 1950

My dear Mr. Schoenberg:

Virgil Thomson allowed me to read the letter you sent him in answer to my communication in his column in the Herald-Tribune of several months ago. My sincere wish to clear up, if possible, any cause for misunderstanding between us prompts me to address you directly. My appreciation of and understanding of the work you have done for music in the past fifty years, and my respect and reverence for the ideals you have upheld for so many years are such that I find it painful to discover that you think of us as so far apart. That is not as I see it, and I take this opportunity to try to clarify my own position for you.

It is clear to me that whoever is reporting my ideas or remarks to you have been doing us both a grave disservice. It is quite untrue, for example, that I have advised students to compose in a "certain style" or that I have recommended "simple intervals." These impressions must have been gained from isolated sentences taken out of context by persons who do not know me well. I do not dictate stylistic choice to my students. In my mind their style should fit their temperament—there is no other way to write honest music. I myself have never followed any formula for composition. I have composed in both a complex and a simple style. Insofar as my compositions exemplify a certain aesthetic[,] other composers may be able to exact useable principles from them, but that is their own affair. It is the teacher's role as I see it, to make evident the expressive and intellectual content of music written in all styles, old and new,—beyond that point the student must work out his own salvation. Can these principles be so very different from your own?

When I was in Hollywood over a year ago I attended an evening of your compositions at the Institute of Modern Art when you were scheduled to speak. That evening I heard you were unwell which discouraged me from making any attempt to renew our slight acquaintanceship. I still recall our conversation at your 69th birthday celebration,—it is a memory, my dear Master, that I shall always cherish.

Most sincerely,

[signed] Aaron Copland

Schoenberg replied graciously on February 21, 1950: "I am always ready to live in peace."

In May and June of 1949, Copland and Erik Johns traveled to England, France, Italy, and Belgium. Copland returned in time for the 1949 Tanglewood season, where he taught for twenty-one summers between 1940 and 1965.

To Irving Fine

IF/LC. als.

[Berkshire Music Center stationery]

March 10 '50

Dear Irving:

This stationary is just to give you a 'saudade' [reminiscence].[1] Yes—you've forgotten—I definitely took the Gettys barn. But how I will eat, if you don't take the Kelleys again[,] is a mystère. The only other possible 'tenant' I know of for you would be Lenny, who is to be at Tanglewood for 4 weeks. I'm afraid thats not much help. . . .

Recently came back from spending 3 days in Urbana. Lectured and conducted Rodeo. Kubly and Binkard[2] were there. The latter frightens me a little—but I suspect he's not quite so 'formidable' as the exterior appears to be. He played some things—somewhat over-intellectualized for my taste, but they included a recent Cummings song that left a good impression. Kubly gives the impression of romancing around, having a hellova good time with all the neuroses of his various students, but not getting much work done, I suspect. We gave a prize to Earl George, who seems to be developing into a prize winner of dimensions. Piece of his none too hot.

Walked into Schirmers the other day and saw your Piano Pieces on display, big as life, right next to Sonny's Sonatas.[3] Made me real sentimental.

Whats whats new? Did I tell you I finished Five Old American Song arrangements?[4] Noone else may like them, but Hawkes is delighted! The Dickenson cycle is done except for a fast song in the middle.[5] (Why didn't you tell me fast songs are hard to write?) Alice Howland is to do the premiere at Columbia's May Festival. I hope she's good—I took her on V.[irgil] T.[homson]'s recommendation.

The Age of Anxiety has come and gone.[6] Lukas [Foss] gave the Masque that Mendelssohn touch. It was charming! The piece itself pleased 'le public,' but I haven't been able to find any musicians around town who really went for it. (Rumor hath it that Auden was not pleased.)

Now that Spring is almost here, even Verna will realize how nice Paris really is. And you'll even start composing for a change, no? Still I'm awfully pleased you'll be back for T— [Tanglewood]. You've heard its to be IBERT.[7] Maybe you'd like to ask around as to what pieces—recent ones—best represent him. Got any bright ideas for lectures for any of us? I'm doing a lecture for Brandeis in early May, and will probably study scores of students then. Tell Verna I scared Durand into giving me back U.S.A. rights to the Cat & Mouse. Now who's 'formidable.' Love to everybody.

Aaron

---

1. Portuguese. Fine would have recognized the word from Milhaud's *Saudades do Brasil.*

2. Herbert Kubly, a writer and professor of drama at the University of Illinois, and composer Gordon Binkerd.

3. Fine's *Music for Piano* and Harold Shapero's Three Sonatas for Piano.

4. The five folk-song arrangements of *Old American Songs I* were premiered by Peter Pears and Benjamin Britten in June 1950.

5. Copland's *Twelve Poems of Emily Dickinson* was completed in 1950. Alice Howland premiered the cycle—with Copland at the piano—on May 18, 1950.

6. Leonard Bernstein's Symphony no. 2, "The Age of Anxiety," loosely based on W. H. Auden's poem of the same title. The piece is a symphony for piano and orchestra. Lukas Foss had played the piano part; "the Masque" is a jazzy section of the second movement.

7. In the summer of 1950, Jacques Ibert was invited to the Tanglewood festival as a distinguished guest composer.

To Thornton Wilder

AC/LC. carbon.

March 28, 1950

Dear Thornton:

I have recently had two talks with Rudolf Bing,[1] the first of the two at his invitation. Both times, you were the main subject of our conversation.

Mr. Bing is an admirer of yours, and particularly keen about OUR TOWN. He visualizes it as an opera for the Met, libretto by you and music by myself. He wants very much to include an American opera in the Met repertory at the earliest possible time, preferably for the season after next, his second. He has urged me to write you now, rather than await your return from abroad, so that we can have your reactions to the idea.

If you think the idea a good one, which I hope you will, then please react to some of the following points:

1. Is the play free of entangling alliances, and able to be used for musical treatment.

2. I've been giving the libretto problem lots of thought and am fairly convinced that the play as it stands would need re-arranging for the best musical results. Does this notion scare you? Would you be willing to undertake the music script (as you did the movie script) with suggestions from me? If not, would you object to someone else taking on the job?

3. I mentioned to Mr. Bing the obvious advantages of a Broadway run for a musical play like Our Town. He seemed to think that a Met 'opening' need not get in the way of a subsequent regular run, and was amenable to the possibility of the one following closely on the heels of the other.

4. I could go on, but I think I'd better wait and see how the idea strikes you thus far. It would be useful to know, however, when you plan to be back.

Have a good European time!

Cordial greetings,

Aaron Copland

---

1. General Manager of the Metropolitan Opera from 1950 to 1972.

Wilder replied: "I'm convinced that I write a-musical plays; that my texts 'swear at' music . . . that in them even the life of the emotions is expressed contra musicam" (C & P II, 214). No such collaboration between Wilder and Copland came to pass.

To Leonard Bernstein

LB/LC. als.

[River Road, Palisades, stationery]

May 27 '50

Dear Lensk:

Your letter caught me in a very sentimental mood. I'd been wondering about you: where you were and what you were doing (precisely), and whether you were having good times. I'd also been wondering about the Kouss—Clarinet Conshirt affair. Is it possible the explanation is that simple?[1]

Your picture of me as having forthcome with no music recently arrives not so à propos because I've just premiered a song cycle of 12 songs lasting 30 minutes at the Columbia Festival.[2] The experts were pleased; but I was roasted in the press, especially by J. D. Bohm ("cerebral" "no feeling" etc.)[.][3] In fact the reviews were so bad that I decided I must have written a better cycle than I had realized. Well, you shall see for yourself in Tangle[wood].

About the Conshirt: Benny had twice signed to play it with Ormandy in '49 and Feb '50, and both times let him down. So as soon as it was clear that Kouss didn't want it at Tangle—, B[oosey] & H[awkes] offered it to Ormandy. He has mentioned in a letter the idea of also doing it in N.Y., Baltimore, and Wash[ing- ton, D.C.]; and Betty [Mrs. Randolph Bean, of Boosey & Hawkes] is on his neck now, trying to pin him down to same. If he doesn't do it in N.Y., of course it's free. In fact its free after Nov 1st—for any other towns than those I men- tioned above, except Los Angeles where Harold Byrns is doing it with his chamber orchestra. Dave O[ppenheim] would probably be happy to do it anywhere you say.

I'm off to MacDowell Monkery for June. E[rik Johns] has a dance tour booked for June in Mid West with a small group, and V[ictor Kraft] is to be in N.Y. Hate to leave the Old Homestead but decided I'd get most work done at Peterboro. Don't know what I'll concentrate on—several things are cookin' . . .

Did you hear? I won an Oscar for The Heiress. Price goes up.

Ashamed to admit I haven't visited P. P. yet.[4] Hope to fit it in. V saw it and liked your share muchly.

Have just finished copying the Short Symphony on thin sheets.[5] Now you can have a copy for yourself. Doesn't a "first concert perf. in U.S.A." tempt you?

You're still my favorite genius.

Love

A—

---

1. Copland had hoped for a premiere of the Clarinet Concerto at Tanglewood in 1950. Bern- stein to Copland, May 21, 1950: "I fought with Kouss valiantly over the Clarinet Concerto, to no

avail. Benny [Goodman] & Tanglewood don't mix in his mind." Copland had finished the Clarinet Concerto in the fall of 1948, but the piece was not premiered until November 1950.

2. *Twelve Poems of Emily Dickinson.*

3. Bohm reviewed the Dickinson songs in the *New York Herald Tribune* of May 19, 1950. The review is negative but contains neither the word "cerebral" nor the phrase "no feeling."

4. A production of *Peter Pan*, with songs by Bernstein, had opened on August 24.

5. Translucent paper with staff lines, capable of being reproduced by the Ozalid process.

To Serge Koussevitzky

SK/LC. tls.

Aug. 29, 1950

Dear Sergei Alexandrovitch:

Ever since our conversation over the telephone about the Clarinet Concerto arrangement the thought has been growing in my mind that I made a mistake in saying 'yes' to your proposal about using the first movement separately as an Elegy for strings. You can see how easy it would be for me to make such a mistake: my natural desire to please you and the thought of the wonderful interpretation you could give such a piece, and the suddenness and persuasiveness of your definite proposal on the telephone.

But thinking it over more carefully I have come to the conclusion that to make such an arrangement at this time would be an even greater mistake, and it is better to admit the mistake before we go any further. I am convinced that to cut the piece in half takes away from the integrity of the Concerto as I originally conceived it, and I am basically unwilling to do that,—at least until the work has had several seasons to make its way as a complete Concerto. No one will be able to understand why, if I am satisfied with the Concerto as a whole, I should be willing now to present only half the work in an orchestral dress in which it was not conceived. Moreover, no one will be able to understand why you should want to present an arrangement of half a work when the entire work is available and has never been heard in its original form in Boston. In the public's mind it can only be understood as an implied criticism of the second movement, and I am unwilling to launch a new work in such a light. Later on, after the Concerto is established as a Concerto, I shall probably feel differently about it. I know that this decision will not make you happy, but try to see it from my point of view, and you will realize that it makes me even less happy.

As an alternative solution I have thought of the following possibility. You may remember that I told you I had recently completed a Song Cycle of twelve songs with texts by the New England poet Emily Dickinson. Without any doubt she was one of our greatest poets. She loved music very much and was a close friend of Thomas W. Higginson at the time he founded the Boston Symphony.[1] (It was Higginson who helped to get her poems published posthumously.) It seems to me that I could compose an Elegy in her memory, based on material from one or two of the songs inspired by her poems. I cannot absolutely promise to have it ready in time, but will do my best to finish it so that you can have it for the December 1st concerts. It would be an Elegy for Strings lasting about 6 minutes,—or perhaps a trifle more.[2]

When you are back in Serenack[3] let me have your reaction. My address will then be: Palisades, Rockland County, New York.

I hope the Hollywood concerts are going well. My affectionate greetings to you both.

Devotedly, as ever,

[signed] Aaron

---

1. It was Henry Lee Higginson, not Thomas Wentworth Higginson, who founded the Boston Symphony Orchestra.

2. This piece was never written.

3. Seranak (for *Serge* and *Na*talie *K*oussevitzky), Koussevitzky's home in Lenox, Mass.

To Nadia Boulanger

AC/LC. als.

[River Road, Palisades, stationery]

Nov 24 '50

Dear Nadia:

What a wonderful letter you wrote me for my 50th birthday! I can't tell you how touched I was. Its almost 30 years (hard to believe) since we met—and I still count our meeting the most important event of my musical life. What you did for me—at exactly the period I most needed it—is unforgettable. Whatever I have accomplished is intimately associated in my mind with those early years, and with what you have since been as inspiration and example. All my gratitude and thanks go to you, dear Nadia.

Perhaps you have heard that I am to spend 6 months (Jan. to June) at the American Academy in Rome. So I hope to see you in Paris in the Spring.

Recently finished a new Piano Quartet which I hope you will like.

Please thank Annette[1] for her nice letter to me.

Always devotedly

Aaron

---

1. Annette Dieudonné was a former student of Boulanger who came to serve as her assistant and companion until Boulanger's death in 1979.

Copland spent much of 1951 in Europe on a Fulbright Fellowship and lived at the American Academy in Rome.

To Irving Fine

IF/LC. als.

[American Academy in Rome stationery]

Feb 8, '51

Dear Irving:

I was about to write you, when the your letter came [*sic*]. Good to hear from you—as always—tho your letter was definitely on the Quiet Side.

By now Sonny[1] has told you more about Academy life than I know—or probably ever will know. I hang out in my corner of the Villa and try to write music. Thats all I know. Musical life in Rome is nice and provincial, so there doesn't seem to be any rush to meet everybody, study their scores, lecture at them etc. All that will come later.

I go to Israel in April (5–27). Orgad[2] is arranging for me to live with 30 composers for 5 days outside Tel Aviv in an 'art colony.' What can I tell them for five whole days?! Pesach I shall have in one of the famous kabuttzim, or whatever they're called. Maybe London at the end of May.

My main news—hold your hat—is that Harvard has offered me the C. E. Norton professorship of poetry (for 51–52)—and I've accepted. (I assume you'll have to keep this severely under your hat until it is officially announced.) Can you possibly explain how they would have arrived at me? I can't. Anyhow I'm it—and so now I must think up a subject for 6 lectures, and feel utterly stumped!

VERY IMPORTANT—where will you be next term? Off on your Gugg[en-heim]? How awful—since I must live in Cambridge from Oct. 1. Life is full of unpredictable things.

Bought a car—a Morris Minor—(Moyshe for short)—and we took our first ride into the country today. Big success. Victor finally got into the center of the Brazilian jungle and photographed those there savages.

Write soon again. Hope Verna is O.K. by now.

Best to you both (plus Claudia)[3]

Aaron

P.S. The more I see of Dallapiccola's music the less I go for it. But he's a charming fellow personally.

---

1. Harold Shapero.
2. Composer Ben-Zion Orgad.
3. The Fines' daughter.

To Elliott Carter

AC/LC. Photocopy of als.
[American Academy in Rome stationery]

Tel Aviv—April 23, '51

Dear Elliott:

I'm writing you this on the eve of my return to Rome, after 2 1/2 weeks in Israel. I've been carrying your interesting letter around with me for 2 months and at last have a moment to write. Your Nancarrow story read like a novel.[1] When you asked who might want to bring out commercial recordings of his newest stuff I immediately thought of the group backing Vladimir Cherniavsky, who is bringing out 'all' Ives. Unfortunately I can't remember the label name or address. (They have issued 'Central P[ar]k in the Dark.')[2] But with all the 'little company' recording that is going on it shouldn't be difficult to interest some group, once we are both back home.

Just now my head is full of Palestine—an incredible mixture of very ancient and very new. Everything about it is highly dramatic and in flux. Most surprising to me were the faces of the younger people born here—wonderfully open, and healthy, and self-assured. No trace of refugee in type or mentality. They were very exhilarating to be with,—jabbering all the while in Hebrew. (I kept wishing I had paid more attention to my Hebrew teacher when I was 13!)

Most dramatic moment was conducting 'In the Beginning' on the shores of the Sea of Galilee with unfriendly Syrians 2 kilometres off. (It was part of a 6 day chamber music festival a la Tanglewood.) The audience came anyhow, tho there are border incidents every night. The country around Jerusalem reminded me very much of Arizona, and the Arab towns looked like Indian pueblos. There are new immigrants everywhere—Yemenites, Moroccans, Iraquis—all Jews, but 1000 years away from the cultivated German refugees. How it will all melt God only knows.[3]

Rome has been absorbing, too. I'm going back until the end of June. Have several concerts to conduct—one with the Rome Radio Orchestra, which is really first-rate. I even do some lectures on Amer. music[,] reading in Italian. End of May I am to conduct the Clarinet Concerto in London.

Have you heard about my Charles Eliot Norton appointment for next term? It means I'll have to live in Cambridge for 5 1/2 months. I'm scared stiff.

Best to you and Helen. And remember me to Nancarrow if you write him.

Aaron

---

1. Conlon Nancarrow, American composer who resided in Mexico. Carter's letter to Copland of February 23, 1951, gives a detailed description of Nancarrow's situation.

2. Polymusic 1001, from a company based in New York. Besides *Central Park in the Dark*, this record contained *Over the Pavements*, *The Unanswered Question*, *Hallowe'en*, the Second Violin Sonata, and the *Largo* for violin, clarinet, and piano.

3. A reference to the "melting pot" of cultural assimilation.

Copland moved to Cambridge, Massachusetts, in October 1951 to begin his six-month residency as the Norton Professor of Poetics at Harvard University. His six lectures were subsequently published as *Music and Imagination* (Cambridge, Mass.: Harvard University Press, 1952).

To Leonard Bernstein

LB/LC. als.

[Harvard University Department of Music stationery]

Nov 5 '51

Dear Lensk:

These old Norton Lectures are paralyzing all my other activities—including letter writing.

It was <u>wonderful</u> to hear from you. Wouldn't want you to be completely swallowed up by marriage![1]

Theres lots to tell—but I'll have to pin point everything. First, as per usual, is Tangle—. Olga [Koussevitzky] told me she wrote about C[harles] M[unch] and the directorship.[2] (All still very quiet.) He really wants you to lead orch. & conducting depts. and says he'll do no teaching if you are with us. What have you decided? I'm waiting breathlessly to hear . . .

Tod & Judd[3] seem to be depending on me a lot since I'm around, but in exactly what capacity, is not clear.

Every stone in Cambridge reminds me of you. Also I. B. Cohen at the Faculty Club. Also (same day) a note from M[uriel] Rukeyser. I don't see anybody as yet because I'm writing my lectures out. Oy, what a headache . . .

E[rik Johns] decided to live in N.Y. on account of dance work at M[artha] Graham's. So we took an ap't in the Willage and I go down weekends. It feels funny to be back in N.Y.—bag & baggage.

V[ictor Kraft] writes very enthusiastic letters from Rio [de Janeiro]. Seems pleased with himself and [his wife] Pearl and Rio and job. Its a miracle, and <u>I'm</u> awfully pleased about it.

In the meantime I get no music written 'since a year' now and finally decided I was on a composing sabattical. Maybe its good?

Did you hear the recording of the Piano Quartet on the backside of the Clar. Concerto?[4] If not, ask Dave to send you a copy. Its out. Soon as the score is out I'll send you one—but it may be 6 months.

I'm jealous of you in Cuernavac. (Have you seen my house in Tepoztlan yet?) But I'm pleased with the upstairs at the Forbes' in Gerry's Landing where I am living. Nice and quiet with a view of the Charles.

Lukas [Foss] was here last week with his brand new wife <u>and</u> Piano Concerto at the B.S.O. It leaves an impression (the Concerto!) (some L.B. in it) but its too long (40 min.)[.] My love to Felicia und abrazos for you

A

P.S. What are you doing with the house in May and June?

---

1. Bernstein had married actress Felicia Montealegre in September 1951.

2. Serge Koussevitzky had died on June 4, 1951. Charles Munch had been conducting the Boston Symphony Orchestra since Koussevitzky's retirement in 1949, and now it was assumed that Munch would also assume the directorship of the Berkshire Music Center.

3. George Judd, manager of the Boston Symphony Orchestra, and his assistant, Thomas D. Perry, Jr.

4. Columbia ML 4421.

To Carlos Chávez

AC/LC. Photocopy of tls.
[Harvard University Department of Music stationery]

Dec. 8, 1951

Dear Carlos:

Awfully nice to have a newly issued score of yours.[1] Thanks so much for sending it to me. Since I had the recordings it was fine to be able to play them and follow from score. It stands up very well I think. Since it is so essentialized and bare there is really nothing there to get stale! And the music, despite the simplicity, is so very much your own kind of thing. Write us more music, please!

You can see from the letter head where I am this winter. Did I tell you that I was appointed to the special professorship that Stravinsky had some ten years ago? It's a soft job—just six lectures,—but one must publish them, so it is like having to write a book. (Stravinsky did the Poetique Musicale[2] as the Norton Professor.) I am calling mine Music and the Imaginative Mind. So far I have delivered three lectures and they seem to have gone well.

Unfortunately I haven't been able to get much composing done. Rome and Israel for six months was very interesting but distracting, and now with this book . . . Well, my appetite is increasing daily, and soon I will be free to do as I like.

Let me hear how you are. Greetings to Blas [Galindo] and [Luis] Sandi and [Pablo] Moncayo.

Always yours,
[signed] Aaron

---

1. Probably the *Sinfonía india*, published in 1950.

2. *Poétique musicale sous forme de six leçons* (Cambridge, Mass.: Harvard University Press, 1942).

To Irving and Verna Fine

IF/LC. acs.

Nov 8 '52

Dear You-all:

I bought a house! Or rather—it's a barn, remodelled—one hour up the Hudson near Croton.[1] Nice country. Nice view of the river. Busy as can be buying furniture, drapes, et al. How are you guys? How did App.[alachian] Spr.[ing] go at B.S.O.? Write me at 9 Charlton. I don't move out till Dec. 1.

Love

Aaron

---

1. Copland called the house "Shady Lane Farm."

To Irving and Verna Fine

IF/LC. acs.

Shady Lane Farm
Ossining, N.Y.
[postmark: December 3, 1952]

Dear Verna & I:

Moved out here on the first and got snowed in on the second! I can't be in N.Y. on Sat. & Sun. as I am still trying to settle in up here. Have no phone as yet—so I am incommunicado, practically. Have no solution for sociability except for you to drive here on your way home.

Best

A

Copland's *Lincoln Portrait* was scheduled on the official concert program for Dwight D. Eisenhower's inaugural in January 1953. When Congressman Fred E. Busbey took issue with Copland's communist affiliations, the piece was pulled from the concert program. The League of Composers, under the guidance of Claire Reis, protested the removal.

To the League of Composers

Reis/NYPL. tls.

Feb 9, 1953

To the Board of Directors [of the League of Composers,]

In view of the public protest made by the League in the matter of the cancellation of my <u>Lincoln Portrait</u> at the Washington Inaugural concert I think I owe our organization a word of explanation.

Because the action taken was necessarily a hurried one, and because the issue concerned the work of one of your own members, I want to urge that the Board today either approve or disapprove what was done in their name.[1]

I want it to be known by you that I read of this incident in the papers, after it was called to my attention by Claire Reis. Imagine my astonishment: this was an attack by an elected official on the patriotism of a private citizen who had never been asked questions by anyone, never been shown any lists, never been requested to explain or justify anything.

I want the League to know that I have no past or present political activities to hide. I have never at any time been a member of any political party: Republican, Democratic, or Communist. I have never joined any organization which did not have as one of its primary purposes the cultural interests of America, especially as related to music. I have never sponsored any cause except as a loyal American, proud of his right to speak his mind on controversial subjects, even to protest when some action seems unworthy of our democratic traditions. Supreme Court Justice [Hugo] Black put it this way in a recently written decision:[2]

"Individuals are guaranteed our undiluted and unequivocal right to express themselves on questions of current public interest. It means that Americans discuss such questions as of right and not on sufferance of legislatures, courts, or any other governmental agencies . . ."

I don't think I need comment on the implications of this little episode, for its sinister overtones must be clear to everyone. We, the intellectuals, are becoming the targets of a powerful pressure movement led by small minds. It is surely a sign of the times that a musical organization like our own should have become involved in an affair such as this.

I shall await your action and be guided by it.

[signed] Aaron Copland

---

1. Claire Reis's telegram on behalf of the League.

2. *Wieman v. Updegraff*, 344 U.S. 183 (1952), held as unconstitutional an Oklahoma law that required state employees to take a "loyalty oath," swearing that they were not affiliated with any communist front or subversive organizations.

On May 22, 1953, Copland received a telegram from Senator Joseph McCarthy, directing him to appear before the Senate Permanent Subcommittee on Investigations. Copland testified in a private hearing on May 26. Although no further action was taken against him, Copland was unnerved by the entire experience.

To John Burk[1]

AC/LC. Photocopy of als.
[Shady Lane Farm stationery]

June 8 '53

Dear John:

I greatly appreciated your sympathetic note about my current tiff with the Senate authorities. All I can say is that it's an experience I never expected to have.

A note such as yours does a lot to help keep one's courage up.

Greetings

Aaron

---

1. John N. Burk, annotator of the Boston Symphony Orchestra programs.

To Prentiss Taylor

Taylor/AAA. als.
[Berkshire Music Center stationery]

Sat. [August 8, 1953][1]

Dear Prentiss:

Here are the tickets.[2] Hope you enjoy the concert.

My permanent address is:

Shady Lane Farm

Ossining, N.Y.

I bought a barn (remodelled) last Dec. so am permanently put.

Thanks for the file of clippings.[3] I hadn't seen half of them and at this distance they actually seemed amusing. But at the time it was no fun at all.

Best to you

Aaron

---

1. Date in later hand, perhaps from postmark.
2. To a concert at Tanglewood at a time when Copland could not attend.
3. Taylor had sent Copland a set of clippings—almost certainly articles from the Washington, D.C., press about Copland's appearance before the Senate Permanent Subcommittee on Investigations—with the note, "I'm enclosing some clippings you mayn't have seen. . for your memory book . . nightmare dept." (Typed card signed, August 5, 1953. Dots are Taylor's punctuation, not ellipses.)

In the spring of 1952, Copland was offered a commission from the League of Composers to compose an opera for television. He accepted and chose Erik Johns as his librettist. The opera, *The Tender Land*, was completed in the spring of 1954 and scheduled for a premiere by the New York City Opera (at City Center) on April 1.

To Mary Lescaze

AC/LC. tls.
[Shady Lane Farm stationery]

March 4, 1954

Dear Mary,

It was awfully sweet of you to offer me a shindig at your home after the opera opening. (The fact of the matter is . . . I haven't finished it yet, but of course I must!)

I want to do everything I can to save you the headache of opening up the house on so confusing a night. Please give me until the 15th, by which time post-opera plans will be clearer. In any case, I'm going to spend it with you— wherever. Operas being what they are—and the City Center being what it is—I shall probably need some heavy hand holding.

Affectionately,
[signed] Aaron

The Tender Land was not particularly well received, and Copland was glad to be leaving town for Europe in April 1954.

To Carlos Chávez

AC/LC. Photocopy of tls.
[Shady Lane Farm stationery]

April 5, 1954

Mr. Carlos Chavez
Mexico, D.F.
Dear Carlos:

I am writing you this just before taking off for a five-week trip to Italy, Switzerland and England.

When I am in London, I plan to speak with Dr. Ernst Roth, who is head of the company of Boosey and Hawkes in London. I have already spoken about you to Mr. Boosey, who gave me a certain amount of encouragement. Much depends on the reaction in London.

The opera was premiered last Thursday. I had finished it a week before! The public response seemed good, but the press was not so good. There was much criticism of the libretto, and the usual complaint about few melodies. My only feeling—that all operatic creation is a great gamble—is borne out by this experience. We shall have a second opportunity to test it under more "normal" conditions in Tanglewood this summer. When you get closer to production of your own work at the City Center,[1] you should consult me about advice as to production difficulties peculiar to that house.

I am ashamed to say I must leave before giving the Symphony #5 my full attention.[2] As for Munch, that will best be taken care of this summer.[3]

Affectionately,

Aaron

[signed] Aaron Copland

---

1. Chávez's opera *The Visitors* had been commissioned for the New York City Center in 1953 but was first performed at Columbia University under the title *Panfilo and Lauretta* in 1957.

2. Chávez's Sinfonía no. 5 for String Orchestra had just been published. Chávez had sent Copland a copy, inscribed "To Aaron, who did, really, commission this piece to me, in memory of old friendship." The symphony was commissioned by the Serge Koussevitzky Foundation.

3. It is not clear what would "be taken care of this summer."

Copland returned to Europe in the spring of 1955, skipping that season at Tanglewood and instead renting a house with John ("Jack") Brodbin Kennedy in the south of France. Copland did not return to the United States until October 1955.

To Irving and Verna Fine

IF/LC. als.

July 5 '55

Dear V & I—

I thought of writing dozens of times,—but you know how it is while one is moving about . . . Now I'm set until Aug 31—found a beaut of a villa up in the hills above Cannes. Have a garden and a cook and a view of the sea. One works in the mornings and evenings—and goes to the beach for the afternoon. It's the perfect existence. Now lets see if it produces any music. . . .

I'm full of questions. How was the Brandeis Festspiel this year?[1] How did Medea go? Who conducts? I'm afraid to ask about my Canticle at M.I.T.[2] I dashed up one evening to hear a rehearsal and (between us) despaired of Liepmann getting any results out of those forces. I wish I could hear it properly presented.

What are you both up to? And where is everybody this summer?

I spent all of May in Paris—mostly correcting Tender Land proofs (B. & H. informs me it is being given at Potsdam, [N.Y.][3] this summer)[.] I thought of you when I visited the Musique Concrete studios. They don't seem to have made much progress in the past few years. Same few composers and same methods. I gave a 1 1/2 hour program of my own things—including 3rd Symph—with the Radiodiffusion Orchestra. Heard Ormandy & [William] Warfield do the Old Amer. Songs at the Opera. Marcelle de M[anziarly] seemed very impressed by the orchestration. I rather liked it myself! Thinking about it later it seems to me I am beginning to mix str.[ings] & w.[ood]w.[inds] in a way that produces a most dulcet effect. Tant mieux!

London was fun. I conducted the complete App. Spr. twice with the BBC Orchestra; gave 2 BBC talks; saw Clurman open his new production of a Giradeaux play;[4] heard Sam B's Prayers[5] (with Sam); lunched with Desmond Shawe-Taylor,[6] etc. etc.—but didn't track down any talk of new geniuses.

Baden-Baden and the I.S.C.M. Festival was not too bad. The Schoenberg Var. op. 31 left the strongest impression—marvellously played by [conductor Hans] Rosbaud & the orchestra. Boulez' 'Marteau sans Maitre' had striking sounds and peculiar rhythms (non-rhythms would describe it better). I worked hard to get him one of the prizes—but lost out in the end.[7]

In the fall I'm full of conducting engagements: Munich, Baden-Baden (I'm doing the Short Symph there), Helsinki, Stockholm, Oslo. Won't be back until the end of October.

Please write. My address: L'ORANGERIE, LES BREGUIERES, LE CANNET, Alps-Mar[itimes], France.

I miss you both.

Aaron

---

1. The 1955 Brandeis University Festival of the Creative Arts included several works by Darius Milhaud, including the American premiere of his "opera in three tableaux," *Médée.*

2. The *Canticle of Freedom,* commissioned by the Massachusetts Institute of Technology (MIT) for the dedication of Kresge Auditorium, was premiered on May 8, 1955, by the MIT chorus and orchestra, under the direction of Klaus Liepmann.

3. Copland's brackets.

4. *Tiger at the Gates,* by French playwright Jean Giraudoux.

5. Samuel Barber's *Prayers of Kierkegaard.*

6. English writer on music.

7. Copland served on the jury in Baden-Baden, and despite his vote, Boulez was not awarded a prize.

To Arthur Berger

AB/NYPL. als.

Address until Aug 31: L'ORANGERIE
(Les Breguieres)
2e CANNES
Alpes-Mar
July 17, '55

Dear Arthur:

I've been thinking of you a lot lately because I've been reading you in Hi-Fi and in The Score.[1] (B[oosey] & H[awkes] had also sent me the Canticle mention.)[2] Did I miss anything else?

I thought the Records resumé was good.[3] You seem to be developing a more 'intime' style in writing—a sort of fire-side-chat-manner which is all to the good, I think. Was especially noticeable in The Score piece, where some of it seemed directed just at the immediate 'family.' I expect you'll be getting repercussions therefrom—so steel yourself! (Only caught one error in the Hi-Fi piece—Webster Aitken plays a D$\sharp$ instead of a D$\natural$—not vice versa.)

I hear you thought the Canticle poorly performed. I'm sure you were right. I heard a rehearsal and, as a result, feared the worst. K[laus] L[iepmann] just ain't no conductor—between us. I'm anxious to hear it properly done some time.

I'm settled for the Summer in a villa overlooking Cannes and the sea. It's just idyllic. But I hope it produces some tough music!

Before that I was mostly in Paris, London and Baden-Baden. I didn't manage to uncover any unsung heroes.[4] I did finally hear a chamber work of Boulez—Le Marteau sans Maitre. (It had to have 50 rehearsals—on dit [they tell me].) I thought it had some music in it—not just fascinating theories of organization. Wm. Glock agreed;[5] but we were definitely in the minority. On the other hand, Henze's Quartet was a mess.[6] New Music in Europe is beginning to take on a moyen âge life,—whatever vitality there is seems to be taking place underground, so to speak. No one at all is interested in 'just music.' First, it must have a sound,—interesting in and for itself; the over-all plan preferably based on some 12–tone-derived gimmick. (How clever of I[gor] S[travinsky] to combine 4 Trbni and 4 Str with diagrams, and yet write his own piece.)[7] Someday, I must try a special sound piece to see what it gives . . .

And what are you-all up to? How is the Louisville piece progressing?[8] How was the Brandeis Festspiel? Write a guy—no?

In the late fall I'm off to Scandinavia. Have concerts and lectures in all 4 countries. Also I'm conducting Short Symph for the 1st time in Europe in Baden-Baden, and the 3rd Symph. in Munich, both in Sept.

Love to Es

Aaron

1. Arthur Berger, "An Aaron Copland Discography," *High Fidelity* 5, no. 5 (July 1955): 64–69; Berger, "Stravinsky and the Younger American Composers," *The Score* 12 (June 1955): 38–46.

2. Berger, "The Pot of Fat Chamber Opera Receives Its Premiere: New Copland Work at M.I.T.," *New York Times*, May 15, 1955. Copland's *Canticle of Freedom* had received its premiere on May 8. (*The Pot of Fat* is the title of Theodore Chanler's chamber opera.)

3. The *High Fidelity* discography.

4. Established composers (not "unsung heroes") who performed at the ISCM Festival in Baden-Baden included Chávez, Dallapiccola, Ibert, Schoenberg, and Carter. The last was relatively new to European audiences, but not to Copland.

5. William Glock, editor of *The Score.*

6. Hans Werner Henze's String Quartet no. 2 (1952).

7. Stravinsky's *In Memoriam Dylan Thomas*, for tenor, four trombones, and string quartet. In the published edition the trombone parts in the Prelude are marked with brackets (the "diagrams") showing their use of the five-note row on which the work is based.

8. Berger's *Polyphony*, commissioned by the Louisville Orchestra, was finished in 1956.

To Goddard Lieberson

GL/Yale. tls.
[Shady Lane Farm stationery]

Mr. Goddard Lieberson
Columbia Records
New York, N.Y.
November 9, 1955

Dear Goddard:

While I was in Europe I read about the July issue of more recordings in our American Chamber Music series.[1] Would you be a good guy and ask your secretary to see to it that I receive a copy of each issue?

Ormandy writes me he is recording Billy the Kid in December. I assume this is for the back side of Appalachian Spring.

Since I am writing you anyway, perhaps I ought to remind you that William Warfield and myself made a recording in August '53 of my second set of Old American Songs. These have never been issued. Bill did a bang-up job, I thought. Isn't there any possibility of combining this second set with the first set already out on one of your 10–inchers?

Hope to see you soon . . .

Yours sincerely

[signed] Aaron

Aaron Copland

1. Columbia Records' Modern American Music Series, which released six recordings a year of chamber music by currently active American composers. The committee for the series consisted of Virgil Thomson, Henry Cowell, Goddard Lieberson, William Schuman, and Aaron Copland.

The eleventh annual Ojai Festival in California featured Copland as composer, conductor, and pianist. Copland made arrangements for his visit with Lawrence Morton, director of the festival.

To Lawrence Morton

AC/LC. Photocopy of carbon.

December 27, 1956

Dear Lawrence,

This is probably as good a time as any to comment on your various communications of the past few weeks.

I'm relieved that you've decided on someone to do the Dickinson Songs. I know they are not easy and the more time a singer has to learn them, the better. I trust your judgment and hope Mrs. MacKay will do a good job.[1]

I've heard Richard Robinson on the Stravinsky record and think he has just the right sort of voice for the Britten Serenade. I'll listen to him at Carnegie Hall on the 10th to get an impression of a live performance.

The most serious problem is the decision concerning Tender Land. I'm sorry you misunderstood or I didn't make clear what I mentioned in our talk at the Harvard Club. Whatever I may have said, what I meant to suggest then was a performance of Act II to be followed by the finale to Act I. I have since given lots of thought to your suggestion of excerpts. Because of the fact that most of the pieces that might be excerpted are comparatively short, I'm afraid that we would get a jumpy and unsatisfactory result, especially when such a procedure is applied to unfamiliar music. Syntheses such as you have in mind would seem to me to work better when applied to familiar scores. Moreover, there is the complication of the parts. Since it is economically not feasible to have orchestral material prepared solely for the Ojai performance, and it is equally impossible to perform excerpts in the order they appear in the score, inevitably a lot of confusion and jumping about would result from an attempt at "excerpting."

As I see it, Act II works fine as a continuous piece, especially with a few minor emendations that I have in mind. I would also not attempt to do the end of the act (Grandpa's cursing-out-Laurie scene, nor the final goodbye of the guests), but would proceed directly from the end of the love duet to the introduction of the quintet finale of Act I. The whole could be programmed as:

The Tender Land; Act II, followed by Finale of Act I.

As far as the audience understanding the dramatic action, it would be my idea, if you have no objection, that I make a few live comments on the action in general with particular reference to what the audience is about to hear. I am delighted we can have a 16-voice chorus. I have made an arrangement of the finale of Act I for chorus which Boosey & Hawkes has published. With them on stage, I can begin the finale with the solo quintet and gradually bring in the 16 voices, which will assure proper éclat for the end of the festival.

I am looking up various possibilities for the string orchestral program and will come up with some suggestions fairly soon.

I confess I am intrigued with the necessity of keeping all this a dark secret from what I took to be the inner circle: Igor [Stravinsky], [Robert] Craft & Co. But what would life be without these little cutenesses!

Best to you

[in pencil] I've decided on Haydn Symph no. 95 in C minor.

---

1. Margery MacKay performed the Dickinson songs on May 25, 1957, with Copland at the piano.

To Lawrence Morton

AC/LC. carbon.

February 15, 1957

Dear Lawrence,

Here is the letter I promised you. I am enclosing the two programs as they now have shaped themselves in my mind. You may not agree 100%, in which case I am expecting you to squawk.

As you will see from the nature of the programs, I am anxious to keep off the beaten track as far as possible.[1] That is, I don't want, whenever it's avoidable, to open myself up to conducting comparisons with Bruno Walter et al. I also am intent on conducting pieces for which I think I have a natural affinity, even though there is a great deal of other music which I admire but wouldn't particularly want to conduct. I've also tried to keep in mind the limited rehearsal time we have and the matter of a limited orchestral instrumentation. When you study the programs, take all the above into account.

The Fifth Avenue Library has no copy of Mendelssohn's string symphonies, so I was unable to consider those.

About Tender Land—I have been going over the Second Act and have decided that my first plan of going from the end of the love duet to Act I finale is unsatisfactory, because it leaves the audience hanging with an unresolved dramatic situation. For that reason, I've decided to continue on into the dramatic scene at the end of Act II, making the move into the Act I finale as follows: cut from the last measure of page 152 to 2 measures before rehearsal number 96 in Act I.

As for the question of minor roles, I am very much hoping that you will be able to use four of the choral singers to fill out the few things they have to do. They could remain within the ranks of the chorus while taking the brief parts of

Mr. and Mrs. Jenks and Mr. and Mrs. Splinters. One could, in a pinch, have three of the minor roles taken by the principal singers; but Mr. Splinters is an essential part of the final dramatic scene and I just don't know how to do without him.

Since I don't plan to make any cuts except as indicated above, I won't have to send you a vocal score as you suggested. I am planning, however, to make use of the chorus in the Act I finale. Boosey & Hawkes, as you may or may not know, has published an arrangement I made for chorus of the final quintet under the title "The Promise of Living." I shall send you under separate cover a marked copy of this choral version, indicating where I should like the chorus to join in with the principals. This is necessary because they will not be singing everything that is indicated in the present printed choral version.

I think Robinson is a good choice for the Britten Serenade. I think he is a possible choice for Martin in The Tender Land, but not ideal. What we need is someone with a more robust and 'operatic' voice. However, I leave that to you. Who, by the way, is going to prepare all those people in their various roles before I get out there?

About the chamber music evening—I think I had better confine my activities to the Dickinson Songs, in view of the time-consuming rehearsals I will necessarily be involved in. I leave it up to you to surround me with whatever other staff you decide on. It is essential, however, that the text of the Dickinson Songs be mimeographed or printed, so that the audience can know what is going on. I've always found that this makes all the difference.

I shall ask Boosey & Hawkes to send you pictures and biographical material. I don't know that I can be helpful with what you call 'story material.' I don't know exactly what that is, and in any case I don't have any of it.

I think I told you that I was leaving New York on February 21st, and will be back about April 1st. My address while away will be Hotel Tamanaco, Caracas, Venezuela.

I am assuming that you will be taking care of getting orchestral materials for the various pieces.

As ever,

Aaron Copland

---

1. Copland conducted his own Clarinet Concerto and scenes from *The Tender Land;* he also conducted works ranging from Purcell's Fantasias for Strings and Haydn's Symphony no. 95 through Fauré's suite from *Pelléas et Mélisande* to Britten's *Serenade* and Diamond's *Rounds*. He also played the piano for a performance of his *Twelve Poems of Emily Dickinson*.

The *Piano Fantasy*, which took Copland the better part of a decade to write, was finished in February 1957. Pianist William Masselos gave the premiere at the Juilliard School on October 25, 1957.

To William Schuman

Schuman/NYPL. tls.
[Shady Lane Farm stationery]

October 1, 1957

Dear Bill:

Thought I'd tell you how pleased I was to read them kind words about the Fantasy.[1]

Last week I heard Masselos play it for the first time in the basement of Steinway's, and I confess it got me. Anyway, I hope your reactions will be borne out at the performance.

I am in cahoots with Mark Schubart about program notes, etc. Having worked so long and so hard on the piece, I thought we might make a little special effort to give it the usual pre-performance buildup.

As ever

[signed] Aaron

---

1. Schuman had written: "Your 'Piano Fantasy' is indeed a fantastic work, replete with all those remarkable Coplandesque features we have come to know so well, plus new tangents in your continuing development. There is no doubt in my mind that this major composition carries an enormous impact."

In the fall of 1958, Carlos Chávez was at Harvard University as the Norton Professor, and Copland was in London, working with the London Symphony Orchestra. Knowing that Copland was looking for a quiet place to compose, Chávez offered his country home in Acapulco, and Copland took up residence in February 1959.

To Carlos Chávez

AC/LC. Photocopy of tls.

Flat 146
55 Park Lane
London W.1.
September 23, 1958

Dear Carlos,

I can't tell you how touched I was to receive your letter about Acapulco. Whether or not I am able to go there I shall never forget your generosity in offering me your house and also the very kind way in which the offer was made. If I am able to take advantage of what seems like a wonderful idea it would be during the months of February and March, and perhaps the first week in April. The second week in April I am due to conduct half a program with the Boston

Symphony[1] so I would hope to have a big reunion with you then in Cambridge. Perhaps if I am lucky I would even be able to hear one of your final lectures. How have they been going? I shall be very curious to read them when they are published.[2]

I have been having an active time since leaving the States immediately after the Tanglewood season finished. I spent ten days teaching at the Dartington Summer School[3] where I had students from the most naive to the most sophisticated. I conducted my Orchestral Variations[4] at the Royal Albert Hall and was pleased at how well they were received. And last week I was in Copenhagen where I presented an all-American program with the Radio Orchestra.

By the way, the Orquesta Sinfonica de Mexico played "Sinfonia India" in Paris and London among other places. People here tell me that in the Mexican repertoire the orchestra sounded very brilliant, and everyone enthused about your piece.

I shall be at the above address until December 1st. As soon as I have made up my mind about Acapulco I shall let you know. I can't be more happy at the prospect if it does come to pass.

Affectionately,

[signed] Aaron

Aaron Copland

---

1. On April 10 and 11 Copland conducted *Appalachian Spring* and the first Boston performance of the suite from *The Tender Land*.

2. Carlos Chávez, *Musical Thought* (Cambridge, Mass.: Harvard University Press, 1961).

3. A "combination of advanced coaching, musical holiday, and concert festival" (Noël Goodwin, "Dartington International Summer School," *Grove Music Online,* ed. Laura Macy [accessed 21 November 2004], http://www.grovemusic.com) held at Dartington Hall near Devon, England.

4. The orchestration of Copland's Piano Variations, made in 1957 for the Louisville Orchestra.

CHAPTER SEVEN

1958 and Beyond

As Copland toured the world conducting and lecturing, he kept in touch with his family and friends, relating bits and pieces of his experiences in short letters. His later years found him involved with conducting and preparing to write his memoirs but were not productive of substantial correspondence. Anniversaries of friends were observed, letters of recommendation written, and the business of the MacDowell Colony—of which Copland was president from 1961 to 1967—continued. Copland wrote of musical matters in letters to Carlos Chávez, up to the year of Chávez's death in 1978.

Through the mid-1960s Copland continued to compose at his previous pace. Among the works from this decade are the Nonet for Solo Strings (1960), dedicated to Nadia Boulanger and their "forty years of friendship"; his final film score, *Something Wild* (1961); and two one-movement orchestral works, *Connotations* (1962) and *Inscape* (1967), Copland's final large-scale pieces. After 1967, he limited himself to writing a few short works, including two *Threnodies* (1971, for Igor Stravinsky; 1973, for Beatrice Cunningham), and to mining earlier sketches for unused material worthy of publication. The *Duo for Flute and Piano* (1971) was born of sketches from the 1940s. His final completed work of any length from new material was the piano piece *Night Thoughts*, subtitled "Hommage to Ives," which was written in 1972 for the 1973 Van Cliburn Piano Competition.

By his eighties, Copland was affected by senile dementia. A variety of staff (of varying quality and reliability) cared for his household, and his personal secretaries—most notably David Walker, who was with Copland from 1952 to 1985, and Ronald Caltabiano—shouldered much of the responsibility for daily telephone calls and correspondence. Copland continued to decline mentally, and his physical health began to fail in the 1980s. Vivian Perlis, who worked tirelessly with Copland in these difficult years to assemble his autobiography, was a particularly devoted friend, as were Phillip Ramey and Verna Fine.

Copland died on December 2, 1990. In the summer of 1991, friends and family gathered at Tanglewood to sprinkle his ashes on the grounds. His papers were left to the Library of Congress. The collection of some 400,000 items includes photographs, music manuscripts, Copland's writings, books, and—of course—his correspondence.

To Eugene Ormandy

AC/LC. carbon.

Flat 146
55 Park Lane
London W.1.
September 23, 1958

Dear Eugene,

I'm late in answering your letter through no fault of my own, because yours followed me to Boston and then to New York and then to London before it reached me. By now I imagine your programs have gone to print, so that this letter may serve little purpose.

As you can imagine, I don't at all like being difficult about the mere title of a piece. After all, the music is the same whatever it is called. On the other hand, I must confess that I never liked the title "Saga of the Prairie," for the simple reason that it sounds too corny to me, and was not my idea in the first place.[1] The best compromise I can honestly allow myself would be to program the piece as "Music for Radio—Saga of the Prairie." I hope that solves this minor complication. I wish I could be back for the performances but my present plans keep me in London until early December.

Some day I hope you will give serious thought to a performance by the Philadelphia Orchestra of my Third Symphony. I say "serious thought" because it lasts almost forty minutes and therefore uses up a considerable part of the program. Perhaps you know that I conducted it last season with the New York Philharmonic.

All my best wishes on the start of the new season.

Yours cordially,

Aaron Copland

1. Copland wrote *Music for Radio* in 1937 on a commission from CBS radio. The audience was invited to submit possible titles and from some 1,000 entries, Copland chose "Saga of the Prairie." In 1968 he retitled the piece as *Prairie Journal.* The work is now generally known as *Music for Radio.*

To Eugene Ormandy

AC/LC. carbon.

Flat 146
55 Park Lane
London W.1.
October 7, 1958

Dear Gene:

I was glad to get your letter of September 25th. And especially glad that the matter of the title has been happily resolved.[1]

It was nice of you to wish me a "good time in Russia," but unfortunately nobody invited me to go there. I was glad to know about the reception to "Quiet City" because the last piece of mine they had heard before that was my "Symphonic Ode" which, I am afraid, frightened them a little bit.[2]

Well, anyway, perhaps I shall get a chance to go with the next bunch of invitees. Maybe you can do something about that.

All my best on the new season,

Aaron Copland

1. Ormandy had written: "I have already done exactly as you suggested hoping that you would agree."

2. Ormandy had written: "Before you go to Russia I want to tell you that your piece, 'Quiet City[,]' had a wonderful reception everywhere we played it [on the Philadelphia Orchestra's Russian tour] and I am sure many Russian composers will talk to you about it."

To Irving and Verna Fine

IF/LC. als.

55 Park Lane
London W1
Nov 5 '58

Dear V & I:

What on earth has happened to you-all?? The silence is thunderous! Or am I imagining things? Not completely, because Sylvia Goldstein of B[oosey] & H[awkes] came thru London with rumors from Rome that you were having ap't troubles. I hope they're solved, by now.

I've been having an interesting time, what with one thing and another. I've

been conducting a bit, here and in Copenhagen and Stuttgart, and lecturing a
bit in Coventry and Brussels; meeting new faces and renewing acquaintances
with Britten, Tippett, [Wilfrid] Mellers, etc. Sorry to report I haven't got much
work of my own done, but foreign towns <u>are</u> distracting, no?

This is mainly to arouse you both to an answer. I only have 3 1/2 more weeks
before going home on Dec. 1. (Next week in Paris.) Best to Alexei [Haieff] and
love to you both.

Aaron

To Carlos Chávez

AC/LC. Photocopy of tls.
[Shady Lane Farm stationery]

January 27, 1959

Dear Carlos:

Finally I have made up my mind to take advantage of your so generous offer
and spend some time in your studio in Acapulco. I am assuming that this is still
convenient for you and that the invitation still is open.

I have a reservation on the Aeronaves for February 11th. I will therefore
plan to be in Acapulco on the afternoon of February 12th.

Could you tell me: 1—The exact address where I should have my mail sent.
2—Shall I bring books or do you have enough reading material in the studio? (I
imagine your main collection is in Chapultapec?) 3—Is there a piano-tuner
available in Acapulco? Can you give me his name and address? 4—Is there a
typewriter, or should I bring my own? (I must write a long speech for the
University of New Hampshire in April.) [added in ink: 5. Also, full name of
your sister with address, just in case . . .]

I hope everything is going well in Cambridge, and look forward to hearing
from you.

As ever,

[signed] Aaron

To Carlos Chávez

AC/LC. Photocopy of als.

Feb 13 '58 [sic, 1959]

Dear Carlos:

I feel like a very lucky fellow today—writing this letter to you from your own
table in your own studio. I am simply enchanted with the set-up, and am most
grateful to you for making it possible. Whats more, I have already written a
page of music on my first morning here, which is a good sign![1]

Chebela[?] has been helpful. I was completely unprepared for your magnificent 'jardin'—and look forward to getting to know it better. She explained it is all your conception, so I expect to discover a connection between your garden and your music. The situation of the house is sensational—it is difficult for me to take my eyes off the landscape.

For the moment I have no car, because they are all rented in Mexico <u>and</u> Acapulco. So I cannot tell much about the surrounding country. Curious detail: just before leaving home my sister called me and told me she was going to Acapulco for five days next week with her husband and daughter, not having any idea I was to be there.

I am still under the spell of the magic change (in less than 24 hours) from the cold and snow of Ossining to the palm-trees and deep blue of the Pacific.

Well, this is merely to tell you, I arrived.

My best to Ottilia

As ever

Aaron

---

1. Perhaps a page of sketches for the Nonet.

In 1960, Copland and Lukas Foss were invited by the State Department to serve as cultural ambassadors to Soviet Russia.

To Irving and Verna Fine

IF/LC. acs.

[photograph: Moscow, view from the Kremlin wall]

Moscow
March 23 '60

Dear Everybody:

Hello from Moscow! Nothing too good for the visiting artist and it's all free: private limousines, operas, circuses, puppet shows, ballets etc, plus jet plane rides to Tiflis and Riga. Our first concert here Friday; 2 others in Riga & Leningrad. Why didn't you warn me about Lukas: he's irrepressible, and a charmer. Love to you all.

Aaron

<u>Write</u> (c/o Amer. Embassy)

To Arthur and Esther Berger

AC/LC. Photocopy of acs.

Leningrad, Apr 6 '60

Dear Es & Arthur:

Greetings from the nicest town so far. We've been in Tiflis, (Georgia) and Riga, (Latvia). Audiences are very cordial and noone turns a hair at our 'modernisms,' 'tho not a word said pro or con about the music itself. Lukas doing his Symphony of Chorales here and me my Statements. First class orchestra. Best to you both. (Sorry to miss the May affair)

· Aaron

After a month in Russia, Copland traveled to London and then to Japan, where he conducted the Boston Symphony Orchestra on its tour of Japan, the Philippines, and Australia.

To Leonard Bernstein

LB/LC. als.

[Green Park Hotel (London) stationery]

May 1 [1960]

Dear Lensk:

Everyone's been writing me how <u>wonderfully</u> you did the 2nd. H[urricane].[1] Also, was sent the write-ups. Naturally I'm tickled pink. Now I hear you're recording it—so I can hear it, and maybe CB[S]-TV will screen it for me when I get back end of June. Anyho this is just to say denks and denks again. (Did you get my wire? I really <u>was</u> all agog.[)]

When you get this I'll be in Tokio! (care Amer. Embassy.)

Had a nice concert here with the London Symphony Orch—big house and lots of enthusiasm. The English—of all ages—tend to spoil me anyhow, so I like it here.

I imagine Lukas has given you an earful about the Russkys. (Some nice lady piano teacher at the Leningrad Cons. asked after you most warmly.) It was an experience I wouldn't have wanted to miss.

Have fun with your new house. And love to you and Felicia.

Aaron

---

1. Bernstein directed a concert performance of *The Second Hurricane* on April 23, 1960; the performance was televised the next day.

To Leonard Bernstein

LB/LC. als.
[Berkshire Music Center stationery]

July 28 '60

Dear Lensk:

A big pleasure to get your letter. On my one day in N.Y. before coming here I had Roger Englander show me the 2nd H[urricane]. That was a big pleasure too—a revival only you could have made so moving. I hope the recording is as good. (Only one reproach: you didn't mention Edwin's[1] name as collaborator.) Goddard had written me about the birthday package and I'm pleased as punch about that too.[2] (He's also bringing out Masselos' performance of the Piano Fantasy which I want you to hear[3]—performance is superb, I think.)

About the TV—Nov. 12; of course I'll do anything you like.[4] Whatever else happens it will give us a reason to 'confer,' i.e., see each other for a change! The only thing I don't want is to be presented as 'grandpa for the kiddies.' One item you might consider is a selection of songs from the Old American Songs. I did them with The Little Orchestra and W[illia]m Warfield 2 years ago. Warfield does them wonderfully and the orchestral versions are fun-things. (You might show the kids the original versions of the songs I worked with.) If you have a quintet of singers the 'Promise of Living' from The Tender Land works fine. (Or that and the Square Dance can be performed in the choral version with orch.) Etc. Etc. . . . . The hard thing will be to illustrate my 'tougher' side, no?

The idea of you watching me conduct for 90 min. struck terror. . . . . After 8 performances of the Symph #1 on tour I think I can trust myself to peek outside 'die score'! Anyway I've been getting lots of conducting practice: in 3 months I've had concerts with 7 different orchestras.

We need you in Tanglewood—but badly. That's a whole chapter by itself. Our summer is enlivened by Luciano Berio who is guest composer and has stirred things up considerably. But otherwise, routine reigns. Too bad . . .

Aside from music, I had a lovely time in London and in Tokio. The only thing I didn't do was write music, hélas!

Love to you always,
Aaron

---

1. Edwin Denby, the librettist.
2. Goddard Lieberson, president of Columbia Records.
3. William Masselos had premiered Copland's *Piano Fantasy* in 1957.
4. Copland and Bernstein appeared together on a Philharmonic Young People's Concert celebrating Copland's sixtieth birthday. The concert was televised by CBS on February 12, 1961.

To Nadia Boulanger

AC/LC. acs.

Dec 8 '60

Dear Nadia:

Its taken me almost a month to thank you for your birthday letter. As you guessed, it was a 'deluge.' Everyone has been very kind. But I still have great trouble making a connection with that number: 60. It seems to have no relation to how I feel. Tant mieux!

I have almost completed the Nonet (3 vls, 3 vlas, 3 vlc.) for Mr & Mrs Bliss.[1] We all agree that you are to be the dedicacee, which makes me very happy—since it will celebrate our 40 years of friendship.

As ever

Aaron

---

1. The Nonet was commissioned in honor of Mr. and Mrs. Robert Woods Bliss for their fiftieth wedding anniversary. It was premiered on March 2, 1961, at Dumbarton Oaks, the Bliss estate. Copland himself was the conductor.

To Nadia Boulanger

AC/LC. tls.
[Rock Hill stationery]

March 31, 1961

Dear Nadia,

First let me say how pleased I am that you will be conducting the Philharmonic next season. I would have answered your letter sooner, but I was conducting at the University of Arizona and have only just received it.

You must know how much I should like to please you in the matter of the "Triptyque de Circonstance."[1] But despite my wishes, facts are facts and they must be faced. The simple truth is that between today and the end of August I have not a possibility of avoiding the various commitments I have made. These [added in ink: are planned 6 months in advance and] include conducting and lecturing engagements in half a dozen cities, not counting England, Yugoslavia and Portugal; the writing of a film score[2] (my first in 12 years); several commissions including the New York Philharmonic and the Philadelphia Orchestra;[3] and my duties as Chairman of the Faculty and teacher at Tanglewood. Moreover, as you know, I am a "slow" composer, who does not dash off pieces just like that. Because of all this, I'm sure you will understand the impossibility of my situation in relation to your request. It is the price one pays for being 60, I suppose!

However, I have two suggestions which may be of some use to you. As you know, the Nonet was written for 9 solo strings; but both Mrs. Bliss and myself thought that it was possible to do with a full body of strings, if one kept the relative proportions: in this case, 9 violins on each of the 3 violin parts, 3 violas on each of the 3 viola parts, and the same for cellos.[4] That would make a string orchestra of 45 players. Since the work is dedicated to you and has never been played in New York, it would be a premiere, (without comparison of other conductors, as you needlessly seem to fear!). The work lasts 18 minutes and is not too difficult to prepare. Boosey & Hawkes tells me they have sent it to you in any case.

The second suggestion I have might be to revive our Organ Symphony in the version without organ (First Symphony). It would be wonderful to hear you do it as conductor after 37 years!! I conducted it with the Boston Symphony last year, both in Boston and on the Far Eastern tour, and audiences seemed to like it.

You can imagine how disappointed I am not to be able to take up your original suggestion.

With all my devotion . . .

As ever,

[signed] Aaron

---

1. Boulanger, in her letter of March 18, 1961, had asked Copland to contribute a brief orchestral movement to a three-movement piece, the other two movements to be by Virgil Thomson and Walter Piston.

2. *Something Wild.*

3. *Connotations* was written for the New York Philharmonic; the orchestral commission for the Philadelphia Orchestra was never fulfilled.

4. Although this hardly seems to "keep the relative proportions" of the parts—augmenting the violins ninefold and the other parts threefold—it does somewhat resemble the recommendation for multiple-string versions in the note to the published score of the Nonet.

To Carlos Chávez

AC/LC. Photocopy of tls.
[Rock Hill stationery]

June 23, 1961

Dear Carlos,

On returning from Europe last week, I was delighted to find the program of the three conciertos [concerts] that were given with the collaboration of Billy Masselos. It pleased me to see that the FANTASY was given twice on the same evening. I am wondering what the reactions of the audience was at the Colegio Nacional.

Since I last saw you, I introduced my NONET in Washington, and heard other performances in Brandeis, Chicago and London. When it is published, I shall send you a copy.

Copland at his Rock Hill home, n.d. Provided courtesy of the Aaron Copland Collection at the Library of Congress.

I went abroad on a State Department trip, conducting in Scotland, Yugoslavia and Portugal. I even managed to sandwich in three days in Madrid where I uncovered an active dodecaphonic school! (Poor Falla[1]—I wonder whether he would have approved.)

At the moment I am heavily engaged in a film score, my first in twelve years; on top of which Tanglewood arrives.

Send me news of you when you get a chance. By the way, I saw a flattering reference to your INVENCION in an English publication apropos of the issuance of the printed music.[2]

Un abrazo. . . . . . .

[signed] Aaron

---

1. Composer Manuel de Falla (1876–1946), leading Spanish composer of the twentieth century.

2. Chávez, *Invención* for piano, dedicated to Copland.

To Carlos Chávez

AC/LC. Photocopy of tls.
[Rock Hill stationery]

September 27, 1962

Dear Carlos:

What a disappointment that you weren't able to come![1] But of course I realized how complicated it might be. In any event, I was just on the point of calling you at the Barbizon when your letter reached me.

I finished my piece just in time to have the parts ready for the first rehearsal. It would have been very nice to have had your reaction. I must say that I myself was surprised how well it was received in view of the fact that the harmonic language was rather severe. Somehow people seemed to be carried along by the fact that the piece has a strong dramatic quality and in some way seemed to fit the solemnity of the occasion and the clean lines of the new Hall. Well—I will send you a score as soon as it is published.

As for the Hall itself, there are plenty of problems acoustically speaking. Even after all these are ironed out, I doubt whether the quality of sound will ever in any way be distinctive. Something in the construction materials used tends to make different orchestras sound the same. This only goes to prove what you and I already know, namely, that the art of the acoustician is a very shaky one.

All my best to you, and good luck on the finishing of the Symphony.

Affectionately,

[signed] Aaron

1. To the opening of Lincoln Center on September 23, with its performance of Copland's *Connotations.*

To Claire Reis

Reis/NYPL. tls.
[Rock Hill stationery]

September 27, 1962

Dear Claire:

Thanks a lot for your nice note.

It is possible that I may be able to take in [Benjamin Britten's opera] "The Turn of the Screw" on November 1st. I'll let you know definitely by October 15th. I hope this will be alright. [Added in ink: (Can't go on Nov. 7)]

I reread my 1953 letter and have decided against publishing it now.[1] My main reason is that in order to make the letter understandable to the reader it would be necessary to explain to the reader what it was all about. I should prefer to save the telling of this tale for a later time in my own reminiscences, if I should ever decide to write them. (Several publishers seem interested!) Also, as a minor point, I notice that the letter is addressed to the Board of Directors of the League of Composers and I was under the impression that all the letters you were publishing were ones to you personally.

All best

[signed] Aaron

P.S. I've had reams of comments about the piece,[2] but not a word from V[irgil] T[homson], R[oy] H[arris], R[oger] S[essions] or S[amuel] B[arber]—all of whom were there! Times haven't changed much, have they??

[in ink] P.P.S. Amused by the gossip in your today's [*sic*] letter. I was invited to serve on the Jury—but will be out of N.Y. during most of the period.

I agree with [Robert] Evett that my letters are dull. That's what we get for talking by telephone so much! I've looked up the letter in C. C. + C. and find it is only an extract—a sentence.[3] Isn't the whole letter publishable as a 'first time' therefore? I hope so, because I don't feel in a serious letter-writing mood!

---

1. Reis was planning to publish a selection of letters to her in *Musical America* as samples of the material to become the Claire Reis Collection in the New York Public Library. She had asked Copland whether she could publish his letter of February 9, 1953, concerning the cancellation of the performance of *Lincoln Portrait* at the Eisenhower Inaugural concert.

2. *Connotations* at the Lincoln Center.

3. Reis had quoted one sentence from a letter Copland had written to her in 1945. See Reis, *Composers, Conductors, and Critics* (New York: Oxford University Press, 1955), 210.

To Claire Reis

Reis/NYPL. als.

Aug 2 '63

Dear Claire:

I received your boat letter and Siena card in the midst of the hecticalities of Tanglewood. The way to solve problems is to stay so busy there's no time to think of them! The big event of the first 4 weeks was the Britten 'War Requiem.' It's brilliantly effective the first time thru;—one wonders about the 10th time, 'tho.

Now I'm back home, (Lukas [Foss] replaced me at Tanglewood) working on my own affairs. I leave for South America on Sept 8th (away until Oct. 20), and have lots to do before then. Last month I conducted a concert at Ravinia with the excellent Chicago Symph.—and had as speaker for the Lincoln Portrait the Governor of Illinois.[1] He did fine, for a Democrat.

I wish I had time to comment on your last letter as it deserves. Your basic advice—"You were good, so just stay good in the same way,"[2] would be OK for Artur Rubinstein, but doesn't work too well for creators. I have no intention of hopping on other people's bandwagons, but the problem remains for any creator—especially sexagenarians like me!—as to how one renews one's self while the big noise is being made by the youngsters up ahead. Still, I didn't mean to look so solemn that evening at dinner—things aren't that gloomy.

Have a good time in London and think of me there.

As ever—

Aaron

---

1. Otto Kerner, a Democrat, was governor of Illinois in 1963.
2. Reis's letter of July 10, 1963, to which Copland's letter is a reply, did not use these words. Copland is paraphrasing the general gist of her letter, which expressed hope that Copland would not feel it necessary to change his style to reflect new trends in composition—"absorb[ing] serial, graph, or electronic methods."

Copland's close friend and fellow composer Irving Fine had died in August 1962, but Copland continued to correspond with Verna. In a letter of November 1, 1963, she wrote with news that she had enrolled at Harvard University to study education.

To Verna Fine

IF/LC. als.
[Rock Hill stationery]

Nov 7 '63

Dear Verna:

Nice to get your letter. I'm 2 weeks back from America del Sur and about to take off again for Europe—2nd trip this year. (I'm a gad-about!) Tanglewood seems far away—as I'm sure it does to Lukas [Foss], too.

Mildly amazed at your new carreer.[1] What's the Education Masters for? (I thought you were a Statistician.) But I'm all for it, anyway. Incidentally it was Lynn Riggs (librettist of Oklahoma)[2] who sang me 'my' version of 'I Bought Me a Cat.['] I've never seen a printed version. Columbia is about to bring out all 10 songs, plus the Clarinet Concerto—the best record I ever conducted. I'll send it to the kids for Xmas.

South America was hard work, but wonderful for the EGO. On Nov 18 I head for Munich to conduct the world premiere of my 'Robbins' ballet[3] at the Bayerische Staatsoper, with side trips to Vienna, Nurenberg and Milan. All in one month. I told you I'm a gad-about. . . .

I've been noticing how well Irving's pieces are keeping up in radio and public performances. It's a pleasure. Sorry I can't be with you Friday eve—but I'll be thinking of you muchly.

Love to you and the girls

Aaron

---

1. Verna Fine had written on November 1, 1963, "Have embarked on a new career. As of this September, I am a Harvard boy! Back getting my masters in education on a part-time basis. Courses are frightful; and my aging brain doesn't seem to respond to all the vague generalities (crap!) that is being thrown at me . . ."

2. Lynn Riggs was actually the playwright of *Green Grow the Lilacs,* the play which was the basis of *Oklahoma!*

3. *Dance Panels.*

To Leonard Burkat

Burkat/Yale. tls.
[Rock Hill stationery]

July 11, 1964

Dear Leonard:

Thanks for sending the congratulatory note about the Medal.[1] Someone should tell Roy Cohn![2]

Thanks too for Red Pony. Nice job, I thought.

Copland conducting, with William Warfield, ca. 1963. Provided courtesy of
the Aaron Copland Collection at the Library of Congress.

Are you dreaming up a beautiful cover for Music for a Great City? We made a good recording in London, I think.[3]

Drop in with Marian if you are ever in this area.

As ever

[signed] Aaron

---

1. The Presidential Medal of Freedom, awarded Copland by Lyndon B. Johnson.

2. Chief legal counsel for the Senate Permanent Subcommittee on Investigations at the time of Copland's appearance, and principal aide to Senator Joseph McCarthy.

3. The cover for the recording (Columbia M 30374), which also included *Statements,* is a handsome photograph of 1960s London, rising to St. Paul's.

To Morris Baumstein

Burkat/Yale.[1] tls.

[Rock Hill stationery]

October 15, 1964

Dear Mr. Baumstein:

Thank you for letting me see the advertising material prepared by Columbia [Records] in connection with the Philharmonic Hall program.

I note in reading the text that accompanies the photographs a reference to my "operatic triumphs." I think in the interest of truth and exactitude the word balletic or ballet might well be substituted for operatic. This is rather a sore point with me in view of the point that the one opera I've composed had a reception which could hardly be called triumphant![2]

Yours sincerely

[signed] Aaron Copland

---

1. Baumstein was no longer working for Columbia Records when this letter was received, and it ended up on Leonard Burkat's desk.

2. Burkat, who answered this letter, noted, "I think of you as the composer of two operas. Have you deleted 'The Second Hurricane' from the canon of your works or do you not count it as an opera?"

To Leonard Burkat

Burkat/Yale. tls.

November 11, 1964

Dear Leonard:

I was amused to get your letter of November 5. I'm not that touchy about the opera. Nevertheless, to refer to them as "triumphs" (which generally re- fers to public acceptance) is to stretch the truth uncomfortably. Since the ad was listing accomplishments, I just thought the word <u>balletic</u> in the place of <u>operatic</u> would be more convincing. As for the SECOND HURRICANE, I'm very fond of it.

I'm enclosing a bit of recent propaganda because of the extract from an intelligent and recent article about it by Wilfrid Mellers.

Alles gutes

[signed] Aaron

To Erich Leinsdorf

AC/LC. carbon.

August 4, 1965

Dear Erich,[1]

I am looking forward as usual to my coming activities in Tanglewood. Since these are the final weeks of the '65 season and the customary period for making plans for next summer, it seems a good time to tell you of my own thinking in relation to Tanglewood.

This being the 25th year since my first association with the Berkshire Music Center, and my approaching birthday marking the normal retirement age, I have decided to tell you of my wish to withdraw from all regular duties at Tanglewood at the end of this season. A formal resignation is not called for since the Trustees of the Boston Symphony Orchestra only make yearly appointments to the faculty.

I take this action knowing what a fine replacement you have in Gunther [Schuller] and fully confident of his ability to carry on the work of the Composition Department if you so decide.

It goes without saying that I shall always be ready to assist in an advisory capacity whenever you wish to call on me.

Yours sincerely,

---

1. Erich Leinsdorf's appointment as Music Director of the Boston Symphony Orchestra in 1962 made him the director of Tanglewood.

Together Virgil Thomson, Lehman Engel, Marc Blitzstein, and Aaron Copland had founded Arrow Music Press in 1937. A year later the press acquired the catalog of Alma Wertheim's Cos Cob Press, and in 1956, Arrow merged with Boosey & Hawkes, Copland's principal publisher. Engel was the president of Arrow Music Press, Copland the treasurer: thus the business of winding up the long-dormant publisher devolved upon them.

To Lehman Engel

LE/Yale. tls.

August 25, 1965

Dear Lehman:

For some time now I've been thinking that the time is ripe for winding up the affairs of the Arrow Music Press. Since it is completely inactive as far as we are concerned, and since we are expending an annual corporate tax of $25 to no purpose, I think the sensible thing to do is to let Boosey & Hawkes undertake the job of signing us off. There is a sum of money in the bank amounting to something like $1800. If you agree with the above, we should get together with Virgil and decide what to do with it. My assumption is that we will apply it to the publication of some young composer's work.

Anyway, what I would like now is an expression of opinion from you as to the advisability of the above.

As ever,

[signed] Aaron

To Lehman Engel

LE/Yale. tls.
[R.F.D. 1, Peekskill, stationery]

September 14, 1965

Dear Lehman,

I had already written to Arnold [Weissberger] about digging the original Arrow papers of incorporation out of his files. If they are nowhere to be found, we shall have to follow Arthur Strasser's advice.

Too bad about Virgil.[1] He seems to have the whole thing mixed up in his mind. We are not giving the Arrow Press to anybody—least of all to Boosey. We are merely dissolving it, since it seems to serve no practical purpose now or in the foreseeable future, unless you and I decide that it should. I think that Virgil thinks he can [added in ink: , if it continues] personally make some use of it, in which case he should start his own press! Our [added in ink: terminal] arrangement with Boosey was signed almost ten years ago and has been running smoothly ever since. In any case, their role would be merely to facilitate winding up our affairs, and that is all.

As soon as the papers are found or reproduced, I'll call Virgil and we will see whether we can persuade him "peacefully" to see matters as they really are.

If this can't be done before I leave for Europe at the end of the month, we'll pick it up again when I get back in December.

As ever,

[signed] Aaron

1. Engel had written Copland: "I saw Virgil by accident a few days ago and he is violently opposed to our letting Boosey have the press as he says that Boosey's is very badly run. Oh, what a perverse one!"

To Nadia Boulanger

AC/LC. als.
[Rock Hill stationery]

Nov 20 1965

Dear Nadia:

Always such a pleasure to get a birthday greeting from you. When I was in Warsaw last week (conducting) we spoke of you constantly, especially with Mycielski.[1] What a charming fellow he is!

I'm sorry my travels didn't bring me to Paris this time, but perhaps next year. In the meantime all my affectionate devotion to you

Aaron

1. Zygmunt Mycielski, Polish critic and composer who had studied with Boulanger.

To Leonard Bernstein

LB/LC. tls.
[R.F.D. 1, Peekskill, stationery]

December 23, 1965

Dear Lenny:

I've been delegated to get in touch with you by our National Institute of Arts and Letters. Thought it might be more 'official' if I wrote instead of just calling up. Also, it will give you more time to think about the matter.

The Institute would like to do something to commemorate Varese.[1] Instead of trying to do it on their own, they thought it would be much more appropriate if the N.Y. Philharmonic wanted to make a similar gesture in conjunction with the Institute.

Miss Geffen[2] indicated that they have some funds which could be expended for such a purpose. I don't think she had in mind anything so elaborate as a separate concert, but rather making it possible to hire extra musicians or perhaps extra rehearsals to allow performance of a work otherwise not performable. What do you think?

Perhaps AMERIQUES could be revived. I don't think it has been performed in a long time. I don't remember the size of the orchestra needed, but it's pretty monster. I notice that Groves lists three other works from the '30's: METAL, for soprano and orchestra; ESPACE, for chorus and orchestra, and a

Symphony with chorus.[3] If you're interested in any of these, I suggest that Mr. Chou Wen Chung be contacted, since he has taken on the part of musical executor and works at the Varese apartment.

Let me know what you think—the sooner the better.

Love,

[signed] Aaron

---

1. Edgar Varèse had died on November 6, 1965.

2. Felicia Geffen, secretary of the institute.

3. Copland was working from the 1954 edition of *Grove's Dictionary of Music and Musicians*, which lists *Metal* and *Espace* and the Symphony as though they were completed works.

To Howard Shanet

AC/LC. carbon.

December 13, 1966

Dear Howard,

Congratulations to you and Bernice on the arrival of the heir and successor to the Shanet fortunes!

In answer to your questions about Damrosch and the Organ Symphony, the remark he made came <u>after</u> the performance, not before it.[1] Just before starting the next piece he turned around and addressed the audience. He had agreed to do the piece in the first place at the request of Nadia Boulanger, who was performing it that day. There was no question as to whether he liked it or not, since he had agreed in advance to play it. He was a great friend of Nadia and, you might say, was stuck with the thing. My idea is that he made the little speech in order to calm the nerves of the elderly ladies in the audience, of whom there were plenty,—and in order to imply that he was on their side of the fence. I don't think you are correct in thinking of him as amateurish or clumsy as conductor. He had years of experience as conductor and was quite competent in Wagner and the usual repertoire. It was mostly the old story of not being sympathetic with the music of his own day. Incidentally, in later years, he always seemed embarrassed when he met me, and more than once said to me, "<u>You</u> understood what I meant by that remark, didn't you?" As a matter of fact, he didn't hesitate to recommend me enthusiastically to the Guggenheim Foundation a few months later, even making complimentary remarks about the Organ Symphony. Perhaps this was just to salve his conscience, but at any rate it did help me to get a (the) first Guggenheim. May he rest in peace!

Best of luck with your book.

As ever,

A.C.

1. After the 1925 premiere of Copland's *Symphony for Organ and Orchestra,* Damrosch had quipped from the stage: "Ladies and gentlemen, I am sure you will agree that if a gifted young man can write a symphony like this at twenty-three, within five years he will be ready to commit murder!" (C & P I, 104).

To Richard Rodney Bennett[1]

Letter file/NYPL. tls.
[Rock Hill stationery]

February 13, 1967

Dear Richard,

It was very flattering to get your letter requesting a 4–hand piano piece! I've never written any 4–hand piano music and it might be fun to try, especially knowing what a good performance it would get.

However, as you can understand, I can't absolutely promise that I will produce a piece I approve of. For that reason, I think we should forget about the question of a fee of any kind, and ["perhaps" crossed out; "just" substituted in ink] just trust to luck for my sake and for your sake something happens.

I'll be over again for another stint with the L[ondon] S[ymphony] O[rchestra] in late September. I hope we can meet again and have a meal together.

Friendly greetings,
[signed] Aaron C

1. British composer and pianist.

To Leonard Bernstein

LB/LC. als.

Aug 2 '67

Dear Lensk:

Just finished the new piece for the 125th.[1] Thought you'd like to know!

I'm calling it 'Inscape.'[2] Of course I don't have to explain to you 'vhat dot means'—but everybody else wants to know. Lasts about 12 min., and ends, (Oy)—quietly.

Kereney[?] is airmailing the score to you on the 4th. I plan to be at the rehearsals. When do you get back? Will we have a chance to giggle over the pages together? Or do you step right from the plane to the hall?? I cant wait to hear you do it. . . .

Have nothing to do while waiting, except 2 weeks at Dartmouth College (for my morale) and an all-me program at the Hollywood Bowl.

Hope you are having a relaxing time at that complicated address.

Love to all

A—

---

1. The 125th anniversary of the founding of the New York Philharmonic.

2. "Inscape" is a word coined by the poet Gerard Manley Hopkins. As Hopkins explains, "No doubt my poetry errs on the side of oddness. . . . Melody is what strikes me most of all in music and design in painting, so design, pattern, or what I am in the habit of calling 'inscape' is what I above all aim at in poetry" (as quoted in C & P II, 348–49).

To Mary Lescaze

AC/LC. als.
[Rock Hill stationery]

Oct 28 '67

Dear Mary:

So nice you heard the new piece,[1] and so very nice that you wrote me about it. Perhaps I should explain that I was there on Monday, having just returned from a 5 week conducting stint in Europe. (I had heard L.[eonard] B.[ernstein] premiere the piece in Ann Arbor in mid-Sept at the start of a pre-season tour during which he gave 9 performances in nine towns. Ain't that 'sumpin'!) Anyway, it was a pleasure for me to hear it so beautifully played at performance #13. And to top it off Lenny tells me he's recorded it.

I had a varied European tour—Vienna, London, Paris, Köln, Venice, Bologna—and as usual the best time was with the London Symphony at Festival Hall. I seem to have a 'thing' going with the British music public which is very pleasant indeed!

Do lets all get together, as you suggest.

My best to Bill.

As ever

Aaron

---

1. *Inscape.*

To Leonard Bernstein

LB/LC. als.
[Rock Hill stationery]

Nov 17 '67

Dear Lensk:

What a <u>beautiful</u> letter you wrote me for my birthday! I shall treasure it always. And what a deep satisfaction it is for me to know that we've sustained our feeling for each other all these many years. It's a <u>joy</u> & that's what it is. And just imagine what it means to me to see you prepare and conduct my music with such devotion and love and musical sensitivity—for that alone I am forever in your debt.

Un abrazo—and love

Aaron

To Leonard Bernstein

LB/LC. als.
[Rock Hill stationery]

Aug 26 1968

Dear Lensk:

I'm late with my birthday greetings—how awful! (Guess I didn't want to get lost in a sea of wires and letters.) I'm just back from conducting at Tanglewood, where your spirit hovers. But it always hovers, wherever I go. American music would have a different "face" without you.

Have a good tour—and always and always I love you dearly!

Aaron

To Nadia Boulanger

AC/LC. tls.
[Rock Hill stationery, "Rock Hill" crossed out]

1538 L. Washington St.
[Peekskill, New York]
October 16, 1969

Dear Nadia,

It's always such a pleasure to hear from you!

I was delighted to know of your interest in my PIANO QUARTET for the Wednesday class. I have sent you by Air Parcel Post a copy of the recording of the work, and added a comparatively recent recording of our ORGAN SYMPHONY on the chance that you don't have that one.

I also wrote to David Adams, the head of the London office of Boosey and

Hawkes, and asked him to send you the pocket scores of the PIANO QUARTET. Since the SEXTET for Strings, Piano and Clarinet is on the same recording with the PIANO QUARTET, I also took the liberty of sending scores of the SEXTET for use possibly on some other occasion. It's a pleasure to present all this avec mes compliments.

Thanks for reminding me about Fontainebleau '71. Fantastic that such a date is coming so soon, no?

Your suggestion about a Concert A.C. is very generous indeed. Naturally I would do my best to be present on such an occasion, but it would be an advantage to have some idea of a possible date.

Affectionately,

as ever. . . . .

[signed] Aaron

P.S. I am to be in London for a concert with the London Symphony Orchestra next month (November 25th) and will remain until December 1st. Any chance of your being in London then? I greatly enjoyed our lunch together last year.

To Nadia Boulanger

AC/LC. als.

[1538 L. Washington Street stationery]

Nov 22 1970

Dear Nadia:

I have two reasons to be grateful to you: one is for the recent birthday letter, and the other is for the extraordinarily generous letter you sent for the Album of Letters from Composers presented to me on November fourteenth.

(Of course I cannot believe I am 70—but rien a faire [nothing to be done],—everyone says I am!)

In re-reading your two letters I have present in my mind all that I owe to you as man and musician.

There is no adequate way for me to express my appreciation for all I learned in those early years of the twenties, and for all the encouragement and help in the years that followed.

Dear Nadia: I look forward to our re-union at Fontainebleau next summer more than I can say.

With all my affection

Aaron

Copland outdoors, 1978. Photographer: King Wehrle. Provided courtesy of
the Aaron Copland Collection at the Library of Congress.

To Lehman Engel

LE/Yale. tls.

February 22, 1972

Dear Lehman:

It has been on my mind for sometime to write you and Virgil on the subject of a definitive close to the inactive Arrow Music Press.

The only matter which really needs to be taken care of is the allocation of the remaining funds which are deposited in the Chemical Bank on 56th [changed in ink to "66th"] Street and Broadway, in the amount of $1,853.86.

At one time, you may remember, we thought of applying this money to the publication of one of Marc's works. Since that time, a Marc Blitzstein Award was established under the auspices of the National Institute of Arts and Letters. The two recipients up to now have been William Bolcom in 1965 and Jack Beeson in 1968. The award is for $2500, "to a composer, lyricist or librettist to encourage the creation of works of merit for the musical theater."

It seems appropriate to me that the comparatively modest sum we have to be presented to the National Institute to be added to the funds they already have. If you agree, would you please sign the enclosed statement. I shall then close the account at the Bank and send the resultant check to the National Institute.

As ever,

[signed] Aaron

To Nadia Boulanger

AC/LC. als.

[1538 L. Washington Street stationery]

Nov 26, 1972

Dear Nadia:

What a pleasure it was to receive your birthday greetings this year, as ever—and in your own handwriting! Many, many thanks.

I have been travelling recently—to conduct and lecture—in Denver, Colorado; Austin, Texas; Indiana University in Bloomington; Johns Hopkins in Baltimore;—wherever I go, students and people generally speak to me about you. "Tell us about Nadia Boulanger" is a familiar refrain. So—you accompany me on all my travels—which is also a pleasure.

I hope soon to get started on an autobiography, mostly in order to tell the story of the development of American music as I saw it in the years '20 to '50. How I wish my memory were better than it is! But I hope to write it for better or worse.

All my affection to you and to Annette [Dieudonné].

As ever

Aaron

With funding from the National Endowment for the Arts, six orchestras commissioned six composers in 1976 for symphonic works to celebrate the national bicentennial. Conductor Eugene Ormandy and the Philadelphia Orchestra were to receive a score from Copland.

To Eugene Ormandy

AC/LC. carbon.

July 30, 1974

Dear Gene:

I'm sorry that I have been so remiss in not communicating with you before this. Actually I had planned to see you during my brief stay in the Tanglewood area last weekend, but was unable to remain for Saturday evening as I had hoped.

The reason I haven't been in touch with you before now regarding the commissioned work is very simple. I have not as yet been able to decide exactly what sort of work I shall be writing. Because of that, it is only natural that I can't tell you the kind of detail concerning the piece, such as length and orchestration, as you would like to have. All that I am able to say right now is that as soon as these matters are determined, you shall be the first to know!

In any event, May 1976, the date you mention for a possible premiere, seems reasonable enough.[1]

As ever,

---

1. Copland never finished his proposed bicentennial piece.

To Vivian Perlis

AC/LC. carbon.

February 3, 1977

Dear Vivian,

I have returned under separate cover the last of the transcripts.[1] Mildly amazed to hear that the total came to 573 pages, and surprised to learn that you think it might make a book.

My problem is that I dream of writing an autobiography and have, in fact, actually written an opening chapter. It is rather difficult for me to imagine how I could be involved in both projects without being glaringly repetitious. No doubt you can come up with some sort of solution and I'd certainly be interested to hear what it might be.

It occurred to me to wonder whether there would be any point in my considering the Ives song volume, for the moment, on "permanent loan" to the library until such time as the law makes it possible to get a tax deduction on the basis of an outright gift to the library. I'm sure this problem must have come up before in the library's affairs, and I'd like some guidance.

Thank you for being such a wonderful host and making things go so smoothly during my recent visit to the University.

As ever,

P.S. When you see Baker, would you please tell him how much I appreciated his driving me to the National Institute in New York.

---

1. Transcripts of Perlis's oral history interviews with Copland.

To Louis and Annette Kaufman[1]

LK/LC. tls.
[1538 L. Washington Street stationery]

December 28, 1977

Dear Louis and Annette:

It was <u>very</u> nice to hear from you; and to know about the reissuing of the violin record of my various compositions.

This is mostly to tell you that the violin version of the Flute Duo[2] will be published by Boosey & Hawkes. Robert Mann of the Juilliard Quartet was kind enough to suggest going over the bowing to assure its violin-ability. I'll certainly send you a copy when this version finally appears. Naturally I'm delighted to know that you think such a transcription is feasible and would interest violinists.

All my best to you both. . . .

As ever,

[signed] Aaron

---

1. Louis Kaufman (1905–94), an American violinist committed to the performance of new music. In the 1940s he arranged Copland's "Waltz and Celebration" from *Billy the Kid* for violin and piano. Annette Kaufman had written Copland (December 19, 1977) that Louis Kaufman's Concert Hall recording "Americana," which featured Copland's "Ukelele Serenade," "Nocturne," and "Hoe-Down," among other works, was being re-released.

2. The Duo for Flute and Piano of 1971, one of Copland's last new works, based on earlier sketches.

To Eduardo Mata

AC/LC. carbon.

September 7, 1978

Dear Eduardo:

I recently received the recording you made with the Dallas Symphony of several of my works.[1] Speaking generally, I think the playing of the Orchestra and your interpretation of the music are excellent.

There is, however, one aspect of the recording which I would someday like to discuss with you at length. Here, to put it briefly, is my concern: the engineers in control of the recording apparatus have to a certain extent <u>un</u>balanced the natural intention of my own orchestration by over-emphasizing certain sections—particularly the brass.

Please understand that I do not mention this to invalidate the importance of this particular recording. I am simply concerned that some control is needed with what engineers are able to do in the control room to distort the composer's carefully calculated natural balances.

I would like of course to have your own reaction to this general point, since it seems to me an important one whenever music is recorded.

With friendly greetings, and much appreciation. . . .

As ever,

P.S. How sad about Carlos![2] Did your homage to him take place while he was still aware?

---

1. *Appalachian Spring, Rodeo,* and *El Salón México* (RCA Red Seal ARLI 2862, 1978).

2. Carlos Chávez had died on August 2, 1978.

To Nadia Boulanger

AC/LC. als.

[1538 L. Washington Street stationery]

July 9 1979

Dear Nadia:

Here, enclosed, are <u>Four Motets,</u> just issued by Boosey, which date back to a <u>very</u> long time ago—1921 to be exact.[1] I had completely forgotten about them. But in some unexplained way a choral director in New York found them among his collection, (a manuscript copy), and assured me that choruses would enjoy singing them. Boosey & Hawkes agreed with him, and so I was persuaded to allow them to be published.

I'm sending them to you as a kind of sentimental remembrance, and with all my affection

As ever

Aaron

1. *Four Motets,* written by Copland in 1921 as an assignment for Boulanger.

Copland's *Two Ballads* for violin and piano were worked up from music composed earlier. His dedicating them to Verna Fine Gordon (she had remarried) was both a gesture to an old friend and an announcement that he was still a part of the world of music. The *Ballads* were never published; the manuscripts are among the miscellaneous materials in the Copland Collection at the Library of Congress.

To Verna Fine Gordon

IF/LC. als.
[1538 L. Washington Street stationery]

7/14/86

Dear Verna:
    I want you to know that I am dedicating my
Two Ballads
for Violin and Piano
to YOU!
Love to you—
Aaron

To Leonard Bernstein

LB/LC. tls, from Ronald Caltabiano.
[1538 L. Washington Street stationery]

May 3, 1988

Dear Lenny,
    I could tell from listening to Aaron's half of the phone conversation that it must have been difficult to communicate. In person things seem to go a little better.
    But do not despair. Aaron seemed to have a very good time, and even now, some two hours later, he remembered that you called. These days that is just about unheard of.
    Thank you for making him happier than I've seen him in a very long time.
Love—
[signed] Ron

Index of Correspondents

Index of Copland's Works

General Index

Concert Hall Records, 248

Conservatoire nationale de musique, Paris, 25

Coolidge, Elizabeth Sprague, 119, 120, 148, 159. *See also* Index of Correspondents

Coolidge Festival (Washington, D.C., *1944*), 163, 166, 169, 170

Coolidge Foundation, 143–144, 145, 154–155, 157

Coolidge Quartet, 122

Coombs, Lillian "Lil", 6, 7, 10, 18, 22, 23, 25, 27, 29, 30, 36

Copenhagen, Denmark, 224

Copeland, George, 13

Copland, Aaron: "Album of Letters from Composers" for 70th birthday, 244; all-Copland programs, 96, 97, 99, 139; and American independence from European music, 87; as autobiographer, vii, x, 2, 248; "best recording I ever conducted," 234, 235 (photo); and the Cold War, 148, 191–192, 208–210; and Communism, 89, 105–106; and composers' isolation, 111; as conductor: 4, 19, 76, 181–182, 184, 191, 192, 194, 199, 205, 213, 216–246 passim; as correspondent, vii, 54, 63, 84–85, 93, 232; and the critics, 89, 90–91, 93; as dean, 191; as dedicatee, 231; and the Depression, 89, 104, 111; and Eisenhower inaugural concert, 192, 208–209; and film music, 118, 119, 120–121, 170, 192 (*see also the following entries in* Index of Copland's Works: *City, The; Heiress, The; North Star, The; Of Mice and Men; Our Town; Red Pony, The; Something Wild*); and Hebrew lessons, 205; as judge, 213; as lecturer, New School for Social Research, 55, 57, 58, 63, 65, 67, 111, 116; as lecturer, Harvard, Norton Lectures, 191, 204, 205, 206, 207; as lecturer, other venues, 70, 78, 183, 184, 185, 192,199, 213, 221, 224, 246; and McCarthy committee, 209–210; and notation of rhythm, 76; as orchestrator, 38, 45, 108, 213; and the Oscar, 121, 148,

192, 201; photographs, 15, 31, 52, 113, 131, 137, 138, 230, 235, 245; plays with Cuban band, 140–141; and political parties, 89, 209; and television, 210, 226, 227; as pianist, 1, 26, 53, 68, 70, 79, 87, 114, 115, 216–218; as publisher, 237, 238, 246; on recording engineers, 249; as sailor, 5–7, 25, 41, 71–72, 74; "severe" and "simple" styles, 89, 153, 191; and World War I, 4, 19; and World War II, 121–122, 129, 145, 146, 147; and Yiddish, 28

Copland, Aaron, travels of: *1921–1924* (Europe), 2, 5–42, 124; *1922* (Italy), 27, 29–30, 33–36; *1922* (Germany and Austria), 38–40; *1926* (Europe), 50–53; *1927* (Europe), 53–57; *1929* (France), 68; *1931* (Europe and North Africa), 81–86; *1932* (Mexico), 89, 92, 94–100; *1936* (Mexico), 114–116; *1937* (Mexico), 118–119; *1938* (London and Paris), 125; *1941* (Cuba) 140–141; *1941* (South America), 141–142, 149; *1944* (Mexico), 158–159, 160–169; *1947* (South America), x, 182–185; *1949* (Europe), 195, 198; *1951* (Europe and Israel), 203–205; *1954* (Europe), 211–212; *1955* (France), 212–215; *1957* (South America), 218; *1958* (Europe), x, 222–224; *1959* (Acapulco), 219–220, 224–225; *1960* (Europe and Japan), 225–226; *1961* (Europe), 229; *1963* (South America), 233; *1963–1964* (Europe), 234; (Europe), *1965*, 238; *1967* (London), 241, 242; *1969* (London), 244

Copland, Aaron, works of: ballets (general), 89, 121, 236 (*see also the following entries in* Index of Copland's Works: *Appalachian Spring; Billy the Kid; Dance Panels; Grohg; Hear Ye! Hear Ye!; Music for the Theatre: as Tragödie im Süden; Rodeo*); choral works (*see the following entries in* Index of Copland's Works: *Canticle of Freedom; Four Motets; In the Beginning; "Lark"; Promise of Living, The; Two Choruses*); film scores (*see*

1 July 2011
Powell's 20% %
Chicago